KU-461-124

Contents at a Glance

Contents

Foreword

In October 1978, I visited Iran on business. I shared the conventional wisdom that Iran was politically stable, a friend and ally of the United States, and a key oil supplier to the world.

My Iranian host, Ali, met me in Teheran. We were to fly south. His wife accompanied him, but there were no introductions and no communication with her. She was covered in her chador, always standing several feet behind her husband.

Ali was a sophisticated, university-educated company manager who spoke perfect English. He made me aware that Iran's religious Islamic fundamentalism was not just a movement representing the "back-country" minority and the poor. Rather, it was vigorous and attractive to many deeply religious middle-class Iranians. Their spiritual leader, Ayatollah Khomeini, had been exiled to Paris.

The next day, while meeting with managers of the National Iranian Oil Company in Abadan, a massive demonstration occurred at the company gates. This was the beginning of a general strike against the government of Shah Reza Pahlevi.

This strike, fomented by the absent Khomeini and his followers, shut down the entire country. Many people resented the Shah's repressive government, extravagances, and self-aggrandizement. The protest was also aimed at the government's secularism and its pro-Western alliances, especially with the United States, which was seen as the "instigator" and major supporter of the Shah. The Western press and Iranians themselves were surprised by the enormity of these demonstrations. Iran was perceived as a rich, stable country with a developing industrial base and a growing middle class.

While waiting to leave, I thought how little Americans (myself included!) knew about present-day Iran, its people, its long and proud history, and its ancient culture. What did we know of Iran's deep religious Shiite Islamic traditions, which seemed to grow throughout the country into real political strength? With its geography, alliances, and oil, how important was Iran to America?

After a week of planning my return to Teheran, I hired a taxi with two drivers. We drove through 500 miles of glorious, high desert mountains. They spoke no English and I no Farsi. Food was pistachio nuts. They made an unscheduled stop at the Ayatollah's mosque in the holy Islamic site of Qom. There, a large crowd of demonstrators faced off with armed soldiers. Fortunately, there was no violence. The next day I flew to London—with my bag of pistachios!

The strikes became more frequent. The shutdown of Iran's oil-producing and oil-refining sectors was effectively stopping the economy. In early 1979, the situation deteriorated. How fast the Shah's government unraveled caught everyone by surprise—even our president, who had spent New Year's Eve in Teheran. Within three weeks, the Shah left. What was allegedly a vacation became permanent, and the government subsequently collapsed. A marginalized interim government was followed by real revolution. The new clerical government executed or exiled key military and government officials. Employees of the U.S. Embassy were held hostage. (At the time, it was reported that only seven Americans inside the Embassy spoke Farsi.) In short order, our countries had become enemies.

Twenty-five years later, can we afford to repeat the earlier mistakes made in our relationship with Iran? We now know that Iran is far too critical a component in the worlds of Islam, geopolitics, and certainly energy. As that country moves into the spotlight once again, a better understanding of its people may ensure a better outcome for all.

Donald H. Harper
June 2003

Donald Harper was a former senior executive with Cabot Corporation. He currently consults internationally with American companies looking to expand worldwide. He is also a partner in Barbin-Harper LLC, an emerging life-sciences company. Mr. Harper is a graduate of Princeton University.

Introduction

Iran is in the news, again. It seems that the image of the glowering ayatollahs is a permanent fixture in our view of the Islamic world. However, limiting our view of Iran to fundamentalist clerics does a great disservice to the vast and impressive history of this complex land. Moreover, Iran does not represent all of Islam—far from it. Iran is a diverse country, yet a vast majority practice Shia Islam, as opposed to the vast majority of Muslims who practice Sunni Islam. Furthermore, the Iran of today is not the same Iran that took American hostages in 1979. In the intervening 25 years, Iran has undergone a series of domestic changes, fought a crushing war, and has endured years of sanctions. The modern Iran is truly on the verge of a new course for itself, and potentially the world.

This book is organized into five parts to help you learn more about the nation of Iran, its history, and its unique position in the world today.

Part 1, "The Basics," gives you the fundamentals on modern Iran, its Persian heritage, and its Islamic present. You'll understand why Iran matters as much as it does to us all.

Part 2, "Ancient Persia to Modern Iran: Long and Turbulent History," fills you in on ancient Persia, the Persian Empire, and Iran's role in the Great Game and the Cold War. You will also find out about the coming of Islam to this region and the emergence of Shiism, a defining element of modern Iran.

Part 3, "The Era of Ayatollahs (1979–2002)," details the coming of the Islamic Republic and the explosion of anti-Westernism in Iran. We also look at the early struggles of the Islamic Republic during the bloody war with Iraq, and the effects of U.S. economic sanctions.

In **Part 4, "Today: Iran's Relationship with the World,"** we look at the challenges modern Iran is facing from the world and the challenges that modern Iran presents to the world. We look at Iran's support of terrorism and efforts to gain nuclear weapons, and its role in the oil economy.

Part 5, "The Future: What Happens Next," deals with the changes that are coming in Iran. We look at the internal and external forces at work, and we focus in on Iranian–U.S. relations in this new century.

At the end of the book, you'll find a number of helpful appendixes.

Extras

As you make your way through the book, you'll notice little snippets of information scattered throughout the pages. They are meant to help you gain an immediate understanding of a specific aspect of the topic at hand. Here's how you can recognize them:

What's It Mean?

These define important words and terms you may not be familiar with.

Bet You Didn't Know

Here are specifics about the items that may not be familiar to you.

Warning!

These alert you to potential misconceptions or problem areas.

They Said It

These define important quotes and speeches relating to Iran.

Persian Perspectives

These boxes provide important details about Persian and Iranian history and culture.

Acknowledgments

I would like to thank my wife, Bernadine Tragert; my development editor, Tom Stevens; my agent, Gene Brissie; and Gary Goldstein.

Special Thanks to the Technical Reviewer

The Complete Idiot's Guide to Understanding Iran was reviewed by an expert who double-checked the accuracy of what you'll learn here, to help us ensure that this book gives you everything you need to know about Iran. Special thanks are extended to Doug Stein.

Trademarks

All terms mentioned in this book that are known to be or are suspected of being trademarks or service marks have been appropriately capitalized. Alpha Books and Penguin Group (USA) Inc. cannot attest to the accuracy of this information. Use of a term in this book should not be regarded as affecting the validity of any trademark or service mark.

Part

The Basics

Okay, so you know that Iran is in the Middle East and is ruled by an Ayatollah, but do you know where the Iranian people come from, what language they speak, and how many there are?

"The lowdown" is the guiding principle for the chapters in Part 1. You'll find out all you need to know to put this complex country into perspective.

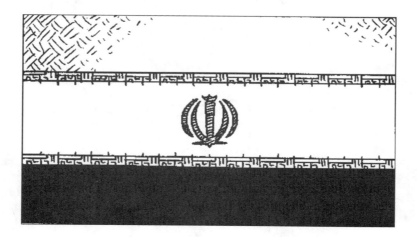

Chapter 1

Why Iran Matters

In This Chapter

- ◆ The historical and cultural significance of Iran
- ◆ On the threshold of change, for better or worse
- ◆ The threat of terror
- ◆ The threat of nuclear proliferation
- ◆ The threat of instability in a volatile part of the world

Iran is one of the oldest and most well-known cultures in the world. Across the centuries, Iran has played a critical role in world events and has provided the world with tools and learning that have contributed to modern science, technology, and art. Iran continues to find itself on center stage. Sometimes the reasons for this notoriety seem less than praiseworthy to the Western observer. Still, Iran unapologetically continues to chart its own course through history.

Strategic Crossroads

Iran has been, and continues to be, strategic. As far back as the time of ancient Persia, the region that is now Iran sat on the borders of East and West. The peoples and empires that came and went in this region flourished as a critical point on the East-West trade routes. The Iranians benefited from this position, and contributed their own value in melding the concepts that came from both sides of the compass. Like they did with goods and merchandise, the Iranians received, stored, re-organized, and forwarded technology and science from one region to another, taking and using it along the way.

In the nineteenth century, Iran became a strategic piece in the competition between the British and the Russian Empires for Central Asian dominance. Later, in the last half of the twentieth century, Iran again became a critical stage for the competition playing out between the United States and the Soviet Union. Today, Iran again is a lynchpin in the emerging competition of radical Islam and the West. (We will look at Iran's strategic position in Part 3, to better understand its current importance.)

Underlying the current strategic importance of Iran, literally and figuratively, is the world's growing thirst for oil. As one of the leading producers of oil in the world, Iran plays a quiet but critical role in the world economy as determined by the price of a barrel of crude. Iran cannot be ignored, despite recent American antipathy toward the ayatollahs who run it.

Source of Culture and Confusion

Iran's culture has always played a critical role in the world's development. From the earliest emergence of civilization on the Iranian Plateau, through the Persian Empire and into the modern era, Iran has straddled Western and Eastern worlds. Iran has synthesized influences from both sides, to create a culture that is unique and that builds upon the best of both. (We will look in more detail at this blending of cultures in Part 2.)

Today, Iranian culture is overshadowed by Iranian Islam. The Islamic Republic of Iran is implementing a complete system of political, economic, and religious constructs that seem at once compelling and confusing to the outside observer. But again, Iran is charting its own course through its contemporary Islamic Republic phase. In fact, the question relating to Iran's future focuses on that term, "phase." Is the current regime just the latest phase in a continuum that stretches back to the earliest days of human history? Or does today's Islamic Republic signal the beginning of a new constancy in the emerging world order? In other words, can the Islamic Republic survive? The leaders of modern Iran, while following a historical roadmap, are pressing ahead into uncharted territory (as we will discuss in Part 4).

On the Threshold

Iran is on the threshold of change, for better or worse. The elements for and against reform of the current fundamentalist regime are growing increasingly forceful, and violent, in their debate on the future of the country. Unlike earlier times, outside forces are essentially powerless to directly determine the outcome, and so can only hope to influence the debate. The Iranian people will sort this one out themselves. (We will look at this internal debate and the forces involved in Part 5 of this book.)

However, this internal debate is no mere sideshow for Western observers. The outcome will affect us all, whether we want it to or not. At the most basic level, if internal unrest disrupts oil production, the world's economy could be impacted quite severely in the short run. The spike in oil prices would be a severe blow economically and remain a sore spot until the rest of the world's oil-producing nations could make up the shortfall.

Beyond the question of secure oil supplies, Iran matters to the West in general and the United States in particular. In fact, the United States and Iran are edging closer and closer together. This increasing proximity will result either in increasing ties to the benefit of both parties, or increasing hostilities, to the detriment of both. The U.S. focus on terrorism, and specifically Islamic terrorism, has fundamentally changed the way the two countries deal with each other.

Take a look at these quotes. They present two opposing views of the increasingly aggressive U.S. stance on combating terror and the Iranian reaction to this U.S. policy.

They Said It

American politicians behave like the masters of the world. They impose sanctions on any place that does not bow to their interests and want to impose their sanctions by force on the world, not just on us .... [The U.S. government] not only puts pressure on Iran. It puts pressure on Europe, Asia, Japan, saying, for example, "If you want to invest in Iran more than such an amount, we will impose sanctions on you." It tries to impose its own domestic laws on the world. That is its domineering way.

The fruit of our revolution is that we have freed ourselves from the yoke of our masters, and we will never submit to any new one.

Those who put coercive pressure on others and resort to force, and world powers that try to make oppressive pressure the basis of their relations with other nations ... they cannot expect anything from the Iranian nation.

—Iranian president Mohammad Khatami, January 20, 1998

There's no question but that there's al Qaeda and folks that are in [Iran]. One of the goals of the war [in Afghanistan] is to go after the terrorists and to stop them and to stop nations from harboring terrorists. There's lots of ways to do that .... We have not found Iran to be a particularly cooperative country in the war against terrorism. I think that would be the understatement of the day.

—U.S. Secretary of State Donald Rumsfeld, in response to a reporter's question about whether Iran was harboring terrorists, February 5, 2002

Simply put, the United States and Iran are on a collision course, which complicates the internal debate already underway in this ancient and compelling land.

Three Flashpoints

Whether it makes the headlines on any given day, Iran matters—if only because of the size of the gap in world views in the two statements you just read.

Iran matters to American policymakers—and to the Western world as a whole—more today, perhaps, than it ever has: more than during the most troubled hours of the Carter administration, more than during the long stretch of scandal and deceit that marked the final years of the Reagan presidency.

Iran matters for three basic reasons:

◆ The prospect of terrorism

◆ The threat of the proliferation of nuclear weapons

◆ The dangers of internal unrest that might destabilize the most volatile region on Earth

Public interest in Iran may rise and fall over time. Yet at any moment, any one of these three factors, or a combination of one or more, could create a crisis that would place Iran at the center of the geopolitical stage.

To begin this book, let's look at these three issues, examine how Iran is involved with them, and find out how they could involve the rest of the world.

Terrorism

The United States regards Iran as a state sponsor of terrorism, which means that the Iranian government actively aids terrorist groups. This assistance comes in the form of providing training facilities, weapons, money, and logistics support to terrorists.

Why do the Iranians do this? While the motivations for any state's policies are complex, the best short answer is that terrorism is Iran's method of choice for influencing the actions of countries it regards as its enemies.

Probably the best-known terrorist group sponsored by Iran is known as the Hezbollah. (Iran is not the only entity that supports the *Hezbollah*, but it is strongly associated with the group.)

What's It Mean? _____

The **Hezbollah** has been engaged in a deadly conflict with Israel for decades. The group is responsible for suicide bombing attacks against Israeli targets, military and civilian, in the West Bank and other Israeli-occupied territories. The Hezbollah's motives are the same as Iran's in this case: Both are dedicated to driving the Israelis out of their settlements in what the Hezbollah and Iran consider to be Palestinian territory.

Ultimately, the Hezbollah and Iran want the same thing: the destruction of Israel itself. (Iran does not officially recognize Israel's right to exist.) Using the Hezbollah to do certain "dirty work" enables Iran to attack Israel without using its own military. The continued attacks and reprisals keep the tension in that portion of the Middle East extremely high and make any peaceful resolution of the crisis extremely remote.

Destabilization as Foreign Policy

This brings us to the other reason Iran sponsors terrorists. Iran is using external terror groups and internal dissidents to destabilize its neighbors and so increase its own sense of security. If the neighbors are distracted, those neighbors will not interfere with Iran. Furthermore, Iran tries to use terrorists to promote its own influence in other regions.

The current leadership of Iran has ample precedent for this practice. The Shah, who ruled before the Islamic Republic was created in 1979, also sponsored rebels inside his neighbors' borders. Iran was a notorious supporter of Kurdish insurgents within neighboring Iraq in the 1970s. Iran is currently supporting factions in Afghanistan that are attempting to overthrow the U.S.–backed government there.

There is, therefore, a long, if not particularly attractive, history of subsidized terror and measures to increase regional instability on the part of Iranian leaders. The leadership today appears to be more than willing to use such policies as tools for exerting influence in the *West Bank*.

What's It Mean? _____

The **West Bank** has been under Israeli control since the 1967 War, when it was administered by Jordan. West Bank settlements are government-supported settlements of Israelis in the West Bank. These settlements are often located in the midst of Palestinian communities and can take the appearance of armed camps. Their isolated locations in the midst of Palestinian populations make them prime targets for campaigns of the Hezbollah, as well as other terrorist groups.

A New American Interest

Following the events of September 11, 2001, the United States has gained a new awareness of terrorism in general and Islamic terrorists in particular. The historic importance of Israel to U.S. policymakers makes the Hezbollah all the more important. The Iranians, as one of the chief backers of the Hezbollah, have taken a new place in the hierarchy of U.S. concerns. The Bush administration has drawn a new line against terrorists and the states that sponsor them. Iran has, in fact, been singled out as a special target of American concern. In early 2002, President Bush made it clear that his foreign-policy intentions extended beyond the borders of Afghanistan (where the Taliban regime had been harboring al Qaeda terrorists) when he declared that Iran was a member of an international "*Axis of Evil.*"

> **What's It Mean?**
>
> Iran, Iraq, and North Korea were singled out by President George W. Bush as a threat to U.S. security and world peace and were deemed the **Axis of Evil**. Iran's support of terrorists helped it make the list.

Iran sponsors terror groups that operate against Israel. Many feel that these terror groups are designed to complicate the U.S. efforts to forge a peaceful settlement in Israel. This is so, the argument goes, because of this cycle:

1. Terror attack (often by Iranian-backed groups)

2. Condemnation of terrorists by the United States

3. Israeli reprisal

This cycle only increases the perception in the Arab world that the United States favors Israel in this conflict and that no fair deal can be arranged with the United States as mediator.

American Targets?

The big question for the United States is whether Iran is or will sponsor terrorists that may attack the United States. If Iran's support of terrorist groups that operate against the United States is proven, there is little doubt that the American response will be swift. The Bush administration has made it clear that the United States will act in its own interest, even if the rest of the international community does not support those actions.

The repercussions of a U.S.–led attack on Iran would be vast and costly. Oil supplies would be affected; countries such as Russia, Turkey, and Pakistan would be drawn in to the crisis; and alliances such as NATO and the United Nations would be severely strained. In addition, U.S. prestige would again be on the line—and with it, the ability for the United States to lead the war on terrorism.

Nuclear Weapons

Iran is apparently working on developing a nuclear arms program under the guise of developing nuclear energy resources. This program, experts say, includes uranium mining near the city of Yazd, a uranium hexachloride plant, a uranium-enrichment facility, and a reactor near al-Bashir. In the words of the International Atomic Energy Agency (IAEA) Director-General Mohamed ElBaradei, the Iranian facility is "much further along than previously thought."

The current state of the development of the Iranian facilities violates Iran's involvement in the *Nuclear Non-Proliferation Treaty.* Under the regulations of the treaty, Iran agreed not to develop its nuclear facilities to the levels they have now apparently reached.

Iran claims that the nuclear facilities are part of its program to develop nuclear energy for civilian use—that is, to build a 500-megawatt reactor for the creation of electricity. Experts say this claim is dubious because Iran is sitting on huge amounts of oil and flares off (that is, wastes) more than enough natural gas to make 500 megawatts of electricity each year. If the country needed the extra electrical capacity, it could much more easily and quickly capture that gas and burn it to create the electricity instead of incurring the massive costs to develop the nuclear facilities.

Iran's work on an apparent nuclear weapons program matters because if the Iranians were to succeed in developing nuclear weapons and had the facility to make enough enriched plutonium for a small nuclear arms cache, the balance of power in the Middle East would shift dramatically. Iran could bring pressure to bear on Iraq, Turkey, Afghanistan, Turkmenistan, Pakistan, Israel, and the oil-rich Gulf states.

Bet You Didn't Know

The Iranian government has been building a nuclear power plant at al-Bashir. This plant is a "breeder reactor." Unlike conventional nuclear plants that produce electricity, breeder reactor nuclear plants are designed to create enriched uranium, which can be used for making nuclear weapons.

What's It Mean?

The **Nuclear Non-Proliferation Treaty** went into effect on March 5, 1970, and 188 countries (including Iran) either have signed it or participate in its reviews. Among other goals, the purpose of the treaty is to prevent the spread of nuclear weapons and weapons technology.

Even more dire, Iran could conceivably provide nuclear weapons to a terrorist group that it sponsors. There is no guarantee that, to forward their own ends, the Iranians would not offer the bomb to one of their proxy terror groups.

Who Is Helping the Iranians?

Iran is getting assistance from Russia, which originally provided the components for the reactor. Russia's motivations for helping Iran can be traced to its traditional interest in influencing Iran and Central Asia. By providing a key technology, Russia gains leverage in the region with an otherwise hostile regime.

It is also quite likely that old-fashioned greed is playing a role. The Iranians are no doubt paying big money to get these technologies, and with the lack of control over the giant Russian industrial conglomerates these days, including the nuclear power plant–building conglomerate, that money is finding many willing takers.

Can the Rest of the World Apply Pressure to Stop This Process?

Unfortunately, the answer is probably no. Iran is already fairly isolated in the world community. It also has a great deal of oil, which the rest of the world needs. It is unlikely that the world oil consumers would agree to boycott Iranian oil, given the well-known consequences of shortages in the oil markets. Aside from that option, the world community can apply little economic pressure on Iran.

One option that has been discussed is military intervention. The United States (or a UN coalition) could attack Iran's nuclear facilities to effectively take them offline. The repercussions of such an act are unclear, but they would certainly create divisions among the United States and its allies, as well as within the United Nations.

The real wild card is Israel's reaction to the existence of an advanced nuclear weapons program in Iran. The Israelis are painfully aware that Iran refuses to acknowledge Israel's right to exist, and of Iran's support for terrorist groups that have repeatedly attacked Israel.

When confronted with a nuclear program in Osirek in Iraq in 1981, the Israelis bombed the reactor, completely destroying it. Saddam Hussein, preoccupied with other issues, did not react militarily to the attack. It is not clear, however, how the Iranians would react if Israel attacked Iranian facilities.

As we have seen, Iran already has a channel for attacking Israel: the Hezbollah. If Israel succeeded in destroying the Iranian nuclear program, the Iranian response could very well be an onslaught of terrorist bombing attacks in Israel.

Another point to consider: If Iran perceived that the United States were involved in any way in a military strike against its nuclear facilities, that could open the door to Hezbollah attacks on the United States.

Internal Unrest

Students in the streets, a ruling government that seems increasingly out of touch with the demands of the middle class, and rising tensions lead foreign governments and embassy personnel to watch with growing concern as demonstrators take to the streets.

This may sound like a description of the days before the overthrow of the Shah of Iran in 1979 and before the establishment of a *theocratic state*. However, the same events are also unfolding in Iran in 2003.

No one really knows what the future holds for the current Iranian leadership, but the prospect of unrest in Iran is a sobering one for the entire region.

Most experts agree that the religious leaders who have held sway in Iran since the 1979 Revolution will have to adapt to a new set of realities. The Iranian people are steadily demanding more personal freedom and latitude in their everyday life. Already, there are indications of popular discontent.

The elected government of President Mohammad Khatami is gently pushing the religious establishment to relax some of the more draconian laws that govern everyday Iranian life. So far, the clerical establishment has resisted any significant reforms.

What's It Mean? _____

A **theocratic state** is one in which practical power rests with religious authorities, as in Iran.

Some kind of reform appears inevitable. The question is whether it will be smooth or rough reform. Will the clerical establishment relent gradually, maintaining control by slowly releasing the pressure on popular discontent? Or will the mullahs move too slowly and find themselves forced to deal with mobs in the streets? If Iran were to become destabilized once again, what kind of government would emerge, and what would the implications be for the region? Would a period of domestic unrest inside Iran invite foreign incursions—as appears to have happened in 1980, when Saddam Hussein attacked Iran shortly following the Islamic Revolution, thus launching the *Iran-Iraq War?*

What's It Mean?

The **Iran-Iraq War** was fought from 1980 to 1988 and was instigated by Iraq under its then new leader, Saddam Hussein. Saddam initiated the war to build his reputation and seize some Iranian territory at the same time. The Iranians responded furiously: The war included gas attacks, bloody "human wave" assaults that included children, tremendous damage to the oil industries on both sides, and massive casualties. There was no clear winner.

A Force to Be Reckoned With

Iran matters to the United States, primarily because of its capacity to affect the agenda of America and its allies. Considering its capacity for sponsoring terrorist movements, its rapidly growing nuclear weapons program, and the geopolitical consequences of internal upheavals within the country, it cannot be ignored. Crises in any or all of these areas could lead to grave problems for U.S. policymakers, among them these:

◆ A disruption in the flow of oil from this vital producer, thus driving oil prices higher and threatening Western economies

◆ The emergence of a more reactionary or hard-line leadership that could be more likely to support terrorist operations on U.S. soil

◆ An increase in the already-controversial U.S. military presence in the region (to prop up unsteady allies)

◆ Intervention by regional powers (such as Turkey or Iraq) in Iranian affairs

The United States, its Western allies, and its allies in the Persian Gulf region all will be affected by what takes place in Iran over the coming years. That much is certain. What's less certain is exactly *how* they will be affected.

In this book, you will get the chance to look at Iran, its culture, its politics, its history, and its current position in the world—and you'll get an idea of the some of the most plausible scenarios for Iran's future.

The Least You Need to Know

- There is a great chasm of mistrust between the United States and Iran, and the relationship between the two countries is tense.

- The U.S. government considers Iran to be a member of the Axis of Evil. (The other members of the Axis are North Korea and up until the middle of 2003, Iran's bitter rival, Iraq.)

- Iran's sponsorship of terrorism, its nuclear program, and its reaction to its own internal pressures all likely will present grave challenges to U.S. policymakers in coming years.

- America and its allies are going to be affected by events in Iran in the coming years; the only question is how.

Chapter 2

Just the FAQs: Common Questions About Iran

In This Chapter

- Where Iran is
- The importance of oil
- Shiites vs. Sunnis
- Common misperceptions

Now that you know why Iran matters so much to stability in the Middle East and, consequently, to the world, you probably have a lot of other questions about this member of the Axis of Evil. In this chapter, we look at some frequently asked questions about Iran's geography, military strength, religion, leadership, and role in the world economy.

Let's start with a very basic question:

Where Is Iran?

Iran lies between the Middle East and Central Asia. It is in the center of a perpetual "hot spot" in world affairs. It's located on the eastern end of the oil-rich Persian Gulf region and the western end of Central Asia. The country encompasses the Iranian plateau, in what was ancient Persia.

Iran's position has been described by its leadership as "neither East nor West." The country is located within the Middle East, but also within Central Asia. It bridges the two regions.

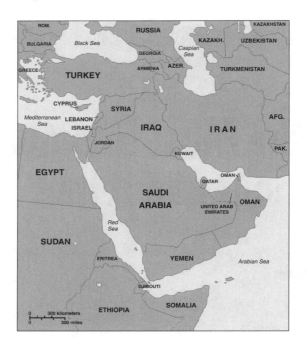

Iran's territory includes oil-rich areas, a long coast line along the Persian Gulf, and a broad central plain flanked by mountains on either side.

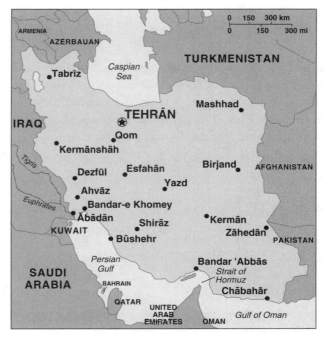

Iran is bordered on the west by Iraq and Turkey; on the north by Armenia, Azerbaijan, the Caspian Sea, and Turkmenistan; and on the east by Afghanistan and Pakistan. Its long southern seacoast is open to the Persian Gulf, the Strait of Hormuz, and the Gulf of Oman (the northwestern-most part of the Indian Ocean). Across the Gulf itself are the oil-producing states of Kuwait, Saudi Arabia, Qatar, Bahrain, the United Arab Emirates, and Oman. Most of the world's oil comes from this region. The United States and the West need to keep this oil flowing predictably and securely. Any instability in the region—either internal to one of the major producers or between one or more countries—would dramatically affect the global economy. If the region erupts into warfare, deliveries would be interrupted, driving up fuel costs and adversely affecting employment and economic conditions across the industrialized world.

Warning! _____

The Middle East is fraught with instability that seems to constantly threaten to blossom into full-fledged war. Iranian internal instability or weakness would certainly draw in neighboring countries, and instability or weakness in neighboring countries would tempt Iran to intervene to its advantage. The Iranians are doing just that in Afghanistan and Iraq in 2003, in the wake of Coalition forces that recently toppled the regimes in those countries.

How Big Is the Iranian Army?

Iran's army is made up of about 500,000 men, one of the largest in the region, with about 350,000 reserves. The heart of the Iranian army is professional soldiers, augmented by recruits and some volunteers. Still, the cadre of experienced combat veterans of the Iran-Iraq War is aging and out of the service. Iran also used poorly trained, ill-equipped volunteers called the Basji who acted as a human wave during the Iran-Iraq War. Any future invasion of Iran would probably have to deal with these zealots along with the conventional soldiers. Iran has tanks and artillery, largely purchased from Russia.

The Iranian air force is still potent and uses fairly modern warplanes from Russia and other nations. In fact, Russia is a primary supplier of all types of weaponry to Iran since 1979. The Iranian navy consists of coastal patrol boats (many purchased from China), but they are capable of creating mischief in the Persian Gulf against unarmed tankers. However, they are no match for the navies of the Western powers. More disturbing to Western oil interests, Iran has purchased a number of antiship missiles from China, which could effectively threaten oil shipping in the Gulf, particularly in the narrow *Strait of Hormuz.*

What's It Mean? _____

The Persian Gulf connects to the Arabian Sea and, thus, the Indian Ocean via the **Strait of Hormuz.** The main shipping channel narrows and makes a right-angle turn. With anti-ship missiles and fast patrol boats, and the entire eastern coastline of the Strait, Iran could make shipping through the Strait very difficult if it wanted to. What is more, Iran has seized two small islands (the Greater and Lesser Tunbs) at the southern outlet of the Strait, which further extends its ability to interdict shipping.

Perhaps not surprising, given its common designation as a member of the Axis of Evil, Iran receives ballistic missile technology from North Korea. This technology is used in Iran's *Shahab* missile program, which we examine in more detail in Chapter 19.

Is Oil Important to the Iranian Economy?

In a word, yes. To a large extent, oil *is* the Iranian economy. Iran has about 89.7 billion barrels of *proven reserves* of oil. This is about 9 percent of all the known oil in the world, and it ranks Iran fourth among all nations in that category. (By contrast, the United States has about 2 percent of the world's proven reserves.) There are roughly one trillion barrels of proven reserves of oil worldwide.

What's It Mean? _____

Oil that has been discovered but not yet pumped from the ground is called **proven reserves.** Proven oil is known to be in a *reservoir.*

The Iranians export about three million barrels of oil per day, ranking Iran fourth among all oil-exporting countries. This amount is Iran's quota, set by the *Organization of the Petroleum Exporting Countries,* more commonly known as *OPEC.* Each member's quota is set through a complex formula that takes reserves, productive capacity, and other factors into account. The amount of slightly less than three million *bpd* (*barrels per day*) is about the maximum that Iran can produce at this point.

The high oil output is due to heavy Western investment in Iranian oil production, which started before World War I and continued throughout the Cold War, up until the Islamic Revolution. As early as 1914, the British wielded great influence over oil production in the region. The Anglo-Persian Oil Company (set up to extract oil from what is now Iran) purchased a large stake in the Anglo-Turkish Oil Company (set up to extract oil from Iraq and other Arab areas). The Anglo-Persian strategy was to develop the production capacity of Persian fields first and hold the other (non-Persian) areas in reserve. This arrangement enriched the Persian rulers, since they received royalties on oil actually produced and sold.

What's It Mean?

The **Organization of the Petroleum Exporting Countries,** or **OPEC,** was founded in 1960 and includes Iran, Iraq, Kuwait, Saudi Arabia, Algeria, Venezuela, Nigeria, Indonesia, Libya, Qatar, and the United Arab Emirates. In 2000, OPEC members controlled some 75 percent of the world's proven reserves, and about 40 percent of world oil production. OPEC found its power in the aftermath of the Arab-Israeli War in October 1973. OPEC agreed to boycott the United States and its allies for their support of Israel during the conflict. Oil prices were increased by 60 percent, creating an oil crisis in the United States.

Barrels per day (bpd) is the basic international unit of measure for oil. A "barrel" equals 55 gallons of oil. Barrels per day is a volume measurement of the number of these barrels that are produced, shipped, or consumed in a single day.

The local leaders in the Arab regions of the Gulf saw less of their potential oil production brought online in the early years. The leaders of the other oil-rich countries received fewer royalties, and this did nothing to increase goodwill toward the English or the Persians.

By the 1970s, Iran was among the top five oil-producing nations in the world. Again, the heavy investments by Western (mainly U.S.) oil companies brought Iran's production to these high levels. By this time, the Iranian oil industry had been nationalized into the National Iranian Oil Company (NIOC), and the lopsided concessions of the early days were abolished. However, Western oil firms were subcontracted to manage operations and develop new infrastructure, and they enjoyed very close working relationships with the Iranian Oil Ministry.

Problems, however, have clouded the export picture. Output in the Iranian oil fields today is a result of this long-lived heavy investment in extraction and production. Simply put, the established and historically most productive oil fields have started to play out—that is, the level of oil left in the most developed fields is diminishing, and it is more difficult to extract what is left. The unrefined crude oil, with the sulfur and other elements in it, is brutal on the infrastructure designed to process it, and heavy ongoing investment is a must. Moreover, if new discoveries are to be brought online, Iran will need outside oil companies to contract to do it with them. Already the French energy company TotalElfFina is involved, as are the Chinese and others. The U.S. oil industry is absent because of U.S. government–imposed sanctions on Iran for terrorism support and nuclear weapons development.

The Iranians certainly are not running out of oil or natural gas, but they are going to have to invest more and incur higher costs to keep up the current volumes. Oil fields in Iran deliver the crude via the natural lift method, where the pressure of the oil under the ground forces it out of the wellhead. This method results in extremely low cost extraction, around $1.50 per barrel as compared to $15 per barrel in the United States (which does not have the high pressure oil reservoirs found in the Middle East). Because the Iranian oil production infrastructure was developed earlier than its neighbors, and so much crude has been extracted, the traditional natural lift process is no longer working as well, because the pressure in the underground reservoirs is diminishing. This forces the Iranians to either live with less production, or spend more money to apply secondary recovery techniques to extract the crude. These techniques include pumping gas or water back into the reservoir to keep the overall pressure up. This process eventually can damage the reservoir, and results in higher downstream refining costs.

Who Are the Kurds?

The Kurdish people occupy a region known as Kurdistan. Kurdistan is divided among Turkey, Iraq, Iran, and Armenia. The Kurds are a minority in each of those countries and have controls placed upon them that are not placed on the majority populations in those countries. The Kurdish people aren't Arab; they are of Indo-European descent. Most Kurds are Sunni Muslims.

Kurdistan is not a nation, but is the name for the region inhabited by the Kurd people.

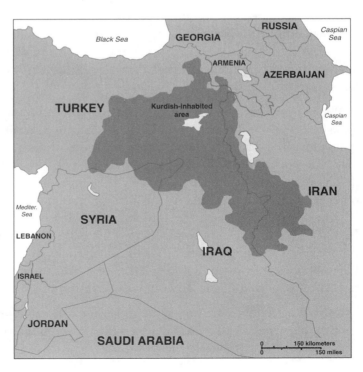

The name of the Kurds is attributed to a name for Babylonian palace guards in 600 B.C.E., the Kardakas. These guards came from the ethnic group that later became known as the Kurds. The highpoint for the Kurds came around 1150 B.C.E. and paralleled the rise of King Saladin. Saladin was himself a Kurd and gained fame in the West during the Third Crusade. Saladin's armies defeated Richard the Lion-Hearted and reinstated Muslim control over Jerusalem. Saladin was credited with showing extraordinary mercy toward the defeated Crusaders in Jerusalem. Rather than slaughtering the Christians (as earlier Crusaders had done to the Muslim inhabitants of Jerusalem when they took power), Saladin spared their lives. Saladin's Ayyubid Empire also defeated the Shiite (Fatimid) rule in Egypt and Syria in 1171. The Ayyubids continued to rule these regions until 1250, when they gave way to the Mamluks, a Turkic group from Central Asia.

As the Ayyubid Empire receded, the relative power of the Kurds receded with it. Over the next centuries, the Kurds were not an integral part of the ruling groups that controlled the region where Kurdistan is located. As a result, the Kurds did not gain political independence.

By the end of World War II, the Kurdistan (the region where the Kurds live) was divided among Turkey, Iraq, and Iran, and no provisions were made to accommodate Kurd autonomy. The Kurds have rebelled against these governments to varying degrees of violence—and varying degrees of outside help—ever since.

The Iranian leadership has consistently suppressed the Kurds. It is doubtful that the Kurds will ever be given real autonomy in Iran or Iraq because Turkey (a NATO member) would not tolerate an autonomous Kurd state on its border, for fear that the Kurds in Turkey would want to break away. The unfolding situation of the Kurd minorities in Iraq following the dissolution of the Saddam Hussein regime is instructive for what could happen in any kind of internal strife in Iran. Experts agree that the best the Kurds can hope for is some increased autonomy and constitutional protections, but not full independence.

Despite the fact that the Kurds are Sunnis, the Shia (also called Shiite) Iranians have repeatedly supported Kurdish opposition groups operating against Iraq over the years. This support follows the Iranian strategy of increasing its own security by weakening its neighbors. In the case of the Kurds in Iraq, Iranian support for the Kurds drew Iraqi military resources away from the Iranian border and into the Kurdish regions.

Who Are the Shiites and the Sunnis?

Shiite Muslims dominate in Iran. However, the Shiites are the minority among Muslims worldwide. About 90 percent of all Muslims today are Sunni. Less than 10 percent of all Muslims are Shiite.

Bet You Didn't Know

Iraq and Iran are the only two Muslim countries in which the Shiites constitute the majority of the population.

Shiism is a result of early political controversies over succession to the Prophet Muhammad. In the ninth century, a caliph was named who was not a direct descendent of Muhammad. The word *caliph* comes from the Arabic word *khalafa*, meaning "he succeeded." This caliph was selected for a variety of practical and political reasons that suited the times and powers in Baghdad (the seat of the caliphate).

A controversy erupted over the appointment of a nondescendant of Muhammad as caliph. The group that opposed this new caliph, and later would be called the Shiites, insisted that the Prophet's authority as the imam (spiritual and political leader) of the community was transmitted in his lineage through Ali, Muhammad's cousin and son-in-law, and thus to Ali's descendants; therefore, only these descendants could lead the faithful. The majority of Muslims held that preservation of the unity of the community and avoidance of difference, even at the expense of acquiescing to less than morally pure (that is, directly related to Muhammad) caliphal rule, was of primary importance. These Muslims argued that the Ulama ("men of religion"), not the caliph, had become the authorities on the proper practice of Islam. This majority group eventually became known as the Sunni Muslims.

Shiism has two major branches: the Twelvers in Iran, Iraq, and elsewhere, who await the return of the twelfth imam who occulted (that is, disappeared from human view in the "great occultation") around 939 C.E.; and the Ismailis, who have a living imam (the Agha Khan). The Twelvers believe that the twelfth imam will reappear as the Messiah when Allah commands.

Bet You Didn't Know

Several groups have splintered off the main body of Islam, but most have not survived the death of their first leader. The Shiite sect is the only major Islamic sect that has persisted for more than 1,000 years in the face of overwhelming Sunni predominance. The Shiites first broke away from the rest of Islam after a series of political and military disputes over the caliphate in the seventh century.

Is Iran a Dictatorship?

Yes and no. Iran is ruled by a Supreme Leader (originally the Ayatollah Khomeini and now the Ayatollah Khamenie) who rules for life. A council of clerics called the *Faqih*, or Assembly of Experts, who are not elected, supports the Supreme Leader and enforces a strict interpretation of Qur'anic law on the population. Almost every major decision is made via these clerics. However, the Majlis (parliament) in Iran is elected. The president (currently Khatami) is elected as well. As we shall see in the chapter on the current domestic situation in Iran, there is some limited democracy. Moreover, the Iranian people do hold demonstrations and counterdemonstrations, which is a form of debate over domestic law and policies, and Majlis is a forum for formal debate and action in the continuing evolution of Iranian civil society.

The most repressive manifestations of the Islamic Republic seem to have faded away. For example, in the early days of the Islamic Republic, there were brutal squads of "religious police" who would immediately and severely punish anyone violating strict Islamic law. If a woman showed too much skin, these gangs were known to brutally beat and even rape that "offender" as punishment. These gangs no longer carry out that brutal repression role, but the state does maintain a strong domestic police force to maintain the observance of the laws. What is more, the legal system strongly favors males over females. Still, there undoubtedly has been a loosening of the strictest constraints of the law. Also, there has been some progress by the more moderate elements seeking to liberalize the Iranian legal system and economy even further. Still, an Islamic Council of Guardians exists to ensure that any laws passed by the Majlis conform to Islamic law.

Common Misconceptions About Iran

Outsiders looking at Iran labor under several misconceptions about this fascinating and diverse country. Iran has many qualities that make it unique, even though these qualities are not well known. Here are some common misconceptions about Iran, and the straight dope on what it is really about.

The Iranians Are Persian, Not Arab

The Persians are ethnically from the Aryan group, which originated in Central Asia. The Persians themselves are a distinct ethnic group. Almost all Persians are Muslims, with smaller numbers of Christians and believers of other faiths. The Persians are mainly concentrated in Iran proper. There are non-Persian Iranians, too, though in smaller numbers.

By comparison, the Arabs are people living in North Africa and the Middle East, from western Morocco to Oman, and from Turkey in the north to Yemen and Sudan in the south. Two hundred fifty million Arabs live in this area, about four million live in Europe, and two million live in the Americas. The Arabic heartland is a region called Hijaz (now western Saudi Arabia). Ethnically, Arabs are mostly dark-haired with brown eyes and medium-light skin. But some Arabs are black and others are blond. These differences are regional and a result of the intermixing and absorption of populations. More than 95 percent of all Arabs are Muslims.

Iranian Islam Doesn't Represent All Islam

Islam is practiced by millions of people across the world. The Ayatollahs running Iran do not represent all of Islam. There are vast numbers of non-Persian Muslims, in places such as western China, Central Asia, Indonesia, the Arab Middle East, and Turkey. As we noted earlier, the Iranian Muslims are mostly Shia, which makes them different from about 90 percent of the rest of the world's Muslims. Even within the Shia Muslim world, the Iranian Shias are ethnically Persian, while the majority of the rest of the Shias is predominantly Arab. So Iranian Islam is, in fact, a fairly small piece of a much larger global religion called Islam.

Terrorists Come from Many Cultures

The escalating conflict between terrorist movements and the civilized nations is taking a new shape. The Bush administration's new doctrine emphasizes U.S. security against terrorism. This policy is preemptive, meaning that the United States has shown that it will attack (unilaterally, if need be) organizations and states that threaten U.S. security. The United States is now leading the international movement to isolate and eradicate terrorist groups wherever they reside. This book examines Iran's role as a possible exporter of terrorism.

However, this is not to say that all Muslims are terrorists—far from it. This book examines terrorism that is sponsored by the Iranian leadership, who happen to be Muslim. Before assuming that all terrorists are Muslim fanatics, one should consider that some of the most persistent terrorists come from countries such as Ireland and Japan, which are certainly not Arab or Muslim.

The Least You Need to Know

- ◆ Iran is located on the Persian Gulf between the Middle East and Central Asia, a strategic location in the largest oil-producing region in the world.
- ◆ Oil drives the Iranian economy.
- ◆ Iran has a potent regional military.
- ◆ The Iranian leadership has created an Islamic republic along strict Islamic law.
- ◆ The majority of Iranians are Persian and Shia Muslim, as opposed to the Arab (or Turkic) Sunnis in the Middle East and other parts of Central Asia.

Chapter 3

By the Numbers: Iran Today

In This Chapter

- ◆ Iran's geography
- ◆ Iran's people
- ◆ The Iranian economy and its unmet potential
- ◆ The government of the Islamic Republic

This chapter serves as an almanac for Iran's geography, people, economy, and government. It provides a no-nonsense framework from which to better understand the following chapters on the history and future of Iran.

Geography

Official name: The Islamic Republic of Iran (*Jomhuri-ye Eslami-ye Iran*) was formerly called Persia (until 1935).

Location: Iran is in the Middle East, bordering the Persian Gulf and the Caspian Sea. The states it borders include Afghanistan, Armenia, Azerbaijan, Iraq, Pakistan, Turkey, and Turkmenistan. Iran is in the middle of the region and sits along the eastern shore of the strategic Persian Gulf, where most of the world's oil comes from.

The Lay of the Land

Size: 1,648,000 square kilometers. Iran is about 10 percent larger than Alaska.

Climate: Iran has an arid and semiarid climate, with a subtropical region near the Caspian Sea. In the lowlands, temperatures swing substantially between summer and winter. The mountain regions have cold winters with occasional heavy snows. Farther away from the mountains, it gets much hotter.

Bet You Didn't Know

About 40 percent of the world's known oil reserves are located in the Persian Gulf region. Iran's coastline extends some 2,440 kilometers along the entire eastern shore of the Gulf. Iran's position dominates the Straits of Hormuz, at a strategic choke point at the lower end of the Persian Gulf. Oil leaving the Gulf by tanker must pass through the Straits.

Terrain: The country is essentially a central plateau ringed by mountains. The central area is a vast plain with deserts and occasional mountains. There are some coastal plains along the Persian Gulf.

Natural resources: Iran's biggest natural resource by far is oil, followed by natural gas and coal. There are deposits of chromium, copper, iron ore, lead, manganese, zinc, and sulfur. Otherwise, there is not much to be had.

Land use: About 10 percent of Iranian territory is arable land for farming. The rest is mostly desert or mountains, and is mainly used for raising sheep and goats.

People and Places

Principal cities: Tehran is the capital and largest city of Iran. Other leading cities include Isfahan, Tabriz, and the holy city of Qom.

Population: Iran has 68,278,826 people (2003 estimates). By comparison, the United States has about 280 million people. In 2003, Iran had a population growth rate of 1.2 percent.

Life expectancy: Males: 68.8 years. Females: 71.6 years. Thirty-one percent of the population is younger than 14, showing the high birth rate in the country. Health standards have declined significantly since the Islamic Revolution, due mainly to poor economic planning and sanctions in response to Iranian policies concerning terrorist group support and nuclear weapons development.

Ethnic groups: Most of the population is Persian (an Aryan ethnic group, originating in Central Asia). The Persians are not Arabs. Persians make up 51 percent of the total, Azeris are 24 percent, and Gilaki and Mazandarani are 8 percent. The Kurds are 7 percent of the population. There are relatively few Arabs (3 percent of the total) and smaller groups of Lur, Baluch, and Turkmen.

The Word on the Street (and in the Mosque)

Language: Persian is spoken by the majority of the population. There are a number of Turkic speakers as well, and the Kurds speak Kurdish. The Lurs and Baluchis each speak their own language.

Religions: The official religion of Iraq is Shia Islam. Muslims make up 99 percent of the population. (Shiites are 95 percent, and Sunnis are 4 percent of the total.) Zoroastrian, Baha'i, Jewish, and Christian groups make up the rest.

Politics: The Lowdown

Governmental divisions: Iran is nominally a theocratic *republic*, with 28 provinces. Tehran is the capital.

What's It Mean?

A **republic** simply defines a type of governmental structure in which the head of state is not a monarch or hereditary ruler. In a republic, a central government has authority over a collection of states. The United States is a republic, as is Mexico and France. Canada is a confederation, in which the provinces have considerably more autonomy than American states. When comparing the Islamic Republic of Iran to the United States, the main difference is that most people think of a republic as a place where citizens have the right to vote and select their representatives to the central government.

Government structure: Iran is a republic style of government, with executive, legislative, and judicial branches. The Constitution of Iran, adopted in December 1979 (and revised in 1989), created an executive branch that featured a Supreme Leader (initially the Ayatollah Khomeini) who would serve for life. He is assisted by an Assembly of Experts (mullahs). The notion of a supreme leader is consistent with the tenets of Shia Islam. The Shiite faith features a strong focus on following a single leader. The leader is both a religious and secular guide for the faithful.

Persian Perspectives

The Islamic Republic of Iran dates its independence from April 1, 1979, when the Islamic Revolution was in its first stages.

The initial constitution envisioned a president elected to four-year terms and a prime minister. Later, in 1989, the prime minister's role was removed and power was concentrated in the presidency. (As we will see in Chapter 11, during the first years of the Islamic Revolution, the prime minister's role in the Islamic Republic was a difficult one in which to succeed.)

The legislative branch consists of a National Assembly, called the Majlis, which is elected by the Iranian people. It is made up of 290 members elected to 4-year terms. The legislature has maintained some degree of vitality even during the Islamic Revolution. Currently, certain members of the Majlis are leading the popular push for reform. We shall see how this tension is mounting in the course of this book. The voting age is 15.

The judiciary features a Supreme Court. In general, the Iranian criminal code is extremely strict and is based upon fundamental Shiite law.

Leadership: The Supreme Leader wields tremendous power. Starting with the Ayatollah Khomeini, this role has become the true power center in the Islamic Republic. However, the Majlis and the opposition party delegates within it are able to exert some influence on policy. Overall, the mullahs in the Assembly of Experts, along with the Leader, are in charge.

The opposition movements are limited and small. Outside of Iran, there are some opposition groups. However, given their distance from the country physically and socially, their ability to represent the Iranian people is limited.

Political parties: There are no legal political parties in Iran, but there are several influential political groups. They tend to toe the line rather than push diverse agendas, however. The major groups in the Majlis include the Assembly of the Followers of the Imam's Line, the Freethinkers' Front, the Islamic Iran Participation Front, the Moderation and Development Party, the Servants of Construction Party, and the Society of Self-sacrificing Devotees.

Money, Money

Economy: Iran's economy is dominated by the oil sector, and the country is a member of OPEC. Oil provides about 85 percent of Iranian foreign exchange earnings. Iran produces almost 3 million bpd. Carpets, wheat and rice, fruits and nuts, iron and steel, and chemicals make up the rest. The economy is basically centrally planned, and the oil companies are state-run. There is significant private-sector activity, particularly in services and small manufacturing. The gray economy functions throughout the country as well.

Currency: The official currency is called the rial (IRR). The official exchange rate in 2003 was about 1,740 IRR = 1 U.S.$; unofficially, the rate hovers nearer to 8,150 IRR = $1. In reality, the black-market rate is very different. The rial is worth much, much less relative to the dollar using that exchange market.

Gross domestic product (GDP): Iran's economy is in the low to medium tier of countries. Iran's GDP was $456 billion in 2002. Over half the population lives below the poverty line.

What's It Mean?

The **gross domestic product (GDP)** is the value of all goods and services produced domestically by a nation's economy.

Industries: Most Iranian industry revolves around petroleum and its peripheral industries. Iran also has chemicals, textiles, construction materials, and food and food-processing operations, based upon imports of raw materials for those industries. Over the past 50 years, Iran has privatized all major national industries. Most are governed by a specific ministry that oversees the management of each enterprise in that sector.

Military: The total size of the Iranian armed forces is about 500,000 men. Iran's regular forces consist of the ground forces, the navy, the air force, and the air defense command; they total about 350,000. The Iranian Revolutionary Guards Corps (IRGC) includes ground forces, the air force, the navy, and Qods (special operations). Also known as the Pasdaran, its members are considered the guardians of the Revolution and number about 120,000. The Iranian forces also include the Basij, which are essentially a mob of poorly trained militia that were used as a human wave in the Iran-Iraq War.

Although it has not been proven, current activity suggests that Iran is working on nuclear weapons.

The Least You Need to Know

♦ Iran is a major oil-producing country at the edge of the major oil-producing region of the world.

♦ Iran is a fundamentalist religious dictatorship, despite its claim to be a republic.

♦ Iraq is a complex combination of peoples (Persians, Arabs, and Kurds) and religious sects (Shia, Sunni, Baha'i, Zoroastrian); Persian people and Shia Islam dominate.

◆ Iran could be a wealthy country, but it struggles due to U.S. sanctions and bad economic policies by the Islamic clerics running the country.

◆ Iran is a leading sponsor of state terrorism and retains a relatively powerful military.

Part  2

Ancient Persia to Modern Iran: Long and Turbulent History

The region of modern Iran was home to ancient Persia, and some of the earliest civilizations on Earth started on the Iranian plateau. From the beginning of history to the so-called "end of history," Iran has played an important role in world affairs.

In these chapters, you trace the series of empires that have risen in this region, the coming of Islam, and the eventual persistence of the Persian culture into the twentieth century.

Chapter **4**

Ancient Persia: A Story of Three Cultures

In This Chapter

- ◆ Civilization emerges in Iran
- ◆ Pre-Persian cultures
- ◆ The Persian ethnic group arrives in Iran
- ◆ Persia gains prominence as a critical link on the east-west trade routes
- ◆ The Persian culture survives within other empires

Iran today is a mix of modern and ancient perspectives that have combined to create a unique contemporary world view, one that cannot be understood properly without understanding Iran's physical and cultural position. Iran is situated between the Middle East and Asia, on the edges of both, but a part of neither.

The story of the rise of what we now know as Persian culture in ancient Iran is one of a sequence of cultures that came to the region and endured, despite outside pressures from their neighbors. In this chapter, you will learn how that culture established itself.

A Separate People

Persians are distinct from the Arabs, Turks, and Central Asians around them. But the Persians came on the heels of two earlier cultures (the Elamites and Medes) who carved out their own places in human history. Building on their foundations, the Persians were able to surpass them both and create one of the greatest empires the world had yet seen. In so doing, they established the myth, if not the reality, of the modern Iranian nation.

The Land Beyond the Mountains

The Zagros Mountains separate the Iranian plain from the Mesopotamian lowlands to the west. These mountains establish the physical and cultural boundary between the Arab world and the Persian world. On the other side of the plain, mountains mark the border with Afghanistan, Pakistan, and the vastness of Central Asia. So depending on how you look at it, ancient Persia (now Iran) is a land apart, beyond the familiar for its neighbors.

The relative isolation of the central Iranian plain from the regions to the east and west meant that cultures could evolve relatively separate from the cultures that evolved around them. From this early accident of geography came the current view of the Persians as a unique culture, apart from their neighbors.

Of course, the culture that first entered the plain between the mountains came into contact with the societies surrounding it, and a vibrant trade in goods—and ideas—took hold.

Domestication and Pottery—Civilization Takes Hold

Thousands of years ago, the first agricultural activity emerged in Iran. Archaeological finds indicate that people were using domesticated sheep and goats in a place called Ali Kosh, in the southwestern part of modern-day Iran, around 8000 B.C.E.

While not as old as the civilizations that arose in Mesopotamia, the early agricultural settlements mark the start of civilization in Iran, and they are among the oldest in the world. Also around this time, clay bowls and figurines were being used in western Iran, around a site known as Ganj Dareh. Over the next several thousand years, these cultures and those that came after them combined to become a unique society, a society with beliefs and practices quite distinct from those of their neighbors.

> **Bet You Didn't Know**
>
> *Mesopotamia* is a Greek term meaning "land between the rivers." This region was the fertile lowland between and bordering the Tigris and Euphrates rivers, in what is now know as Iraq. Most scholars agree that civilization as we know it emerged in this region more than 10,000 years ago, and the first cities took hold here. Ancient Mesopotamia is even considered to be the possible location of the biblical Garden of Eden, further attesting to its primary place as the "Cradle of Civilization."

These settlements represented peoples from a variety of cultures, ethnic origins, and languages. These scattered and diverse groups in the Iranian plain gradually established more permanent settlements and eventually came together to create cities. Around 3900 B.C.E., the city of Sialk (near modern Kashan) was founded on the Iranian plateau. It was apparently the first significant city in that area.

Along the Far Shore—the Elamites Emerge on the Western Lowlands

As the scattered agricultural settlements on the Iranian plain began to consolidate, a relatively more advanced society began to emerge along the eastern border of Mesopotamia, to the west of the Iranian plain. These people were living on the eastern side of the great Tigris and Euphrates rivers, in an area now called Khuzestan. Remember this name—you will encounter it again in the course of this book.

In this relatively fertile and hospitable region, a stronger society eventually emerged. Its beginnings were tumultuous. The society was called Elam, and its inhabitants were centered in the cities of Susa and Anshan (Susa was in the lowlands west of the Zagros, and Anshan was nestled in the mountains). The Elamites came into contact with the cultural, economic, and military powers in Mesopotamia, including the Sumerians living around their cities, such as Ur and Lagash.

> **Bet You Didn't Know**
>
> Khuzestan is the region of Iran that borders central Iraq. Geographically, Khuzestan is contiguous with the central Iraqi lowland, not the central Iranian plain, and historically has been a buffer region between Iran and its neighbors. Saddam Hussein targeted Khuzestan when he invaded Iran in 1980. A large portion of Iran's oil lies under Khuzestan.

Elam.

Persian Perspectives

Susa was a site built on a mud-brick platform in the midst of a cluster of agricultural settlements. The central site was probably some sort of religious and commercial locus for this group of people. Numerous artifacts have been found in graves near the site. Susa was not a city in the same way that Ur was a city, with a defined wall. Still, over time, Susa became the center of a powerful society of its own.

Enter the Mesopotamians

The Sumerians and the Elamites traded, learned, and fought with each other. The Elamites, who came after the Sumerians, took up several Sumerian innovations, including writing. Ancient pottery uncovered in a place called Hajji Faruze resembles artifacts uncovered in Mesopotamia, which indicates trade in manufactured goods between the two cultures. By 4000 B.C.E., archaeology shows that the Elamites were using their own form of pictographic writing that appears to have been adopted from the Sumerian cuneiform.

The superior organization and technology of the Sumerian societies eventually overwhelmed the Elamites but, at the same time, contributed to their eventual success.

The Conquered Become the Conquerors

The Elamites were *hegemonized* by the Sumerians and the Akkadians of Mesopotamia during the period of 3000 to 2000 B.C.E. This period also marks the acquisition of Sumerian art, religion, building practices, and literature. The Elamites, like the Akkadians, took the best of the Sumerian culture and made it their own.

In borrowing from the *Akkadians* (who, in turn, were borrowing from the Sumerians), the Elamites began to make great strides in technological innovation and culture of their own. The Elamites also borrowed from the Central Asian–derived cultures that were taking shape in the highlands to their east.

As the Elamites became more advanced, they also became more powerful. Finally, by 2000 B.C.E., the Elamites were able to turn the tables and attack their masters. The Elamites succeeded in consolidating their strength enough to attack and sack the city of Ur. This action thwarted threats from these Mesopotamian cultures and gave the Elamites the breathing room to create a powerful civilization in their own right.

Over the next 15,000 years, the Elamites' power went through periods of ascent and decline. They seized Mesopotamian cities and then relinquished them. They fended off the Persians, the Medes, and the Scythians, to their east and north, but also traded with those cultures. They did the same with emerging Mesopotamian city-states such as Babylon. In fact, Susa became a target for conquest, much as Ur had been before it. In 1000 B.C.E., the famous Babylonian king, Nebuchadnezzar I, sacked Susa.

What's It Mean?

Hegemony is the cultural or political domination by one people over another.

Persian Perspectives

The Akkadians were a Semitic people, which means they were related to the Hebrews and the Arabs. They were the first people to unite the Mesopotamian city-states into a single cohesive empire around 2300 to 2100 B.C.E. They also pushed into the Medes' land to the north of the Elamites, weakening the Medeans. The most famous Akkadian king was Sargon I.

Persian Perspectives

The following succinctly summarizes Elamite history:

◆ The Elamites first emerged on the eastern edge of Mesopotamia around 4000 B.C.E. This was the first group to define a unique culture that was separate from yet influenced by the Middle Eastern and Central Asian cultures around it. This pattern defined Iranian culture from that point forward.

◆ First dominated by the Akkadians and Sumerians, the Elamites later conquered them in 2000 B.C.E.

◆ The Elamite dynasty ruled Mesopotamian lowlands off and on from 2000 to 600 B.C.E. The Elamites defeated the Kassites of Babylonia in 1157 B.C.E. to more firmly establish their reign.

◆ The Elamites finally succumbed to the powerful Assyrians in 646 B.C.E.

Over the centuries, though, the Elamites finally met their demise. They eventually succumbed to a new power coming out of Mesopotamia, from a new empire centered on their old rival, the powerful city-state of Babylon.

Enter the Aryans

Even as the Elamites began to stake their claim to the western edge of what is now Iran, other groups began to enter the Iranian plain from the east. These people were nomadic tribes from Central Asia. This was the first of many such incursions from Central Asia into Iran over the centuries.

> **Persian Perspectives**
>
> The Aryans originated in Central Asia, on the plains near the Caspian Sea. They spoke a language linguistically similar to Sanskrit. They spread south into modern Iran and Afghanistan and northern India. In fact, the names Iran and Iranian are derived from the word *Aryan*.

From 1500 to 800 B.C.E., these nomads were moving into the region to escape wars, find more open land, and find greener pastures (literally) for their horses. While several groups moved on the Iranian plain, two groups moved across the region to set up camp in and around the Zagros Mountains on the central plateau's western edge. Along with the Elamites, these two groups, the Medes and the Persians, defined early Iranian culture for the next several centuries. The Medes and Persians were ethnically part of the Aryan people.

The Medes were located more in the northwestern areas, and the Persians settled in the southwest, including the northern border of the Elamite lands. These groups began to found cities of their own and establish themselves in their new home.

First the Medes ...

While the Elamites were flourishing and (eventually) failing on the eastern edge of the Mesopotamian lowlands, the Medes were emerging as a power on the Iranian plateau. They came under pressure from the Assyrian Empire in northern Mesopotamia. By 900 B.C.E., the Assyrians were writing accounts that indicated the Medes and Persians were threats to their empire.

> **Persian Perspectives**
>
> The Assyrians were a highly militaristic society that ruled in northern Mesopotamia from 1200 to 612 B.C.E. They came up with such military innovations as the battering ram, iron swords, and body armor. Their key figures were Sargon II, who conquered Israel, and Ashurbanipal, who built the great library at Ninevah. The 30,000 tablets of Sumerian writings gathered there are a key source of information about ancient Mesopotamia and Iran.

The Medes Expand

The Medes also encountered the raiders from Anatolia (today's Turkey) but managed to fend off all invaders as they set up their own power base. The Medes started to push outward toward Mesopotamia after 800 B.C.E.

The Persians laid low in their southwestern settlements and were content to pay tribute to their Medes cousins. They watched as the Medes began to spread out, gaining power and prestige over the years. Finally, they conquered Ninevah in 612 B.C.E. This event signaled the end of the Assyrian kingdom (at least for a while) and ushered in a new era for the Aryan cultures on the Iranian plateau.

Protecting the Persians

The Medes' empire was centered on its capital city of Ecbatana (near modern-day Hamadan), in what is now Iran. The Medes' holdings stretched from the Black Sea in the north to the Persian Gulf (and so included the Persians themselves). The Medes encountered the Chaldeans in central Mesopotamia and raiders from Anatolia (modern Turkey), both of whom sapped the strength of the Medes' empire.

From the Persian perspective, the Medes were the ideal buffer; they gave the Persians the room they needed to set themselves up as a power of their own. With the Assyrians out of the way for a while and the Medes running interference against potential enemies from Mesopotamia and Anatolia, Persian society thrived and refined itself. The Medes were content to exact tribute from (but not sack and pillage) the Persians, further enabling them to grow stronger and more capable in their own right.

> **Persian Perspectives**
>
> The Medes were an Aryan group that settled in the Iranian plateau. They grew to power around 600 B.C.E. They were able to push back outside rivals, and they provided a buffer for the Persians to their south.

The Persians Take Center Stage

Only about 60 years after the Medes sacked Nineveh and established their own empire, the Persians emerged as a power of their own. Unhappy about the hefty tribute they'd been paying to the Medes, the Persians finally rebelled against their masters. Their decision to do so laid the foundations of the Persian Empire, an empire that eventually eclipsed all those that had come before it.

Cyrus Becomes Great

The Persians began their path to empire by means of a leader who came to be known as Cyrus the Great. Cyrus led an army of Persian peasants against the powerful Median king, Astyages. By 608 B.C.E., Cyrus had defeated Astyages and taken control of the Median kingdom. The Persian star was on the rise.

The Great Gets Greater

Alarmed by the Persians' rapid rise to power, the other regional powers united against what they perceived as the common enemy. The Babylonians, Egyptians, Lydians, and Spartans combined to attack the mounting Persian threat to their lands. But it was too late to turn back the Persian onslaught.

The Persian peasant army, led by Cyrus, continued to score impressive victory after victory and to expand its holdings across the region. By 546 B.C.E., the Persians had disposed of the Lydians, sacking their capital at Sardis and capturing their king, Croesus. Babylon fell next, in 539 B.C.E., in a surprisingly quick campaign.

Cyrus did not try to sweep away the cultures, local customs, and laws that he encountered. Instead, he indulged them, acquired what he could from them, and allowed them to continue on. This style of governance enabled the Persians to control a relatively large and far-flung empire.

Good and Evil on the Persian Plain

The Persians adopted a new religion and brought it with them as they moved across the region. Founded by the prophet Zoroaster, this new religion saw the world as the struggle between good and evil. The religion, which had a profound influence on Christianity, introduced a number of familiar modern religious concepts: duality of good and evil, mankind's free choice between the two alternatives, messianic redemption, resurrection, a final judgment, heaven (the word *paradise* comes from a Persian word), hell, and the concept of an almighty, kind, loving, and forgiving God.

Zoroastrians (Zoroaster's followers) believed salvation comes through good thoughts, good words, and good deeds. They believed in the final victory of the good, as manifested in the ultimate good deity, Ahurah Mazdah. The Zoroastrians saw other gods as allies in this struggle between good and evil. The Persians under Cyrus adopted Zoroastrianism, and it spread with them into Mesopotamia. It enjoyed a brief period of importance in the region.

When Cyrus and the Persians conquered Babylon, they encountered the Hebrews who were being held in captivity there. They also encountered their god, Yahweh. The Zoroastrian Persians saw Yahweh as a "good" god and an ally of Ahurah Mazdah. Cyrus liberated the Hebrews and let them return to their homelands in Israel. The Books of Ezra and Nehemiah narrate this portion of Hebrew history.

Cyrus as Hebrew Hero

Remember that the Persians allowed local cultures to co-exist with their own. This principle applied to the Hebrews whom the Persians encountered in Babylon. In fact, the Hebrews regarded Cyrus as a great king. In the Book of Isaiah, Cyrus is described as an instrument of the Lord because of his decision to take action to liberate the Hebrews.

Persian Perspectives

The Hebrews refer to Cyrus no fewer than 25 times throughout their scriptures. For example, in Book of Isaiah (45:1–2), Cyrus is described as the right hand of God:

> Thus sayeth the Lord to his anointed, to Cyrus, whose right hand I have holden, to subdue nations before him; and I will loose the loins of kings, to open before him the two leaved gates; and these gates shall not be shut.

This passage also refers to the account that the Persians conquered the heavily fortified Babylon relatively easily.

Cyrus's Ego Trip

For his part, Cyrus tended to regard himself as something akin to a perfect ruler. When he took Babylon, which was in many ways his crowning achievement, he had this inscription made:

> ... when I, well-disposed, entered Babylon, I established the seat of government in the royal palace amidst jubilation and rejoicing .... I did not allow any to terrorize the land of Sumer and Akkad. I kept in view the needs of Babylon and all its sanctuaries to promote their well-being. The citizens of Babylon ... I lifted their unbecoming yoke. Their dilapidated dwellings I restored. I put an end to their misfortunes ...

This inscription, preserved in the British Museum, is hailed as an example of Cyrus's administrative philosophy and proof of his "enlightened" reign.

Perhaps the best testament to Cyrus comes from the Book of Isaiah: "I will raise up Cyrus in my righteousness: I will make all his ways straight. He will rebuild my city and set my exiles free, but not for a price or reward, says the Lord Almighty." (Isaiah 45:13)

Cyrus himself died in battle in 530 B.C.E., fighting on the northern frontier of Iran. This event did not, as it turned out, signal the end of a great empire; instead, it opened the door to an even greater empire, that of Cyrus's eventual successor, Darius.

The Least You Need to Know

- Civilization may have started in Mesopotamia, but it emerged fairly soon afterward in what is now Iran.

- The cultures that emerged in the region set themselves up as distinct and apart from their neighbors to the east and west.

- The Persians followed in the footsteps of the Elamites and Medians before them.

- The Persians launched a great empire, starting in 550 B.C.E., led by Cyrus the Great.

- Cyrus's death in 530 B.C.E. signaled the start of an even greater empire that eclipsed all that had come before it.

Chapter 5

The Persian Empire: The Heritage of Modern Iran

In This Chapter

- The Persian Empire continues to grow in greatness
- The Greeks stop the westward spread
- Alexander the Great shows he is greater still
- Alexander's legacy reshapes the old empire
- The Parthians take up the crown

The Persian Empire is the predecessor of modern Iran in two key ways: It established the Persians as the dominant ethnic and cultural group in what is now Iran, and it defined the separate relationship of the Persians toward their neighbors on all sides. Even as the empire expanded, contracted, and then endured the invasion of Alexander, the Persian culture survived.

The Great Made Greater

In 530 B.C.E., Cyrus the Great was killed in battle when fighting nomadic raiders (the Massagatae) in what is now northern Iran. By the time of his death, he had built up the greatest empire the world had known and had established the Achaemenid dynasty. Cyrus's tomb was built in Pasargardae, the capital city at the time.

Cambyses Picks Up Where Cyrus Left Off

Upon his death, Cyrus's son, Cambyses, continued to expand the empire his father had so gloriously begun. With the conquest of Babylon and the rest of Mesopotamia, the only other great rival in the region was Egypt. Led by Cambyses, the Persians were able to conquer the Egyptian army of Psamtik III in 525 B.C.E. After Psamtik was defeated, Cambyses received the surrender of Lybia and Greek city-colonies on the North African coast.

> **Persian Perspectives**
>
> The Achaemenids took their name from Achaemenes, a revered warrior who is credited with training the Persians and who was an ancestor of Cyrus the Great. The dynasty of rulers that followed Achaemenes was given his name.

Stymied on the Edges of Egypt

Cambyses then set out with his army to take the Greek outpost at Siwa, farther out into the desert from the Nile region. The expedition was a colossal failure, with Cambyses losing 50,000 troops in the effort. He suffered further losses trying to take the former Egyptian ally kingdom of Meroe. Cambyses gathered up the rest of his army and headed back toward the Persian home base.

Civil War and the Rise of Darius

Cambyses was not as popular or powerful of a ruler as his father had been. After the conquest of Egypt and the subsequent setbacks in North Africa, Cambyses's administration was beset with intrigue and division. In 520 B.C.E., Cambyses died (some scholars say he was murdered) while passing through Syria on his way home to Persia. His brother Smerdis became the new king, but this move was not accepted by all the ruling elite of the empire. A brief civil war erupted around the question of succession. Finally, a general named Darius overthrew Smerdis and made himself the new king. Darius was related to the Achaemenid family line and had earned his rank as commander of the *Immortals*.

> **What's It Mean?**
>
> The **Immortals** were the cream of the Persian army. They were regarded as the finest fighters, and their reputation was fearsome.

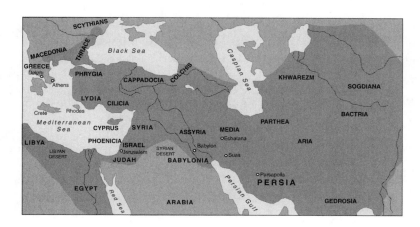

The Persian Empire, as it appeared in 500 B.C.E., eclipsed the empires that had come before it in size and sophistication. Its vastness was managed by excellent roads and a localized form of rule.

Darius the General Becomes Darius I

Darius spent the next five years fighting to maintain his claim to the throne. He eventually prevailed and was crowned Darius I. Darius went on to lead the Persians to even greater heights than they had already achieved.

Satrapies and Pony Express Help Keep It Together

As big as the Persian Empire became during the reigns of Cyrus and Cambyses, Darius continued to expand its borders. By the height of Darius's reign, the Persian Empire stretched from the eastern edge of northern India, across Mesopotamia, and around to the Nile Delta. To put it into perspective, traveling from one end of the empire to the other was the same as traveling from New York City to Los Angeles.

The Persian Empire was able to survive through a combination of advanced infrastructure and roads, and a localized system of government. The empire was divided into a number of satrapies, each run by a Satrap, or local governor. The satrapy system enabled central authority but allowed local autonomy for day-to-day decision-making. In addition, the localization of administration enabled the conquered peoples to maintain their customs and cultural traditions. This practice, in turn, gave some release to popular discontent within the empire.

The Persians built an excellent road system and utilized an ancient version of the Pony Express as a messenger system to link the far-flung

> **Bet You Didn't Know**
>
> The Greek chronicler Herodotus described the Persian messenger system under Darius in these words: "Nothing stops these couriers from covering their allotted stages in the quickest possible time—neither snow, rain, heat, nor darkness." Heard that before?

reaches of the empire to the center. In fact, one royal road was more than 1,500 miles long. Messengers, riding in relays, could cover the entire distance in less than 10 days, as compared to the months it would have taken without the road or an effective horse-relay system.

Darius also built up Persepolis, in what is now south-central Iran, as his seat of government. All satrapies owed annual payments to Persepolis. These payments were made in the spring (sort of an ancient tax time), during a large festival. The result of the roads, ports, and the canals, along with the messengers and the satrapies, was an enduring means of empire building and stability.

Bet You Didn't Know

As part of his empire building, Darius completed a canal that linked the Mediterranean Sea to the Red Sea, an early precursor to the Suez Canal. He actually took up the work started by an earlier Egyptian king, Necho II, in 610 B.C.E. Archaeologists in the nineteenth century came across a buried stone post, one of several that marked the course of the channel: "I am a Persian. I commanded to dig this canal from a river by name of Nile which flows in Egypt .... After this canal was dug, ships went from Egypt through this canal to Persia, thus as was my desire." This post was left by Darius's men in his name.

The stability brought with it other technological innovations. The Persians continued the practice of copying and improving on the best practices of the regimes they conquered. For example, the Persians sent a team of scribes to Egypt to write down the Egyptian legal code to bring it back to Persepolis. Eventually, that legal code became the basis of imperial law. The Persians also utilized irrigation and agricultural methods taken from the Mesopotamians and other empires they conquered. What is more, they brought these innovations from one satrapy to another and so spread knowledge and technology throughout the empire and to the cultures beyond.

To facilitate the spread of commerce, Darius instituted a coinage system, called the darik, that was accepted throughout the empire, and also a sophisticated banking system. (In fact, the word *check* is derived from the Persian language.) He also created a system of standard weights and measures that were used throughout the Empire. These dual innovations of universal currency and universal standards became cornerstones for expanded trade. Persia prospered, with wealth and ideas flowing back to Persepolis. The splendor and might of the Persians grew to unprecedented heights.

Darius I Becomes Darius the Great

Of course, Darius I was not content just to hold on to what others had made. He, too, wanted to be great, and he set out to make a name for himself, at the head of the vaunted Persian army. Starting in 520 B.C.E., for five years Darius pushed the frontiers of the empire eastward into northwestern India.

Continuing on, in 513 B.C.E. Darius assembled a huge army and navy to assault Scythia to his north. The campaign ended in failure when Darius was unable to get the Scythians into the open field before his supply lines were almost cut.

Darius continued his expansionist work. Also in 513 B.C.E., he crossed the *Bosporus* and set out on an expedition into southern Europe. He again relied on the Ionians for assistance, crossing over to Europe on a bridge of Ionian boats. Eventually, Darius pushed the Persian frontier all the way to the banks of the Danube.

Still, the huge size of the empire, unprecedented in the world at that time, meant that central control was often challenged and that the central government was continually trying to devise ways to manage its unruly satrapies. Already, revolts were suppressed in Babylonia and Egypt. In fact, Darius had executed the Egyptian satrap for his inability (or unwillingness) to keep order there.

What's It Mean?

The **Bosporus** is the narrow strait that separates Europe from Asia. The modern city of Istanbul (formerly Byzantium and then Constantinople), in Turkey, is located here.

Greek Tragedy

In 498 B.C.E., the Ionian colonies along the Greek coast rebelled against the Persians.

In 500 B.C.E., Aristagoras, the leader of the Ionian city-state of Miletus, led a revolt against the Persian garrison there. History tells us that Aristagoras actually had pushed the Persians to attack the neighboring kingdom of Naxos (to increase his own stature). The campaign failed, and, fearing for his position due to resultant Persian wrath, Aristagoras initiated a rebellion to save his own skin.

Bet You Didn't Know

The Ionian colonies were Greek settlements on islands of the Aegean Sea and the western coastline of Asia Minor. The region and the islands are still called by that name. The Persians had subdued these city-states and had utilized their resources in their military campaigns against the Scythians and in Europe.

The other Ionian cities and the island of Cyprus soon followed suit, and by 499 B.C.E., the local Persian satrap had lost control of the situation. In 496 B.C.E., the Greeks burned the imperial center of Sardes. The Ionian states and Cyprus were in full rebellion.

Knowing that Darius and the Persian army would come to get him, Aristagoras appealed for help from the great Greek city-states, including Athens and Sparta. Eretria and Athens sent an army and navy to support Aristagoras, but Sparta refused to help. Without sufficient military resources of their own, the Ionians were doomed. The Persians were able to retake Cyprus with the help of the Phoenicians and then to defeat the rebels in a pitched naval battle of Lade in 494 B.C.E. Aristagoras was killed, Miletus was razed, and the survivors were exiled to Mesopotamia. But this was not the end of Persians fighting Greeks.

The Persian Wars

The Persians, in the area anyway and looking for revenge, continued on to subdue the Greek peninsula, something they had been unable to do before. The campaign began well enough for the Persians, who succeeded in taking Thrace and reasserted their presence in Macedonia by 492 B.C.E. The Persians then moved south to punish Eretria and Athens for their role in supporting the Ionians. In 490 B.C.E., the Persians took Eretria but were stopped on the road to Athens, at a little place called Marathon.

Phidippides Runs Into History

In 490 B.C.E., the outnumbered Greeks defeated a much larger Persian force at the Battle of Marathon. The Greeks used superior tactics to overwhelm the Persians. At the end of the battle, the messenger, Phidippides, ran 26 miles back to Athens to spread the word of victory, collapsing when he reached the city. While the battle itself was relatively small in overall scale, it was essential in the development of Greece and Persia. The Persians were stopped for a time, and Athens was saved (again for a few more years). More important, the vaunted Persians had been defeated. The myth of invincibility was broken.

> **Persian Perspectives**
>
> When Darius died, he instructed that the following be inscribed on his tomb: "By the favor of the great God I believe in justice and abhor inequity. It is not my desire that the weak man should have wrong done to him by the mighty."

Darius the Great died in 486 B.C.E., but the fighting in Greece paused only for a brief respite. After

Xerxes, Darius's son and successor, dealt with rebellions in Egypt and Babylon (again), the Persians again swept down the Greek peninsula, in what came to be called the Second Persian War.

Xerxes Reaches the Highwater Mark

In this second invasion of the Greek peninsula, the Persians were able to overwhelm the Spartans at Thermopylae (despite legendary Spartan resistance) and sack Athens (by then deserted in the face of the advancing Persians). However, that was as far as Xerxes got. In 480 B.C.E., in the Bay of Salamis, the Greek navy under Themistocles won a stunning victory using the novel tactic of ramming the Persian triremes and setting them ablaze with "Greek fire."

The Athenians and Spartans had united to form the Hellenic League to counter the Persians. While it had not stopped the sacking of Athens, it did lead to a combined-forces victory over the Persians at Plataea. The Greeks followed that victory with another at Mycale, where the remainder of the Persian fleet was soundly beaten. The Persians retired back to Asia Minor.

The Greeks Keep Coming

Not satisfied to see the Persians leave the Greek homelands, the Greek city-states formed the Delian League, with the goal of driving the Persians out of all Greek colonies on Asia Minor.

The Persians continued to reel from the Greek pressure. The Greek fleet retook Cyprus and then Byzantium on the Bosporus. In 475 B.C.E., the Greeks took the city of Eion, and in 466 B.C.E. they defeated the Persian navy at the mouth of the Eurymedon River. The Persians were being forced back off Asia Minor and farther away from Greece year by year. Perhaps not surprisingly, Xerxes was assassinated the following year, and his son, Artaxerxes, took the crown in 465 B.C.E.

Bet You Didn't Know

Asia Minor is the name for the region between Europe and the mass of the Asia continent. Turkey now occupies this region.

The Greeks Finally Go Home

The Greeks then backed another rebellion in Egypt. The rebels, with Greek assistance, took the capital of Memphis in 460 B.C.E. Artaxerxes eventually retook Egypt by 454 B.C.E. After some more fighting between the Delian League and the Persians in Egypt and Cyprus, the fighting began to wind down between these two rivals. Finally, the Greco-Persian Wars ended with the Peace of Callias in 448 B.C.E.

The Persians Keep the Lid On

Athens and Sparta began to fight between each other in 431 B.C.E. Over the next 150 years, the Persians played both sides against each other, to maintain their own power around the edges of the Greek territories. With the Greeks out of the way, the Persians turned inward to deal with some internal squabbling.

In 424 B.C.E., Artaxerxes died, and two of his sons, Xerxes II and Sogdianos, were assassinated in succession. Ultimately, Artaxerxes's other son took the crown and assumed the title of Darius II. After his reign, which was marked by the successful maintenance of the balance of power between the Greeks and the Persians (Darius II backed the Spartans over Athens in 407 B.C.E. to keep the Athenians in check), the crown passed to his son, Artaxerxes II.

The Spartans, now empowered by their victory over the Athenians, sent an army to Ionia to support the colonies there against the Persians. Artaxerxes responded by supporting Sparta's rivals—Corinth, Athens, Argos, and Thebes—during the Corinthian War in 395 B.C.E. In 387 B.C.E., Artaxerxes mediated the "King's Peace" between Athens and Sparta, ending the wars between the two city-states. Upon his death in 359 B.C.E., Artaxerxes III emerged as the new king (after going through the now usual intrigues and assassinations).

Bet You Didn't Know

Phillip II was killed while attending a public ceremony. He was set upon by his own guards, in the presence of hundreds of his subjects. Many historians suspect that Alexander himself had Phillip killed, in order to assume the throne.

Then, just three years later, in 356 B.C.E., Alexander III (soon to be Alexander the Great) was born to Philip II of Macedon and his wife, Olympias. This event marked a critical date for the Persians, as we shall see in the next chapter.

Artaxerxes then reasserted Persian authority in Anatolia and took back Egypt. Upon Artaxerxes II's death in 336 B.C.E., his son Oarses took over. Then, at Oarses's death, Darius III took the Persian throne, and Alexander III became King of Macedonia at the same time (at the dramatic death of his father, Phillip II). These two leaders would find themselves on a collision course in short order.

Alexander Challenges the Persians

Alexander III started out to create an empire of his own. After assuming the Macedonian crown and consolidating his home base, Alexander set out after the biggest force in his way: the Persians under Darius III.

In 334 B.C.E., Alexander and his forces landed at Gallipoli and promptly defeated the Persian army in battle at the Granikos River. Darius III then led his army against Alexander, but found himself on the losing end again, at the Battle of Issus in 333 B.C.E.

Alexander's Macedonians, with their phalanx formation and long spears, consistently defeated the Persians. Alexander captured Gaza and Tyre along the Mediterranean coast, and then defeated Darius III again at the Battle of Gaugamela. From there, Alexander went on to Babylon in 332 B.C.E. Finally, five years later, in 327 B.C.E., Alexander razed Persepolis, the seat of the Persian Empire, signaling the end of organized resistance from that army.

> **Persian Perspectives**
>
> Oarses came to power when a eunuch named Bagoas poisoned Artaxerxes II, in an intrigue at the imperial court. Bagoas struck again, killing Oarses, which ultimately paved the way for Darius III to take the throne. Darius then had Bagoas killed—probably to make sure he was not number three!

Like the Persians before him, Alexander appreciated the best practices of the cultures he conquered. In the case of the Persians, he was a fan of Cyrus the Great and paid homage at his tomb. Also, while he executed many Persian leaders and allowed his troops to plunder, he married Roxana, a Persian noblewoman. Alexander was so taken with all things Persian that he ordered 10,000 of his men to marry Persian women in a mass ceremony.

After the failure at Babylon, Darius was killed by his own generals, and the way was open for Alexander to take Susa and Persepolis, which he did.

Luckily for the Persians, Alexander followed their policy of allowing local cultures to retain much of their own identity. Just as the Persians had indulged, studied, and synthesized the best of conquered cultures, the Macedonians followed the same tactic with the Persians. As a result, despite the failure of Persian arms, their science, commerce and culture, and administrative techniques survived.

Seleucis Takes Up the Crown from Alexander

In 323 B.C.E., Alexander died in Babylon. His empire, vast and unruly, was unable to survive without him. Alexander's empire was divided among some of his generals. The area that became Iran, which included Persia, was taken over by Seleucis. He established the Seluecid dynasty, which lasted until 64 B.C.E.

The Seleucids set up their capital at Ctesiphon, on the eastern bank of the Tigris River, in Mesopotamia. This move to a city more oriented toward the East, showed the Seleucid focus on Asia, as opposed to Mesopotamia, for this new empire.

Ctesiphon also symbolized the role the Greek/Macedonian elites played in controlling the empire, particularly in the decades immediately after Alexander's death. These elites tended to create their own enclaves in newly built cities, rather than assume positions in existing conquered cities. Gradually, however, the Persian administrators rose to positions of importance in the administrative apparatus.

However, this dynasty came under pressure from within and eventually succumbed to the Parthians, who established a new dynasty of their own. Still, the Parthians never achieved the heights that their predecessors gained.

The Least You Need to Know

- ◆ The Persian Empire was gathered by Cyrus the Great. He is regarded as the first and, in some ways, most admired Persian king.

- ◆ Darius continued Cyrus's work, expanding the empire still farther. He encouraged standards of weights, volume, and measures, as well as a banking system.

- ◆ The Persians' westward march stopped in the Greek Peninsula (even though they eventually managed to sack Athens).

- ◆ Alexander the Great disposed of the Persian military machine on his sweep through the region. Important for modern Iran, the culture, language, and traditions of the Empire were allowed to survive.

- ◆ Upon Alexander's death, the portion that included Persia was allotted to Seleucis, who founded the Seleucid Empire that eventually fell to pressures from within.

Chapter 6

The Path of the Prophet

In This Chapter

- A career like no other
- Muhammad and the Qur'an
- Trial, opposition, and triumph
- A new religion is born

The event that had the greatest impact on the development of the nation today known as Iran also had a determining influence on billions of non-Iranians throughout the course of history. It is regarded as the hinge-point of history by approximately one out of every five humans currently living on Earth. For many centuries, the event was misunderstood or, more often, completely ignored by many Western historians and social analysts. Yet, ignored or studied, misrepresented or properly understood, the implications of this event continue to reverberate throughout the world. The event in question was the mission of the Prophet Muhammad, which was conducted in Arabia nearly 14 centuries ago.

In this chapter, we focus on the mission of the Prophet himself. The reason for this is simple: No understanding of Iran is possible without a basic understanding of Islam, and no understanding of Islam is possible without a basic understanding of the life and mission of Muhammad.

Man on a Mission

Muhammad's mission, pursued over a period amounting to a little more than two decades, has to be ranked as one of the most influential undertakings in all of history. That may seem to be an extravagant statement, but consider that Muhammad's faith and leadership have affected billions of people over the centuries and continue to affect believers and unbelievers alike to this day.

Not long ago, Muhammad was selected as the single most influential human in human history by author Michael Hart in his book *The 100: A Ranking of the Most Influential Persons in History.* The purpose and outcome of his mission are essential to know for anyone interested in understanding social, political, and religious institutions in Iran or anywhere else in the Islamic world.

Whatever the reason, most Westerners know little about Muhammad, yet his life was unlike that of any other historical figure. This chapter gives you a very brief overview of Muhammad's extraordinary career. Let's begin by looking at *why* that career was unique.

A Career Like No Other

You should know from the start that Muhammad's was a career like no other. That career allowed one man to combine the roles of religious leader of the *Muslims*, soldier, emperor, and interpreter of the law—and to succeed at a truly astonishing level in all four roles. No other figure in history has been so successful on all four fronts.

To begin to get a sense of the real dimensions of Muhammad's historical role, we have to begin by thinking of a religious leader of primary importance—say, Jesus or Moses or the Buddha—and then imagining that this same religious leader somehow managed to establish himself as the most powerful political and military leader of a given era. We then have to think of that person exercising a supreme political power not unlike that of, say, the great Roman emperor Augustus Caesar; or William the Conqueror, who conquered what is now England; or Charlemagne, who established the Holy Roman Empire.

> **CAUTION**
>
> **Warning!**
>
> *Muslims* generally reject the notion of Muhammad as "founder" of *Islam* because they regard their religion as timeless and as having been founded by no human. And the idea is troublesome for another reason: It gives outsiders an unrealistic and very limited picture of what the man actually did.

To understand the scope of Muhammad's career, one has to take into account two remarkable facts about the man, his mission, and its long-term impact.

What's It Mean? _____

Islam translates as "submission." *Muslim* means "one who submits" and is an adherent to the teachings of Islam. The emphasis in Islam is on submission to the will of a single God, Allah. The "five pillars" of this faith are as follows:

1. Confession of faith in God and his prophet, Muhammad ("There is no God but God; Muhammad is the Prophet of God")
2. Ritual worship
3. Almsgiving
4. Fasting
5. Pilgrimmage

Fact #1: Muhammad's Message Was Written Down

Traditions concerning the life of Muhammad appear to be more accurately preserved than those of most (or perhaps all) of the great religious figures who preceded him. This means that Muhammad's actual decisions on legal and social questions, as well as his observations on the proper conduct of everyday life for the individual, are not only known, but are still observed today by believers. These traditions are regarded by Muslims as second in importance only to the word of Allah himself and are of primary importance in determining the meaning of the Islamic scriptures.

Bet You Didn't Know _____

Allah is the one God, according to Muslims. This God is the same God of Abraham in the Jewish faith, and God the Father in the Christian faith. The difference is that Muslims consider Abraham and Jesus as prophets. To the Muslims, Jesus is not the Son of God, but is instead a revered prophet who came before Muhammad. According to Muslims, Muhammad is the final prophet, carrying on the work begun by the prophets before him.

It's important to note here that Muslims *do not* worship Muhammad. They do, however, revere him as Allah's final prophet and celebrate him as the wisest and best possible human role model.

Not surprisingly, then, those traditions regarded as Muhammad's authentic recorded sayings and actions constitute not only examples for correct behavior, but very often binding legal precedents for the world's 1.1 billion Muslims. In practice, this means that, although Muhammad died 1,400 years ago, he remains the most important "jurist" of all for roughly one fifth of the world's population.

Think for a minute about what that means. During their lifetimes, Augustus Caesar and Charlemagne may well have had extraordinary influence on the legal and social systems of their lands. No one, however, is particularly interested in following their decrees today! With Muhammad, it is different.

Muhammad has played a unique moral and legal role in the daily lives of Muslims throughout the history of the faith, and he will continue to play that role as long as it is practiced. Imagine for a moment that you are holding a book that contains all of the authenticated, authoritative decisions of a great deliberative or judicial body—say, the U.S. Supreme Court. Now imagine a book of comparable legal authority, but one that takes the form of written accounts of the words and actions of a single man, a man regarded by over a billion people as having been divinely guided in his decisions. You'll then have some sense of the immense impact of the record of Muhammad's actions and instructions to his global community followers, collectively known as the *Sunnah*.

What's It Mean?

The **Sunnah** is the body of traditional Muslim law. It is based upon the teaching of Muhammad, and it is observed by orthodox Muslims. This should not be confused with the term *Sunni* which is the name given to majority of Muslims worldwide. While the terms are derived from the same root word, the designation of Sunni has a broader context and serves to define these Muslims as apart from the Shia Muslim sect.

The actual instructions of other major religious leaders in world history are often revered, and they are sometimes even observed, but they have rarely, if ever, guided whole societies or determined social and legal precedents in essentially the same way for centuries at a time. Authenticated traditions related to Muhammad's life, by contrast, continue to serve as consistent, practical guides in the daily resolution of important questions relating to religious rituals, community standards, and legal interpretation.

Fact #2: Muhammad Created a Community of Believers Whose Fundamental Ideas Are Basically Unchanged

The second remarkable thing about Muhammad's impact has to do with the group of people who followed his guidance. There is a powerful sense of community in the *ummah*, a sense of continuity of tradition and practice that has endured from

Muhammad's day to ours. And this is an extraordinary achievement. The overwhelming majority of today's Muslims eat, pray, and dress in accordance with interpretations of law that issue from Muhammad himself.

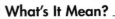

What's It Mean?

An **ummah** is a community of people. The term is used to refer to Muslims who share the common beliefs of Islam.

And that's not all. Despite the many undeniable divisions, military conflicts, and disagreements that may exist in the Muslim world, the movement of Muhammad nevertheless still inspires an extraordinary unity of purpose and outlook. Consider it this way: A Greek Orthodox Christian and an ecstatic, snake-handling Pentecostal Christian are unlikely to greet each other as brothers or to describe each other as members of the same nation. Yet this is exactly how Muslims from far-flung regions, embracing different philosophies or schools or thought, regard themselves: as members of a single nation. Although that nation has not, in political terms, expressed a single leadership ideal for many centuries, it nevertheless sustains a powerful and enduring set of social and cultural institutions.

Fourteen centuries later, the shared perspective and mutual support shown by Muslims to fellow Muslims as members of the ummah is an extraordinary legacy— a legacy that is attributable to the mission of Muhammad.

So Who Was He?

Muhammad was born in the south of Arabia sometime around the year 570 C.E. Both of his parents were members of the dominant Quraysh tribe. He was orphaned very soon after he was born, and in his youth (and for much of his life) he received the protection and support of his prominent uncle Abu Talib.

Warning!

Depiction of the likeness of the Prophet Muhammad is forbidden within Islam. In February 2003, editors at *Newsweek* magazine, apparently unaware of this restriction, reproduced an "undated Turkish manuscript" that featured an illustration depicting Muhammad and the Angel Gabriel. The graphic ran as part of a story exploring similarities and differences between Christian and Islamic religious scriptures. Condemnation of *Newsweek* from Muslims around the world was quick and intense, and the issue was pulled from some newsstands.

Tradition tells us that Muhammad was illiterate, which does not mean that he was ignorant (later events demonstrated that he was anything but ignorant). He simply was one of many people of the era who did not possess facility with the emerging Arabic notation system. At the age of 24, Muhammad married a significantly older woman, the widow Khadija. At the age of 40, Muslims believe, he was visited by the Angel Gabriel (Jibreel) and ordered to "recite" certain verses composed by Allah. This was the first portion of the *Qur'an,* or recitation, which Muslims believe to be the literal word of God. The various portions of this revelation, which form the central holy book of Islam, were completed over the balance of Muhammad's life.

What's It Mean? ——

The **Qur'an** is the collected sacred texts of Islam. Muslims believe that the Qur'an contains Allah's revelations to Muhammad.

There Is No Doubt in It

Non-Muslim historians and analysts usually acknowledge that Muhammad "sincerely believed" (or some such formulation) that the verses he attributed to a series of visions were directly received from the Almighty. What such a description of the revelation of the Qur'an does not accomplish, however, is to make clear the dramatic difference in tone and structure between the recorded sayings of Muhammad and the extraordinary language of the Qur'an itself.

Not surprisingly, a number of Westerners have concluded that the Qur'an is simply a poetic formulation of Muhammad's views, held by many to be "inspired" in the same way that Christian scriptures are held to have been "inspired." The view in the Muslim world is very different indeed.

The fundamental teachings of the Qur'an—whose author Muslims consider to be Allah, not Muhammad—are straightforward enough to be summarized concisely:

◆ There is one God, who will summon each individual human to an accounting for his or her deeds.

◆ Those who rejected the prophets sent by Allah in years past were punished severely.

◆ Muhammad is the final prophet of Allah.

◆ Starkly differing fates—paradise or hell—are waiting for those who accept or reject Muhammad's message.

Summaries of these apparently simple ideas, however, do absolutely no justice to the text. The basic themes are replayed and reexamined in hundreds of different ways and from hundreds of different narrative perspectives throughout the Qur'an, delivering the strange sensation that a message is both new and old, repeated for the hundredth time and discovered anew as though one were encountering the message for the first time. The lines are delivered with an extraordinary eloquence and power—a level of expressiveness and persuasive power that has moved such non-Muslims as Leo Tolstoy, Johann Wolfgang von Goethe, and George Bernard Shaw, to name just a few, to sing the work's praises.

Regardless of one's personal assessment of the Qur'an as a religious or literary document (and it has been called the greatest masterpiece of the Arabic language), one should understand that Muslims are not merely skeptical of claims that Muhammad "wrote" the Qur'an, but are openly hostile to such claims. It is a central tenet of the faith that the verses of the Qur'an reflect the viewpoint of no man, but of the one God.

It is unlikely, of course, that non-Muslims would accept such a claim at face value. Not surprisingly, debates over the nature of the authorship of the Qur'an, and its similarity to or difference from other religious scriptures, have been the order of the day for most of its approximately 14-century-long history.

Bet You Didn't Know _____

The influence of the Qur'an, like Muhammad's role as its chief advocate and defender, is beyond dispute. Here are a few representative passages:

> This Book, there is no doubt in it, is a guide to those who guard (against evil). Those who believe in the unseen and keep up prayer and spend out of what We have given them. And who believe in that which has been revealed to you and that which was revealed before you and they are sure of the hereafter. These are on a right course from their Lord and these it is that shall be successful. (2:2–5)

> Allah is the light of the heavens and the earth; a likeness of His light is as a niche in which is a lamp, the lamp is in a glass, (and) the glass is as it were a brightly shining star, lit from a blessed olive tree, neither eastern nor western, the oil whereof almost gives light though fire touch it not—light upon light— Allah guides to His light whom He pleases, and Allah sets forth parables for men, and Allah is cognizant of all things. (24:35)

> Say: He, Allah, is one. Allah is He on whom all depend. He begets not, nor is He begotten. And none is like Him. (112:1–4)

Trial and Triumph

For a few years, Muhammad shared his revelations only with his wife (who offered him unyielding emotional and financial support) and with other close family members. Sometime around the year 613, he began to preach publicly and to win both followers and the attention of the authorities. Sensing that his attacks on the region's traditional practices of pilgrimage and idol worship could be costly in both political and economic terms, the powerful leaders of his home city, Mecca, decided that he was a dangerous man.

A pattern of persecution emerged. In the year 622, Muhammad and his modest band of followers were forced to flee for a city now known as Medina, where the first Muslim community was founded. This migration out of Mecca and into a new community that hailed Muhammad as a leader marks the initiation of the Muslim era.

A staggering series of events played out after Muhammad established himself in Medina. In 624, he led an utterly improbable military campaign against the Qureysh at the Battle of Badr. Somehow—believers insist that it was by means of divine intervention—he won. Following a defeat at the Battle of Uhud, Muhammad consolidated his position and reinvigorated his community of believers at Medina. Then he stormed back to defeat the Meccans at the Battle of the Trench. In 630, he took control of Mecca without bloodshed and completed what must stand as the greatest personal ascent in human history. In 622, he was the well-connected but essentially powerless leader of a tiny religious fringe group; eight years later, he was the emperor of Arabia and had laid the foundation of a new religion that would sweep the globe.

By the time he died in 632, Muhammad had …

- Brought monotheism to a pagan land.

- Utterly defeated his enemies (turning many of them into converts to his faith).

- United the previously scattered Arab tribes.

- Delivered a literary and religious masterwork.

- Established the first constitution in history and laid the foundations for a body of law that endured for a millennium and a half.

Warning!

Muslims believe that Muhammad did not "create" Islam. Muslims consider Muhammad to be God's final prophet, but he did not invent the faith, which exists eternally and was revealed by Allah.

To put the matter briefly, he was a political and religious leader of a caliber that the world had not seen up to that point—and has not seen since.

His ummah, or community of believers, was established. But the task of following in the path of the prophet would prove more difficult, and more divisive, than his first generation of followers could have possibly imagined.

The Least You Need to Know

- Understanding Iran means understanding Islam, and understanding Islam means understanding Muhammad and his mission.

- Muhammad's teachings were recorded in the Qur'an.

- Muhammad did not have it easy, and endured severe trials and tribulations following his path.

- By the end of his lifetime, Muhammad had launched Islam, the newest of the major religions in the world.

- Muhammad's followers launched an empire that would stretch across the Middle East, across northern Africa, and into Europe.

Chapter 7

Shiism and the Path of Imam Hussain

In This Chapter

- ◆ The caliphs
- ◆ The tragedy at Karbala
- ◆ The rise of the Shia movement
- ◆ Opposition to the new school of belief

In this chapter, you learn about the origins and guiding principles of the Shia movement—the second-largest division of Islam, and the predominant form of Islam in Iran.

The Tragedy of Imam Hussein

Thirteen centuries ago, in what is today the city of Karbala in Iraq, a human tragedy of extraordinary dimensions played out. This gory episode marked the formal beginning of a long-standing rift within Islam—a rift that gave rise to the current Sunni/Shia division.

A Crime Against the Grandson of the Prophet

Even before the advent of Islam, military action was prohibited on the Arabian peninsula during the first four months of the lunar year, which were regarded as sacred. This tradition persisted under the rule of the Prophet Muhammad (although occasional exceptions were made in extraordinary situations involving the defense of the empire).

The observance of nonviolence during the sacred months was an important stabilizing factor. It was, therefore, a bloody breach of custom, religion, and humanity when a massive military assault was unleashed against Imam Hussein, the grandson of the late Prophet Muhammad himself, in 680 C.E.

Muslims believe this was a grave crime and an incalculable tragedy for the faith. Its implications are still being felt in the twenty-first century.

How Could It Have Happened?

To begin to understand the massive implications of that fateful assault upon Muhammad's grandson, one must understand that the Prophet Muhammad had managed, through diplomacy, personal charisma, and (believers maintain) divine guidance, to reconcile various warring factions in his empire. His successors—known as *caliphs*—were not as successful.

What's It Mean?

The English word *caliph* corresponds to the Arabic word *khalifa*, which is, in turn, a compression of the phrase "Khalifa Rasulil-lah," meaning "successor to the Messenger of God." The first four successors to the Prophet Muhammad as leader of his empire and the Islamic faith are known as the "rightly guided" caliphs. (The split between Shia and Sunni Muslims involves, among other things, a dispute about who should have been named as the first successor to the Prophet.)

To begin to understand what made the tragedy at Karbala possible—and what its implications for the development of Islam were in Iran and elsewhere—we must look briefly at each of the four men who followed Muhammad as caliphs, or leaders of the Islamic community.

Persia Joins the Fold

The title caliph was first bestowed upon Abu Bakr, the Prophet's father-in-law. Abu Bakr was the man elected to lead the people of Islam after the death of the Prophet; he was the first of four caliphs whose legitimacy is beyond dispute among modern-day Muslims. Abu Bakr consolidated Islam's authority and put down several rebellious tribal movements. He died of natural causes and was replaced by Umar, the second caliph.

Umar Takes Charge

Umar conducted a series of astonishingly successful military campaigns that extended the new empire's reach to Syria, Egypt, and Iraq. Most significant for our purposes, he also launched the initial conquest of Persia.

Umar's successful assault on the Sassanid dynasty in Persia led to the fall of Ctesiphon, the Sassanian capital, in 637. The Persians were dealt a series of military defeats, including the Battle of the Chains (so named because the Persians were chained together so they would not run, a practice that re-emerged in the Iran-Iraq War). Finally, in battle at Al-Qadisiyah (near Baghdad) in 636, the Sassanian general in charge of the troops was killed, and the leaderless Persian army capitulated to the Arab invaders. The collapse of organized Sassanian resistance brought about a trans-formation of the once-mighty Persian Empire from a highly class-conscious kingdom based on Zoroastrian religious rituals to the newest outpost of the egalitarian-minded Islamic state. Many of the lower strata of society (and even the lower rungs of the elite) quickly embraced the new religion.

Persia's entry to the Islamic fold was fateful indeed. Umar's conquest and conversion of this great—and non-Arab—land demonstrated once and for all that the message of Islam was not merely a matter of one man's rule and not merely an Arab move-ment, but a much larger phenomenon with cross-cultural—and eventually global—influence. Still one of the fastest-growing religions, Islam is practiced by just over one billion people from northern Africa through the Middle East, to Central Asia, west-ern China, and Indonesia. But there was soon to be dissension in the ranks of the faithful.

Enter Uthman

Although it was under Umar that Persia first became part of the extraordinary spiri-tual and temporal empire of Islam, the consolidation of Islamic rule in Persia was not concluded until the caliphate of Umar's successor, Uthman.

As the third caliph, Uthman continued the expansion of the empire into other lands: to Morocco in the west, to Afghanistan in the east, and to Armenia and Azerbaijan in the north. Persia was no longer the outpost of Islam, but was a central region of the empire.

Persian Perspectives

During Uthman's caliphate, a complete and authoritative written version of the (orally delivered) Qur'an was set down. In fact, Muslims consider only the Qur'an in its native Arabic to be the true word of God. The divinity of the word is lost, literally, in the translation to other languages.

The first half of Uthman's 12-year caliphate was a period of glowing success on the military, political, and religious fronts. The second six-year period, however, was marred by internal strife. Popular rebellions and factionalism severely undercut his authority, and Uthman was reluctant either to abdicate or to use military force against those Muslims who opposed him. He was slain by rebels in the year 656.

The Prophet's Son-in-Law Assumes Authority

Following a few days of uncertainty, Muhammad's son-in-law Hazrat Ali was eventually chosen to succeed Uthman. Although he considered himself the rightful heir to the caliphate after the death of his father-in-law, he was passed over and bided his time until this point in history, at which point he became the fourth caliph.

Ali is a crucial figure in Islamic history, but not because of his accomplishments in office. He was able to implement a number of important civil reforms, but he was ultimately overtaken by a tidal wave of civil strife and political opporession. During Ali's five-year period of leadership, it's safe to say that chaos had a field day. Trouble in Arabia led to the capital being moved to Iraq. Old conflicts resurfaced in various parts of the empire, and rebellion and power-grabs became the norm.

Never truly in control of his empire, Ali made an unfortunate compromise with a rebellious Islamic governor in Syria, Muawiya, after having led an inconclusive military campaign against him. Ali acknowledged the authority of Muawiya's rebel government. The fraying-away of the influence of the Prophet's companions could no longer be denied.

Later, Ali and Muawiya, as well as another leading figure of the day, Amr bin al-As, were targeted for assassination by a group known as the Kharijites. The plots against Ali and Muawiya failed; the one against the Prophet's son-in-law succeeded. Confusion and civil disorder within the empire grew to new dimensions.

The Rise of the Ummayads and Their Conflict with the Prophet's Family

After Ali died, he left two male descendants, Hasan and Hussain. Hasan abdicated the caliphate rather than ignite civil war with Muawiay, the rebellious governor of Syria who had given Ali so much trouble. Muawiya established a new dynastic line, the Ummayad dynasty.

Eventually, Hasan died. The other son of the previous caliph, Hussain, did not hold the title of caliph, but he was the ruler of a portion of the empire—the portion that we would today call Iran.

Many Muslims came to believe that the line of leadership inspired by the late Muawiya was irretrievably corrupt. One group, in particular, pinned its hopes for the future on the descendants of Ali. In fact, for some years members of this group had been calling themselves the followers, or *Shia*, of Hussain's late father, Ali.

What's It Mean?

Shia means "follower or partisan," and Shia Muslims are those who "follow" the authority of the Prophet's son-in-law, Ali, and his descendants.

The first rightful caliph, this group argued, was Ali. The second had been Hassan. Now the mantle fell to the younger son, Hussain.

Many Muslims prayed that Hussain was the man who would restore Islam to its rightful direction—the leader who would restore the proper moral direction to the (now vast) Islamic empire. At this stage, the Shia movement was primarily political. It was all about who would or would not lead the empire, but Shiism was not to be an exclusively political movement for long.

The Place of Sorrows

After the caliph Muawiya died, his son Yazid succeeded him as caliph.

Believers in a small town called Kufa—located in an Umayyad-controlled portion of the empire in present-day Iraq—called on Hussain to establish himself as the leader of their community. This overture constituted a serious challenge to the new Yazid regime and attracted its attention. Yazid ordered his governor, Ibn-e-Ziad, to deal with the problem. The new caliph faced a serious challenge of legitimacy because Hussain and other members of the second generation of the Prophet's family refused to acknowledge his authority.

Soon Ibn-e-Zian obtained intelligence that Hussain, his family, and a small group of followers were headed for Kufa. The governor's forces moved quickly, and a force of thousands of Umayyad soldiers surrounded the grandson of the Prophet and his small band of followers at the site of the present-day town of Karbala. Despite the sacred time of year, which prohibited military action, the governor's forces surrounded the tiny party. A standoff of some days followed.

Hussain refused to pay the required tribute to Yazid. The Umayyad eventually tortured and slaughtered all the members of Hussain's party. The head of the Prophet's grandson was severed from his body. His surviving family members were led in shame behind a procession that featured 72 heads set on the points of lances.

> **Bet You Didn't Know**
>
> The traumatic events at Karbala are commemorated with great grief and passion each year at Karbala in Iraq by Shia Muslims on the tenth day of the month of Muharram. The very name of the town means "place of sorrows."

The travesty unfolded during the lunar month of Muharram; the slaughter of Hussain's party is today known as Ashura. A shrine to the event stands in Karbala, the spot where it took place.

At this point in history, the Shia movement began to acquire a religious dimension.

A New Page in History

The Umayyad dynasty was consolidated, but at a terrible cost. Throughout the Muslim world, believers grieved at the loss. The partisans, or followers, of Ali were moved to particularly bitter tears.

> **Persian Perspectives**
>
> All Muslims—Sunni and Shia alike—regard Hussain as a martyr and revere his memory. Only Shia Muslims, however, regard him as the rightful successor to the Prophet Muhammad—the second Imam.

They are still grieving to this day. The Shia movement started out as a political dissent, but it gradually evolved into a potent and frequently oppressed alternate school of belief. That school has endured for centuries despite often bloody persecution.

The tragedy at Karbala was the turning point in the movement. More than 13 centuries after the fact, the massacre still inspires (quite genuine) howls of grief and rage—and the kind of tears that can perhaps be shed only by people who have known oppression.

Sunni and Shia

The major difference between Sunni (traditional) Muslims, who today make up 85 to 90 percent of all Muslims, and Shia (followers of Ali) Muslims (who make up 10 to 15 percent) has to do with the nature of the imam.

Shias regard Ali (the fourth caliph) as the first Imam, his eldest son Hasan as the second Imam, and his martyred son Hussain as the third Imam. Note the use of the capital *I!*

Sunni Muslims regard an imam (lowercase *i*) simply as a teacher and the person who leads community prayers. Shia Muslims, on the other hand, view the role of the imam in a very different way.

Shiites believe that the Prophet Muhammad explicitly appointed his son-in-law Ali as the sole spiritual and political authority in the community, that he did so under divine guidance, and that he therefore transmitted a kind of distinctive authority that has been compared with that of the apostolic succession in Christianity. (Today's Shia clerics in the most predominant section of the school act in the place of and on the authority of the last Imam.)

Shias and the Imamate

For Shia Muslims, the doctrine of an institution known as the Imamate takes on something like central importance within the faith. When you spell the word with a capital *I* you are not talking about the Sunni figure who leads prayers at a mosque, but instead about a figure within the Shia tradition who is recognized as the designated successor to the Prophet.

Other distinctive elements of Shia Islam include the following:

- ◆ Its conception of a continually revised and expanded set of Islamic practices

- ◆ Its emphasis on the religious importance of specific shrines and sites

- ◆ Its interpretation of divorce law (which tends to be somewhat more permissive toward the rights of women than Sunni interpretations)

- ◆ Its status and history as a (frequently repressed) minority sect

Over the centuries, there have been a number of movements within Shia Islam, including Twelver, or Ithna-Ashari, Shiism (the main branch of the school); the Isma'ilis; the Zaidis; and the Fatimids. As a general rule, Shiites adhere to the Jafri school of legal thought, in contrast to the Sunni preference for the Hanifa, Shafi, Hanibal, and Malik schools.

The Twelver movement within Shiism is the most numerous group. Twelvers regard the (disappeared) twelfth Imam as the only legitimate authority over human society; any political initiative that excludes or evades his influence is regarded as futile and unproductive. The Twelfth Imam is believed by the Twelver Shia to have disappeared from human view in 939 C.E. The Twelfth Imam is still present, just not in physical form. The Twelver Shia believe that the Twelfth Imam will reappear in physical form when Allah commands it to happen.

Other Movements Within Shia Islam

There have been and are other movements within the Shia school besides the Twelver. These include the following:

- ◆ **Zaydis** (prominent in Yemen). They are also called "Fivers" because they recognize only the first five Imams recognized by most Shias.

- ◆ **Ismailis** (prominent in Pakistan, Syria, India, and Yemen). They are also called "Seveners" because they recognize only the first seven Imams recognized by most Shias.

Shia Islam's Survival Instinct

Today followers of the Shia movement form numerical majorities in Iran and Iraq. In Iran, faced with decades of abuse under the rule of the Shah, an activist school took a new approach to the practice of Islam beginning in the 1970s—formulating a doctrine that Islam was meant to be not simply a means of personal spiritual purification, but a tool for the liberation of downtrodden people. The resonance of such an ideology with Shia history was powerful, and the result of the ideology was the first openly Islamic state of the twentieth century. It brought a theocratic model of government back to the forefront of the world of Islam and created a government willing to support the cause of Muslims perceived as enduring trial, persecution, and torment beyond the borders of Iran.

This survival instinct in part explains the hostility of the Shiite leadership in Iran, such as the Ayatollah Khomeini (you will learn about him in Chapter 11 on the Islamic Revolution). These clerics saw the Shah as just the latest in a long line of oppressors of their "true" faith—and, of course, they saw the United States as the supporter of that oppression.

However, before the United States came on the scene, the newly Islamic Persia had to deal with overthrowing its Arab rulers, absorbing the shocks of Mongol and

Central Asian invaders, and eventually balancing the actions of a pair of superpowers engaged in their own game of global dominance.

The Least You Need to Know

♦ The Shia school of Islam emerged in a violent schism in 661 C.E., when Muhammad's cousin (and son-in-law) and last of the "Rightly Guided Caliphs" was assassinated and a nonfamily member was made caliph.

♦ This massacre at Karbala is a defining element of the Shia faith; the event is a religious observance, and the place itself is a holy shrine.

♦ Shia Muslims place much more emphasis on individual leaders than do Sunni Muslims.

♦ Persian rulers adopted Shiism during the ensuing strife.

♦ Shia Muslims make up the majority of Muslims in Iran and Iraq, but they are only about 10 percent of all Muslims worldwide.

Chapter 8

From Arab Conquest to the Great Game— Persia Perseveres

In This Chapter

◆ Shia Islam, the second defining element of modern Iran, takes hold in Persia

◆ The Safavids (Persians) assert themselves after the shocks of the Mongol and Tamerlane

◆ Persian shahs encounter Russian and British power and influence in the nineteenth century

◆ Persian elites attempt to set up a constitutional monarchy

In 644 C.E., after resisting for 10 years, the Sasanians finally succumbed to the Arab armies under the Rightly Guided Caliph Umar at the Battle of Nahavand. The Sasanian king, Yazdegerd III, fled to Merv (far to the east in what is now Turkmenistan). The conquering Arab armies brought their new religion, Islam, with them. With the advent of Islam, Zoroastrianism was no longer supported officially, and most Persians adopted the new religion. Whether at the point of a sword or because of divine inspiration, Islam quickly took hold in the former Sasanid territories.

Flourishing Under the Arabs

By 750, the Abbasid Empire established Baghdad as its power base, and this move put Persia right in the thick of the action. Persian technicians and bureaucrats were able to flourish in the new state structure, and the flow of ideas and inventions went through Persia to and from Baghdad and the Far East.

The Arab Empire, at its greatest extent, around 850 C.E. It reached from India in the east to Spain in the west. Baghdad was its heart, and at the time was unparalleled in its sciences, art, and literature.

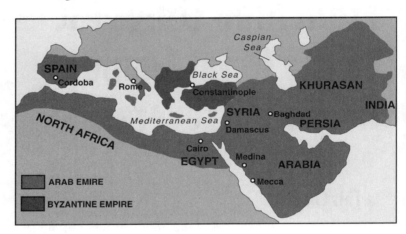

By 900, the "Golden Age of Baghdad" had reached its height. The Arab Empire had reached a grandeur and sophistication that rivaled the Byzantines and far eclipsed medieval Europe. Persia, too, benefited from the art, science, mathematics, and commerce that flourished during this era.

Persian Perspectives

The Samanids, who controlled the Khorasan region, created a unique blend of Persian and Islamic art and architecture. Their distinctive style is still present in eastern Iran and parts of Central Asia. The Tomb of the Samanids in Bukhara, located in modern Uzbekistan, is an excellent example of the synthesis of cultures and building styles.

Fraying at the Edges

At the same time, the military might of the Abbasids had begun to wane. At the farthest reaches of the Arab Empire, in Spain, northern Africa, and eastern Persia, independent kingdoms began to carve themselves out of the larger realm.

In eastern Persia, the Saffarids, Buyids, and Samanids seized local control. These smaller kingdoms still adhered to Islam, and their rulers continued to build on the cultural foundations provided by the

Abbasids. The Samanid capital at Nishapur in what is now eastern Iran became its own center of learning and commerce.

The Buwayhids Look East

At the same time that the Samanids were consolidating their power to the east, the Buwayhids rose up and moved westward toward Mesopotamia. They seized Baghdad in 945. Although the Abbasid dynasty lasted for another 300 years, the power of the Abbassid caliphs was reduced to a purely spiritual role as the leaders of Sunni Islam. The Buwayhids maintained the caliphs in this state, like the Mamluks had before them. Political, commercial, and military power in the Abbasid Empire was managed by the Buwayhids and the groups that came after them rather than the caliph.

Under Buwayhid authority, the arts and sciences continued to flourish in Baghdad. Ibn Sina (called "Avicenna" in Latin) was a leading physician and philosopher. His books and teachings were translated into Latin and became seminal works for European medical science. Abu Ja'far Muhammed ibn Musa al-Khawarizmi is another example of the blending of East and West that developed under Buwayhid oversight, within the embrace of the Abbassid Empire. Al-Khawarizmi discovered some of the fundamentals of algebra and introduced the Hindu (Eastern) concept of the zero to Middle Eastern and Western mathematicians.

> **Persian Perspectives**
>
> The Mamluks were Turkic warrior-slaves who had taken control of the empire from within. Originally brought to Baghdad as guards, these slaves became increasingly involved in the daily matters of the empire. Finally, the Mamluks were able to rule from behind the throne, directing the actions of the caliph but not appearing to be in control.

> **Bet You Didn't Know**
>
> Al-Khawarizmi wrote a mathematics text called "Kitab al-jabr w'al muqabalah" ("Restoration and Balancing"). The text introduces several algebraic concepts. The title itself, "al-jabr," gives us the modern word *al-gebra*.

Shiism Spreads into Persia

The Buwayhid rulers adopted Shiism, and it seems likely that their subjects also adopted the new school. Of course, the caliph in Baghdad was the leader of the Sunnis, but the Buwayhids did not interfere with his role in that regard.

In 1040, another Turkic group from Central Asia, called the Seljuks, emerged to challenge the Buwayhid control of Baghdad. In 1055, the Seljuks seized Baghdad. While not Arab, they were welcomed by the Arabs there because they were Sunnis instead of the Shiite Buwayhids. Still, like the Buwayhids before them, the Seljuks retained political and economic control of the Abbasid Empire, leaving the caliphs to run the moral and spiritual affairs of the empire.

Mongols Crash the Party

By 1221, the Mongols had made their way to Persia and had taken control of the region. Over the next 30 years, they proceeded to first sack and destroy the major cities in Persia (and beyond), and then foster commerce and cultural exchange between the Eastern and Central Asia regions and their Middle Eastern and Western holdings.

The Mongols divided their vast holdings into more manageable units, and the Ilkhanid dynasty was given control of what was to become Iran. In 1258, the Ilkhanids finally closed the book on the Abbasid Empire. They formally dissolved the empire (in fact, it was gone already) and set up a capital in Tabriz, in what is now northwestern Iran. They ruled the region until 1353, when the Jalayirids took up the mantle of authority. The Jalayirids were also a Mongol dynasty, and they moved into the power vacuum that was being created by the Ilkhanids' decline when the last Ilkhanid Khan died. They ruled over northwestern Iran and Mesopotamia until they were swept away by one who was as fierce as the Mongols themselves had been.

What's It Mean?

An **atabeg** was a regent who served a local prince under the Mongol system of administration. The atabeg usually controlled a city that then was controlled by a prince and, ultimately, the Khan. The atabegs had great local autonomy.

The Lame Newcomer

Around this time, a Turkic *atabeg* named Timur came from Central Asia and swept westward across Iran into Mesopotamia. Timur was lame in one leg and was known as Timur the Lame or Tamerlane.

Tamerlane's armies performed a repeat of the Mongol plunder and pillage, and a repeat of the subsequent fostering of East-West commerce and ideas. Tamerlane used Samarkand as his capital, way off to the east in what is now Uzbekistan. The Mesopotamian and Iranian lands quickly reasserted their local autonomy as Tamerlane's empire fell apart at the time of his death.

More Turco-Mongol Dynasties in Persia

The Timurids (so called because they were the local rulers designated by Tamerlane who was also known as "Timur the Lame") ruled Iran after the death of Tamerlane in 1405. They ruled first from Tamerlane's capital of Samarkand, and later they shifted westward to Herat in modern Afghanistan. Despite this attention toward Persian lands, the Timurids eventually were pushed out by other Turko-Mongol dynasties.

First came the Qara Quyunlu (1406–1469), ruling from the old Mongol capital in Tabriz. They were supplanted by the Aq Quyunlu dynasty (1469–1508). Continuing the tradition of East-West trade, the Aq Quyunlu even made trade contact with Venice, in far-off Italy. Venetian accounts of the time mention a large and beautiful Aq Quyunlu palace in Tabriz.

> **Persian Perspectives**
>
> The term *Qara Quyunlu* is Turkic for "black sheep"; *Aq Quyunlu* means "white sheep." Why these dynasties took these names is not clear.

The Safavids Take Charge

In the early sixteenth century, the Safavids consolidated these smaller regional dynasties. This dynasty became the final and lasting legacy of the Turko-Mongol rule in Persia, although they gradually assumed the name and mantle of "Persian" themselves. The Safavid Empire can be considered the starting point for modern Iran. The current borders, Persian culture and language, and Shia Islam were all solidified into the Iranian edifice during this era (1501–1795).

Starting in what is now Azerbaijan, the Safavids wrested control of Tabriz from the Ab Quyunlu in 1501. That same year, their leader, Safavi, was crowned Shah, starting the Safavid dynasty that lasted until World War I. The Shah also declared Shia Islam to be the official religion of the empire and "encouraged" conversion to the Shia faith by evangelization and threats. While Shia Islam had been practiced in Persian lands as far back as the Buwayhid times, this was the first official declaration of its primacy in that region.

> **Persian Perspectives**
>
> The Safavids were named for their first leader, Ismail Safavi. His followers were called the Qizilbash, or "Red Heads," for the red caps they sported.

The Shia Concept of Authority

Safavi anointed himself as Shah and was revered as the "perfect guide" and manifestation of the godhead on the earth. He was considered the temporal and spiritual leader of his empire. In this context, his subjects did not differentiate among the types of authority Safavi embodied. Religious, administrative, political—it was all one. This concept has survived even to this day, as it is embodied by the current Iranian leadership.

The Ottomans Contain Safavid Expansion

During the next century, the Safavids found themselves fighting the newly emerged Ottomans for control of Anatolia, Mesopotamia, and their northwestern Iranian homeland itself. The Ottomans even seized Tabriz, forcing the Safavids to relocate their capital to Qazyin in 1555. Eventually, the Safavids managed to push the Ottomans out of Iran proper, and the modern Iran-Iraq border became the dividing line between two coalescing camps: the Shia Safavids and the Sunni Ottomans. In 1533, the Ottomans forced a treaty that specified the northern borders in Azerbaijan, which have remained constant almost to the modern era.

> **Persian Perspectives**
>
> The Safavids coveted southern Iraq because the Shia holy cities of Karbala and An Najaf are located there. They were able to seize the region in the early seventeenth century, only to be finally expelled by the Ottomans in 1638. The ongoing fighting set the tone of conflict between Shia and Sunni that has persisted in that region to this day.

At the same time, marauding Uzbek tribes threatened the northeastern frontiers of the empire and effectively limited Safavid expansion north of the Oxus River (now called the Aru Daryia). With the borders along the Mespotamia, Anatolia, and Caucasia set by the Ottomans, and the border along the northeast set by the Uzbeks, the boundaries of the modern Iranian state were starting to take shape.

Persian Influences Take Hold

Meanwhile, the Safavids continued to enjoy a cultural flowering, as the best of the Qara Quyunlu, Ab Quyunlu, and Timurid cultures (which also incorporated Persian influences) were blended to create a distinctive Safavid presence. Through the early seventeenth century, the Safavids (most notably under Shah Abbas) continued to improve their commerce infrastructure, building roads, bridges, and caravanseries (trading complexes) to improve the flow of goods across the empire. At the same time, the capital was shifted westward again to Isfahan in southern Iran, centering the Safavids in the Iranian region. Persian became the dominant language and cultural base, and it remained so into the modern Iranian state.

So at the same time the Pilgrims were erecting crude wooden huts and trading for corn with the Native Americans at Plymouth Plantation in what would become

Massachusetts, the Safavids were constructing the magnificent Royal Square and Royal Mosque ensemble in Isfahan and trading for silk, textiles, and gold with Europe on one side and China on the other.

The Qajars Take Up Where the Safavids Leave Off

By the mid-eighteenth century, Safavid power was beginning to wane. Drained by fighting with the Ottomans and Uzbeks, and beset by internal rivalries, the last Safavid Shah finally was overthrown by invading Afghan tribes in 1735. A period of internal squabbling, followed by a loose reunification under Karim Khan, lasted until 1779, when Khan died.

At Khan's death, infighting again broke out among the tribes inside the old Safavid empire. The Qajar tribe, led by Agha Mohammad Qajar, eventually emerged victorious, and Agha made himself Shah and launched the Qajar dynasty. This dynasty ruled Persia until 1925, when it gave way to the Pahlavi dynasty. The Qajar Shahs continued the concept of the Shah as the "shadow of the godhead" on the earth, and they retained absolute authority over their administrators. However, the relationships with the tribes were less stable. The Shahs ruled but did not totally control the various tribal factions. Also, the army consisted of levies from each tribe. It was not a national army loyal to the Shah, but rather a collection of tribal warriors. The Persian army in the nineteenth century was formidable, but it was no match for the organized European armies of Britain and Russia.

The European Challenge

As the Qajars were hemmed in to the west and north by the Ottomans, they continued to look eastward, into Afghanistan and beyond for power and influence. However, as the nineteenth century began, the Qajars found their designs in Central Asia superceded by the designs of two new powers: the Russians to the north and the British (in India) to the east.

During the latter part of the eighteenth century and into the early part of the nineteenth, Tsarist Russia began to press south into the Caucasus region. Over a 15-year period, the Qajars were soundly defeated by the Tsar's armies. After these two lopsided defeats at the hands of the Russians, the treaties of Gulistan (1812) and Turmanchay (1828) ceded all of its lands in the Caucasus. Later in the nineteenth century, Russia forced the Qajars to cede any claims to their former lands in Central Asia.

As part of their uneasy relationship with the Russians, the Shah had agreed to allow the Russians to set up consulates anywhere in his empire they wanted. With a consulate in place, the Russians could set up commercial and military relationships that would further align Persia with Russia—and not with rival Britain.

The Crimean War: Opportunity Lost?

The Russians and British collided (some would say inevitably) over the Crimean portions of the faltering Ottoman Empire in 1853. War erupted late that year and eventually ended with a British victory of arms. However, the Russians were hopeful that the Persians would support them against the British. First, the Russians wanted to march across Persia and Afghanistan to threaten British India. However, the Russian high command realized that the likelihood of a successful march across these two rival states—neither of which had any real love for the Russians anyway—was unlikely. The Russians instead pushed for the Persians to make mischief for the British by pressing into Afghanistan.

The Lure of Herat

The Afghan city of Herat beckoned the Shah. The Qajars had coveted the strategic city, located in the western region of Afghanistan, as a new eastern extension of their empire. The city had been part of the old Safavid Empire but had been lost during the period of internal strife before the Qajar ascendancy. In 1839, the Persians had tried to take the city but had been convinced to stop by a British naval and army expeditionary force that was dispatched to the Persian Gulf. Since that failed attempt, the Persians had been stymied by British support for the Afghan ruler Dost Mohammed, who saw Herat as part of his domain.

With the British otherwise occupied fighting the Russians, and with Russian prompting, the Shah finally moved against Herat in October 1856. It is unclear what prompted the move in the end, whether it was fear of the Russians or a perceived weakness of the British. Either way, the Persian army was in Herat at last. The British responded immediately. They were concerned that if Herat became part of the Persian holdings, the Russians would set up a consulate there and increase their threat to British India. Following their previous tactic, the British sent a squadron to the Persian Gulf and proceeded to bombard (and occupy) the Persian coastal city of Bushire. After doing the same in two other Persian Gulf cities, the Shah finally relented. The Persians pulled out of Herat, and the Shah renounced all claims to the city in the Treaty of Paris, signed with Britain in 1857.

The Shahs Watch the Great Game

The Russian Empire was expanding across Siberia and slowly progressing southward. The southern sphere of influence for Tsarist Russia steadily moved closer to the northern fringes of British India.

While the Russians were moving south in Central Asia, the British were consolidating their grip on the Indian subcontinent. Through the middle of the nineteenth century, the British crown tightened its control over India, taking over for the British East India Company in 1858 after suppressing the Indian Mutiny. The British East India Company had dominated most of India for 200 years, but with the increased threat from Russia, the crown assumed complete control over administration of the colony.

The British recognized the Russian threat and began to push northward, co-opting India nobles in the north and currying favor with the Afghan rulers to the northwest as they went. The *Great Game* was underway.

What's It Mean?

The **Great Game** is the term for the regional "cold war" between the British and Russian empires, from the end of the Crimean War to the outbreak of World War I, when Britain and Russia were allied against Germany. The Game was played out in Central Asia and focused on both Russian expansion southward toward India and British maneuvering to thwart that expansion and preserve their grip on the Indian subcontinent.

For most of the Great Game, Persia was a side show, albeit an important one. Both sides wanted to bolster their positions by bringing Persia in on their side. The key was Afghanistan. Both the Russians and the British saw Afghanistan as the route from Russia into India. Herat was considered a strategic point on that potential invasion route. One of the critical elements in the Great Game was the British effort to subdue Afghanistan and maintain it as a buffer against the Russians. The Persians were seen as a potential counterweight to Russian pressure on Afghanistan. So once Persian designs on Afghanistan were halted by the Treaty of Paris, the British began to curry the favor of the Shah. Through bribery, negotiation, and veiled threat, the British steadily made economic inroads into the Qajar regime. In return for British protection against Russian encroachment, the Shah gave favorable concessions to British commercial and financial interests.

The Western Powers Alienate the Clergy—Act One

During the late nineteenth century, the corrupt business dealing between imperial Britain and Naser ad Din Shah outraged the clerics. For example, a railroad concession was granted on suspicious terms to the British, and a tobacco concession also was granted, each case creating outrage among the Qajar religious and political elites. The Shia clerics issued a fatwa (religious order) against smoking, which effectively forced the Shah to cancel the concession. Popular discontent driven by the Shia clerics was playing a role in Persian internal and foreign policy. This trend continued until 1980. The targets of clerical animosity were the Shah and the British.

The Shah Loses His Grip

Growing discontent with the Western leanings of the ruling class, bureaucratic corruption, and oppression fomented increasingly open rebellion to the regime. Eventually, tax collections failed and the Shah's ability to finance his power base in the government was severely limited. The unrest culminated in Naser ad Din Shah's assassination in 1896.

Unfortunately, Nasar ad Din's son, Muzaffar, was no better than his father. Continued corruption and financial crises, along with continued favoritism in granting concessions to the Europeans in return for bribes, led the Persian elites to launch the Constitutional Revolution in 1906. By the fall of that year, succumbing to popular pressure, Muzaffar ad Din Shah authorized the creation of a constitutional government. In October 1906, the Majlis was assembled and the new constitution was signed by the Shah on December 30, 1906. Perhaps overcome by the events unfolding around him, the Shah died just a week later.

The Short-Lived Constitutional Monarchy

His successor, Mohammad Ali Shah, set out to undo the gains of the constitutional monarchists and reassert the absolute authority of the Shahs. In June 1908, Mohammad Ali Shah called out the Persian Cossacks to close the Majlis building. Resistance sprang up across the country, and the Shah was deposed and forced into exile (starting a familiar pattern) in July 1909. However, the constitutional monarchy did not survive much longer.

The British and the Russians, taking advantage of the civil war and weakness inside Persia, effectively split the country into two zones of influence. As World War I began, despite their efforts to remain neutral, the British and the Russians fought the

Ottoman Turks in Persia, with the British and the Russians emerging victorious. A provisional, pro-German government was formed but failed to rally much support, and it quickly collapsed at the end of the war.

With the Russians now focused on their own revolution, the British were left to extend their domination over Persia. They attempted to get the Persian prime minister, Vosuq od Dowleh, to ratify the Anglo-Persian Agreement of 1919, giving Britain effective control over the country. The Majlis, discovering the large bribes the British were offering Dowleh, refused to ratify the treaty. However, the British soon found a willing ally in a Persian Cossacks Brigade officer, Reza Khan, who seized power in a coup in February 1921. Reza Khan eventually launched the Pahlevi dynasty that produced the last Iranian Shah.

The Least You Need to Know

- Persian culture managed to survive the Arab conquest and the subsequent invasions by the Mongols and Tamerlane.

- The Safavids laid the groundwork for the modern Iranian state. Modern borders, Persian language and culture, and Shia Islam all were firmly established during this dynasty.

- The Qajar dynasty experienced the emergence of British interest in Persia, starting with the Great Game and extending into the post–World War I era and beyond.

- The power of the Shiite clerics to rouse popular opinion against the Shahs (largely for the Shahs' corrupt dealings with European powers) was also established.

- The first constitutional "experiment" failed in Persia with the coup by Reza Khan.

9

Iran Between the World Wars: Oil and Empire

In This Chapter

- ◆ As the Great Game winds down, Persia takes on a new importance as an oil source to the British

- ◆ The Persian elites try to limit the absolute power of the Shahs

- ◆ Persia, the British, and the Russians jockey for power in the decades leading up to World War II

- ◆ The British and Soviets invade Iran at the start of World War II and make Reza Muhammad Pahlevi the new Shah

In this chapter, we look at the consolidation of British control over Persia and the emergence of oil into the schemes of empire.

In the Bulldog's Grip: British Attention Shifts to Persia

During the Great Game era (from the 1890s to the onset of World War I), Persia and its rulers attempted to navigate a path between the British and the Russians. Generally, the Persians feared the Russians more than the British, but they sometimes opposed the British if it suited their own ends. (You'll recall, for instance, that the Persians coveted the city of Herat in western Afghanistan and adjusted their foreign policy to suit that objective.)

The British, for their part, tended to view Persia as a means to an end. It was part of the connection between London and India, and it was through this lens that British policymakers typically saw their relations with Persia. However, as the Great Game concluded and World War I loomed, the British soon learned to look at Persia in a new and pragmatic way. The British view of Persia changed because of one thing only: oil.

During the first decade of the twentieth century, the British gained a new appreciation for the oil that had been discovered in Persia in the latter part of the nineteenth century. This shift in viewpoint did not take place by chance. Up to that point, the Royal Navy had used coal to power its fleet. As the new technology of internal combustion engines reached the navy by means of factories of England, however, oil became militarily and strategically important to the British Empire—and, ultimately, to the entire industrialized world.

Bet You Didn't Know

Oil became a strategically important commodity for the West beginning in 1911, when the first Lord of the Admiralty—a bright young gentleman by the name of Winston Churchill—made the decision to switch the ships of the Royal Navy from coal-powered engines to oil-powered engines. Almost overnight, the British government's interest in oil in general, and the Anglo-Persian Oil Company in particular, increased significantly.

Suddenly, Persia took on special importance in British strategic planning for the region. It was no longer an abstract region on a map, a connecting point for an imperial power to traverse on its way to India. Persia became a focal point for British imperial interests.

Before long, the Russians followed the British example. They, too, realized the industrial and strategic importance of Persian oil reserves.

Oil Makes Its Mark

All of this interest in oil—an interest that drives geopolitical debates today—began with an entrepreneur named William Knox D'Arcy, a wealthy Englishman. D'Arcy got the idea to drill for oil in the Middle East.

Oil had been taken from *seeps* since ancient times. But in 1901, D'Arcy got the idea that there was oil under the ground in Persia. On May 28, 1901, he gained a 60-year concession with Mozaffarol din Shah that gave him access to southern Persia. D'Arcy also agreed to build a refinery on Abadan Island, at the head of the Persian Gulf. D'Arcy's concessions were limited to southern Persia, thanks to the emerging dividing line that was being drawn across Iran by the British and the Russians.

At the same time D'Arcy was poking around in the sand, the two superpowers were negotiating what eventually came to be known as the Anglo-Russian Agreement. This agreement frankly divided Persia into two spheres of influence—an arrangement that brought global powers into the business of exploiting Persian resources. The agreement set into motion a fateful sequence of events whose repercussions have been felt ever since.

What's It Mean?

Seeps are natural emissions of oil from underground sources. Oil has been gathered from such locations for much of human history.

Persian Perspectives

The Anglo-Russian Agreement, signed in 1907, effectively partitioned Persia between London and Moscow. It locked out the Germans (who were beginning an attempt to establish their own influence in the region). However, the agreement did not end the jockeying for position and influence with the various tribal leaders in the region.

Central Government? What Central Government?

Not surprisingly, perhaps, the Shah did not play a leading role in the negotiations surrounding the first exploitation of Persia's most important natural resource. (Later, he made his presence felt.) D'Arcy's deal was instead negotiated with Sheikh Khazal, who ruled the lands in southern Persia where the refinery was to be located. The central government played no role in the negotiations.

After seven long years, D'Arcy finally struck oil at Masjid-e Soleiman. With his concessions and his gusher, D'Arcy established the Anglo-Persian Oil Company in 1909.

D'Arcy Avoids a Cash-Flow Crisis

D'Arcy's problem was that he and his backers had run low on funds by the time he finally found the black stuff. To keep the company alive, they had brought in the Burmah Oil Company as an investor. As a result, when the Anglo-Persian Oil Company was formed in 1909, Burmah Oil owned 97 percent of the shares of the new company. The new company negotiated favorable concessions—this time from the Shah—and began extraction operations.

England Avoids an Oil-Flow Crisis

Led by Winston Churchill, His Majesty's Government quickly became a big customer for Anglo-Persian's oil. On the eve of the war, however, the British government became deeply concerned about accessing that oil. To safeguard that access, the British government invested £2 million in the Anglo-Persian Oil Company, gaining effective control of the company.

With government backing, the Anglo-Persian Oil Company increased its operations. At the same time, the Anglo-Turkish Oil Company began to do the same in Turkey and Mesopotamia (now Iraq). Oil had vaulted Persia into the limelight once again.

Persian Perspectives

Oil concession agreements in Iran were negotiated to maintain Anglo-Persian's position—by propping up the Shah. First, there was a commercial agreement between the Anglo-Persian Oil Company and the Persian government. Second, there was a political agreement between the British government and the Anglo-Persian Oil Company (which was something of a conflict of interest, considering that the British government was the majority owner of the company). Finally, the Shah endorsed the whole arrangement, knitting the company, the crown, and the Shah together. The money that eventually flowed to the central Persian government enriched the Shah and enabled him to strengthen his power base.

The End of Absolutism—Maybe

As British interest in Persian oil increased, so did the efforts of the Persian elites to gain power for themselves.

As the Great Game in Persia wound down with the signing of the Anglo-Russian Agreement, the Persian nobility established a constitutional monarchy.

The constitution limited royal power that had been considered absolute for the past 500 years by creating a parliament. Following the death of the Shah, the crown prince, Muhammad 'Ali Mirza, was named the constitutional king. He was deposed, however, after imprisoning political opponents and revoking the constitution. His son was placed on the throne, the constitution was reinvoked, and a regency was established.

The entire chaotic period is known as the Constitutional Revolution of 1906 to 1911. What's important to remember is that the *Persian elites'* attempt to establish a constitutional monarchy ultimately ran up against the daunting obstacle of British interests in the region.

What's It Mean?

The Persian elites included tribal leaders and wealthy city-dwellers. These groups pushed for constitutional limits on the Shah's power so as to protect their own positions of privilege and counter the threat of arbitrary action by the Shah.

Bet You Didn't Know

The 1906 constitution derived its legitimacy from the people and placed a great deal of importance on the rights of the Iranian nation and emphasized the idea that serving the people is the foremost duty of those in charge of the government.

—From a 2003 press release from the Iranian government marking the ninety-seventh anniversary of the Constitutional Revolution of 1906 to 1911

The British Set Up Shop in Tehran

As the British became increasingly interested in Iranian oil, they came to realize how much they would stand to gain if they could find a single compliant leader to work with. They needed someone who would protect their interests and speak with a single voice; they did not relish the idea of working indefinitely with a fractured and potentially hostile assembly of local legislators.

In pursuing their interests—and perhaps to perpetuate existing divisions—the British continued to curry the favor of local tribal chieftains and sheikhs. Among these was Sheikh Khazal, the man who had agreed to have the refinery constructed on his territory.

World War I: Neutrality Compromised

The Persian government attempted to maintain neutrality during World War I. However, the British and the Russians eventually occupied the country, and they faced little resistance from the Shah when they did so.

The Allied powers wanted to preserve their holdings (particularly their oil investments) in Persia. As a result, they occupied the country to keep the Germans and their allies out. Compliance with this state of affairs was an odd kind of neutrality, but this was nevertheless the label to which the Persian government clung.

Persian Perspectives

The British and Russian occupation of Persia during World War I was prompted by a German saboteur who wrecked a portion of the pipeline that ran from the oil well field at Masjid-e Soleiman to the refinery at Abadan. The pipeline was put out of commission for five months. The British could ill afford to lose the Anglo-Persian Oil output, so they moved troops into Persia. Russia, their old Great Game rival—and current ally against Germany—moved troops into the northern portion of Persia as well.

The occupation rankled the Persian elites and exposed the weakness (or, at least, the pro-British bias) of the Shah. In addition, the occupation showed how ineffective the Assembly was when it came to actual day-to-day governance of the country.

The Dawn of the Pahlavi Dynasty

Given the obviousness of British maneuverings, military muscle-flexing, and deal-making with local chieftains (not to mention the generally weakened status of the Shah and the National Assembly), the dream of the 1906 to 1911 Revolution didn't really have much of a chance to become reality. The grand constitutional monarchy never gathered the strength that Persia's constitutional reformers had envisioned.

Less than a year and a half after World War I concluded, on February 22, 1921, Reza Khan Pahlavi overthrew the ruling Shah and took power in a coup. Khan was a Persian army general. The coup effectively ended the Qajar dynasty, which had been established more than a century earlier in 1794.

By 1923, Pahlavi was in firm enough control to re-create the government in his own image. He managed to get himself elected prime minister by the Constitutional Assembly in that year.

On December 12, 1925, the parliament voted to give him the crown of Iran, and he was henceforth Reza Shah Pahlavi. This consolidation of power—which granted an ancient and honored title to the perpetrator of a twentieth-century military coup—launched the Pahlavi era, the last of the Shah lines to rule Iran.

On April 25, 1926, the new Shah was crowned as ruler of Persia. His eldest son, Muhammad Reza, was named crown prince. In future years, Muhammad Reza Pahlavi did just about everything imaginable to suggest that his genealogical claim to power extended far back into the mists of Persian history. In fact, it extended only as far back as the Western era of Lindbergh, flappers, and Prohibition.

Between the World Wars

Following World War I, the British continued to develop the Anglo-Persian oil holdings. However, they soon found that they were dealing with a much tougher Shah. Pahlavi cracked down on the local chieftains and refused to recognize the concessions that granted the refinery on Abadan. Reza argued that the deal struck by Anglo-Persian Oil and Sheikh Khazal was not valid because it did not include the signature of the central government.

Under the reign of the new Shah, the government of Persia embarked on a number of modernizations and industrial development campaigns, as well as a general Westernization of the country. During the same period, the government made life difficult for those perceived as threats to the Shah.

Arrest of Opponents—and a Challenge to John Bull

In 1925, Reza Khan arrested Sheikh Khazal and placed him under house arrest in Tehran. Khazal lived the rest of his days under arrest, and the power of the central government was gradually ratcheted up.

Thanks in part to the Russian Revolution in 1918, the Soviets withdrew from Persia in the 1920s. (They also repudiated Czarist debt claims against Persia.) They were back before many more years passed, however.

Germany's defeat in World War I and Russia's temporary exit from the ranks of the region's geopolitical players left the British as the only world power still involved heavily in the inner workings in Persia.

In the late 1920s and early 1930s, the Reza Shah government flexed its muscles against the British and tried to renegotiate the concessions with Anglo-Persian Oil.

Shah to His Majesty: "Pay Up"

The Persians wanted to get a 25 percent share of the Anglo-Persian Oil Company, impose a surcharge on each barrel of oil exported, and reduce the size of the original concession by 75 percent. In effect, the Persians wanted to take back those concession areas where the Anglo-Persian Oil Company was not extracting oil at the time of the negotiations. The Shah wanted nothing less than a complete restructuring of the relationship.

The British did not want to agree to these demands, and they punished the Persians by reducing output (and thus payments on exports). After a while, the Shah decided he had had enough and simply declared the D'Arcy concession invalid. The British responded by moving ships into the Persian Gulf and appealing to the League of Nations.

Hammering Out a New Deal

The League's response was to suggest that the two sides negotiate a new agreement between themselves. The negotiations resumed, first in Europe and then in Tehran. The talks dragged on until the Shah intervened in 1933 and extended the D'Arcy concession (due to run out in 1961) by another 30 years.

The new deal that accompanied the extension was better for the Iranians, but not by much. Anglo-Persian Oil still maintained advantages in pricing for oil exports and still had tight control over the refineries and oil wells already in production.

The British and Russians Intervene (Again)

Still, this Shah was no puppet. Like the Shahs who ruled in Iran during the era of the Great Game, Reza Shah Pahlavi tried to maintain his own course. It was not always a pretty course.

As Nazi Germany began to emerge in the 1930s, Reza Shah Pahlavi became increasingly enamored of Adolf Hitler. This sympathy toward Nazism first annoyed and then alarmed the former Great Game rivals, Russia (now known as the Soviet Union) and Great Britain.

In 1941, the Shah's Nazi sympathies became too much to bear, at least in the eyes of the Soviets and the British. With war raging in Europe, the British and the Soviets invaded Iran and jointly occupied the country.

> **Persian Perspectives**
>
> In 1935, Reza Shah Pahlavi formalized the name change from Persia to Iran. He was looking to modernize Iran, and he figured that Persia was an old-fashioned name.

The (now-allied) British and Soviet governments certainly wanted to keep Iran out of the Axis. They also wanted to ensure access to oil during the war.

With those goals in mind, they deposed the Shah and set up his son, the crown prince Muhammad Reza Pahlavi, as the new (and, as it turned out, final) Shah of Iran. From the beginning, Muhammad Reza Pahlavi was beholden to the Allies, who guaranteed his status as leader during their occupation of Iran during the war years—just as he was to become beholden to the Americans, who took on the responsibility of maintaining his regime during the Cold War. In other words, the final Shah was a creation of the outside world. For four decades, the Allied powers had longed for a Shah they could control. In 1941, they got one.

Bet You Didn't Know

The Axis was the World War II alliance whose chief members were Nazi Germany, Italy, and Japan.

The Least You Need to Know

- The superpowers' interest in oil shifted British and Soviet attention from Central Asia to Persia.

- The Persian elites attempted to curtail the absolute power of the Shahs by establishing a constitutional monarchy.

- An attempt to create an effective constitutional monarchy was thwarted by a coup led by Reza Khan, who made himself a new Shah and limited the power of the Constitutional Assembly, essentially reasserting the power of the monarch in Persia.

- The British, under the auspices of the Anglo-Persian (after 1935, Anglo-Iranian) Oil Company, extended the Iranian oil infrastructure and continued to extract oil on extremely favorable terms.

10

Iran and the Cold War

In This Chapter

- ◆ The geopolitical picture changes after World War II
- ◆ The United States takes sides in Iran
- ◆ The Shah and SAVAK
- ◆ The Shah's grip on power increasingly depends on U.S. public and covert support

American observers often remark that the Iranian Revolution of 1979 was the result of the rise of fundamentalist Islam in that country. They also argue that anti-Americanism in Iran (whenever it has appeared after 1979) can be attributed to the teachings and the political influence of Muslim clerics in Iran who are hostile to the United States. Strictly speaking, both of these statements are accurate, but they are also serious oversimplifications of the history of U.S. involvement in Iranian affairs after World War II.

In this chapter, you learn about some of the often-overlooked events of the Cold War period, events that help explain *why* the Iranian populace eventually supported a fundamentalist Islamic regime. You also get an idea of *why* Iranians at all levels of society began embracing an anti-American world view and why that world view has endured for as long as it has.

A Geopolitical Agenda

To get an understanding of how things went so disastrously wrong in the U.S.–Iranian relationship in the late 1970s, you have to understand what was most on the minds of senior American decision makers in the early 1950s: the demands of a larger geopolitical agenda than that of the Middle East. The real agenda was that of the *Cold War.*

> **Bet You Didn't Know** _____
>
> The **Cold War** was a long-running conflict pitting the United States and its allies against the Soviet Union and its allies. The Cold War did not take the form of direct military conflict between the Warsaw Pact (the Soviet alliance) and NATO (the western alliance), but it did see proxy wars between Communist and non-Communist forces, such as those of Vietnam and Korea, as well as competition in the realms of economics, propaganda, espionage, and culture. The duration of the Cold War is generally accepted as late 1945 to December 26, 1991, when the Soviet Union was formally dissolved.

Truman Draws the Line

The United States and the Soviet Union had been uneasy allies during World War II, joining forces to defeat the forces of Germany in the 1940s. At the very end of the war, the Soviet Union made a formal declaration of war against Japan, thereby joining the cause of the United States and speeding the end of the bloodiest and most costly military conflict in human history. Anyone who believed that the Soviet declaration of war against the Japanese marked the beginning of a new era of U.S.–Soviet cooperation, however, was gravely mistaken. In the aftermath of the war, the situation polarized, and spheres of U.S. and Russian "influence" emerged.

Soviet "influence" over the countries of Eastern Europe led very quickly to Communist governments that took orders from Moscow. American "influence" in the post-war period meant that the United States assumed a pre-eminent role in world affairs, a role that corresponded roughly to the role played previously by Great Britain. In fact, the British and their empire were in serious decline, both economically and politically. The Americans, on the other hand, were on the rise, and the mobilization of American industry for the war effort had reinvigorated the once-moribund U.S. economy.

The Americans assumed leadership of what eventually became known as the "Western alliance." That leadership was first expressed by means of a policy known as the Truman Doctrine—a policy that was first implemented in Greece and Turkey but that had a fateful impact on the relationship of the United States and Iran.

Standoff in Iran

At the end of World War II, the Red Army still occupied a portion of northern Iran. Though they originally were supposed to withdraw at the end of the war, the Soviets remained. They even created a People's Republic of Kurdistan and the Republic of Azerbaijan. These two Soviet puppet states claimed portions of Iran. Truman insisted that they leave and through channels made it clear that he would drop an atom bomb on the Soviets in Iran if they didn't. (At this point, the Soviets did not yet have the Bomb.) Stalin took the hint, and the Soviets pulled out. Once the Red Army was gone, the Kurdistan and Azerbaijan states fell apart almost immediately. However, this was not the end of conflict between the United States and the USSR. Indeed, it was just the beginning.

Crisis in Greece

Although popular imagination records the surrender of Japan in August 1945 as the final event of World War II, President Truman did not formally declare an end to the hostilities of this conflict until December 31, 1946. Very shortly thereafter, a new global conflict began. Its first stirrings were detected when the British and the Americans found themselves faced with a serious problem in Greece.

At the beginning of 1947, the British announced that, because of growing Communist influence in the country, they would not recognize the government of Greece after March 31. Later in the year, American policy experts concluded that the Soviets had embarked on a worldwide campaign to propagate Communist doctrines and establish Communist governments.

The response from the American president, Harry Truman, was to meet the challenge head-on. He went before Congress, condemned Communist influence and agitation in Greece, and asked for $400 million to support American interests in the region.

Truman got what he wanted and managed to turn back Communist influence in both Greece and Turkey. In the process, he established an American policy that became known as the Truman Doctrine. This doctrine held that America would challenge Soviet ambitions on a global level.

The Truman Doctrine thrust the United States onto the world stage at precisely the time that the British were leaving it. A State Department official is said to have remarked of the British request for American help in Greece, "Great Britain had within the hour handed the job of world leadership ... to the United States."

The Enemy of My Enemy Is ... Okay, I Guess

In hindsight, it's easy to conclude that adherence to the Truman Doctrine delivered a major geopolitical success four and a half decades later: the collapse of the Communist regime in Russia and the emergence of its many satellite states from Communist dictatorships. It's also important to acknowledge, though, that U.S. appeals to the Truman Doctrine are associated with some of the worst mistakes in the history of American foreign policy. Most of these mistakes involved a prevailing American attitude best described as "The enemy of my enemy is my friend." One of the most dramatic of those mistakes occurred in Iran in the early 1950s.

Means to an End

In opposing Soviet expansion wherever and whenever it reared its head (or seemed likely to rear its head), American policymakers sometimes embraced an ends-justifies-the-means mind-set that had grave implications in its relationships with nations in the Middle East—and with the people of Iran, in particular.

You'll recall that Reza Shah Pahlavi leaned toward the Axis powers during World War II, and he found his nation occupied by the Americans and the Russians as a result. He was subsequently deposed in favor of his son, Mohammad Reza Pahlavi. This son—the second and last in the Pahlavi line—emerged as a pro-Western leader. He is, in fact, the Iranian leader (after the Ayatollah Khomeini) with whom most Americans are usually most familiar. This is the man who was eventually overthrown by the Iranian Revolution of 1979.

Yet it would be a mistake to see this second Shah in the Pahlavi "dynasty" as assuming office with the same activist philosophy that his father had brought to the conduct of state affairs. To put the matter bluntly, the new Shah was a timid and untested figure—one easily manipulated by others. His early "rule" is best filed under the word *figurehead*.

The new Shah's influence rose only when he was chosen as a means to a particular end—a pro-Western, antinationalist end favored by the CIA and by major Western oil companies. His transition from figurehead to despot was made possible by American interests and was the result of the American obsession on winning dependable "allies" in the face of growing Soviet influence around the world—even if securing such allies meant ignoring the democratic values that were supposedly at the heart of the Truman Doctrine.

Mossadeq and Nationalism

In 1951, Mohammad Mossadeq was elected as the prime minister of Iran. Mossadeq promoted a modest and extremely popular brand of Iranian nationalism, but he was no fanatic. More to the point, he had been elected to lead a legitimately elected government—a government chosen by the Iranian people in free and fair elections.

The sequence of events that eventually led to the Shah's ascent to power—and to a bitter hatred of the United States on the part of many Iranians—began to unfold shortly after Mossadeq's election. In April 1951, under Mossadeq's leadership, the Iranian parliament voted to nationalize the country's oil industry. This meant that the Anglo-Iranian Oil Company was rather unexpectedly shut down.

The fact that Mossadeq offered the company considerable compensation for its holdings is often overlooked by Americans recounting these events. The plan to nationalize the oil industry was nothing more or less than a purposeful effort to change the balance of economic and political power in the industry. It was not, however, an attempt by the government to "seize" the Anglo-Iranian Oil Company's assets without recompense.

Britain was having none of it. It refused to purchase Iranian oil, which threw the Iranian economy into turmoil, and it appealed to the Americans—in the form of the Central Intelligence Agency—to find a way to oust Mossadeq.

The West Takes Sides

There followed a fateful power struggle between the Shah of Iran—the figurehead leader installed by the Allies during World War II—and the legitimately elected prime minister of Iran. Mossadeq had the advantage of massive popular support. The Shah had the advantage of the Central Intelligence Agency, which boasted deep pockets and a profound commitment to evicting Mossadeq from authority in Iran.

In 1953, with the backing of the U.S. intelligence establishment, the Shah stripped Mossadeq of his powers and appointed his own prime minister to lead the country. The immediate result was a series of massive street demonstrations against the Shah's move. Seemingly terrified at the complexity of his situation, he left the country with the howls of his countrymen ringing in his ears and landed in Rome. (As it turned out, this 1953 departure served as a precursor of his similarly shameful flight from

Iran in 1979 in the face of even more intense public opposition—a departure that turned out to be permanent.)

The Shah may have gotten cold feet, but the CIA appeared to be playing for keeps.

Protestors for Hire

Possessed of a seemingly limitless budget, the CIA paid for pro-Shah demonstrators to mount street demonstrations. These "rented" demonstrators took over a radio station and announced (falsely) that Mossadeq had been overthrown and that the Shah was on his way back to Tehran. The truth of the matter was that the fall of Mossadeq only came about after a tank battle endorsed by the CIA. The Iranian military, in the form of Gen. Fazlollah Zahedi, fell in line with the U.S. intelligence operatives and Western oil interests.

The coup was successful, and the Shah was installed as the leader of Iran. His consolidation of power was entirely dependent on the covert actions of foreign powers and business interests. He took over leadership of the state in exchange for his total subservience to the wishes of Western oil executives and strategic planners eager to install an anti-Soviet regime. He remained utterly obedient to those interests for the balance of his time in power.

Unchallenged Authority

The tank battle that imposed the Shah's authority in Iran was undertaken at the cost of several hundred lives. This violence, however, was only a modest preview of coming attractions for the Iranian people.

In 1963, the Shah set out on a campaign to "modernize" (or depending on your point of view, "Westernize") Iran. It was known as the White Revolution, and it incorporated land reform and social and economic measures. The reforms were not popular in all corners of Iranian society, however, and organized opposition to them was soon evident. In response to this opposition, the Shah began to rely more on surveillance and intimidation carried out by his secret police force, SAVAK—which had been trained by the CIA. The SAVAK's methods included torture and murder.

Persian Perspectives
SAVAK was founded in 1957 under the direction of American and Israeli intelligence officials.

The Shah thus maintained his hold on power by means of brutal suppression of both real and perceived political opponents. In doing so, he authorized a number of brutal "interrogation" methods that had been shared with his security forces by none other than the U.S. government.

Persian Perspectives

Over the years, SAVAK became a law unto itself, having legal authority to arrest and detain suspected persons indefinitely. SAVAK operated its own prisons in Tehran (the Komiteh and Evin facilities) and, many suspected, throughout the country as well. SAVAK's torture methods included electric shock, whipping, beating, inserting broken glass and pouring boiling water into the rectum, tying weights to the testicles, and the extraction of teeth and nails. Many of these activities were carried out without any institutional checks.

—From "Ministry of Security: Savak" on the Federation of American Scientists website (www.fas.org/irp/world/iran/savak)

The bottom line: The Shah's was a regime that owed both its existence and its endurance to two factors. The first was its willingness to support the desires of its Western interests on matters of oil and anticommunist ideology. The second was its willingness to shed human blood to silence popular opposition.

Persian Perspectives

The Shah's personal security force, known as SAVAK, trained by the American Central Intelligence Agency, was a human-rights nightmare. In 1976, Amnesty International (AI) issued a report that cited Iran's SAVAK as the institution with the worst record of human-rights abuses on the face of the earth. In its condemnation of the activities of Iranian security forces, AI wrote that the diversity and cruelty of abuses in Iran were "beyond belief."

Twenty-Six Years of Abuse of Power

The Shah's backing by the United States, which instructed him in "security" matters and turned a blind eye to his horrific human rights abuses, is not likely to be forgotten soon by Iranians who lived through the 1953 to 1979 period, a stretch of time whose excesses and brutalities have been compared to those of the most oppressive regimes in history. Although it is certainly true that opposition to Soviet expansionism in the Middle East and elsewhere was a noble and worthwhile goal, it is also true that in the pursuit of that goal, American policymakers frequently lost sight of basic human and democratic values. Iran was such a case.

In response to these points, many in the diplomatic and intelligence establishment have argued that the world is not a tidy place, that allies are not always admirable, and that geopolitical concerns sometimes eclipse regional ones. All these are valid points, but some difficult core truths remain. The hatred for the United States now entrenched in Iran took root and thrived not because of some strange aberration of the people, their culture, or their religion, but in response to clear abuses of basic human values.

To put it another way: By installing and supporting a leader with a taste for bloody suppression, the United States reaped a whirlwind in Iran. In fact, many analysts believe that the hard-line Islamist regime that rules Iran today could never have assumed power or implemented a theocratic state if the people of Iran had not been deprived of their democratically elected leader in 1953—and seen him replaced by a brutal tyrant whose chief (and perhaps only) "virtue" was his willingness to accede to Western interests.

The Least You Need to Know

- The threat of Soviet expansionism led the U.S. government to adopt a policy of opposition to global Communist influence, spelled out in the Truman Doctrine.

- The United States orchestrated a coup in Iran that Western officials believed promoted its geopolitical and economic interests.

- This coup, which consolidated the power of the Shah of Iran, replaced a democratically elected leader that the West did not like with a dictator that it did like.

- The human rights abuses of the Shah's security apparatus were horrific.

- These events must be taken into account in any discussion of Iranian–U.S. relations.

Part 3

The Era of Ayatollahs (1979–2002)

Most of us have strong images of the Islamic Revolution in Iran, and were surprised to hear the Ayatollahs call the United States the "Great Satan." The rise of fundamental Islam defines the internal and foreign policies of Iran, and conditions the way the rest of the world looks at them.

The chapters in this section are a "how and why" of the Islamic Republic. We take a look at what makes this lonely Islamic state work—and not work.

Chapter 11

The Ascent of Fundamentalism

In This Chapter

- ◆ Resentment of the Shah
- ◆ The radicalization of the state
- ◆ The United States helps keep the Shah in power
- ◆ Laying the groundwork for the Islamic Republic

In this chapter, you'll see how the stage was set for the entrance of fundamentalist clerical power as the most important political force in Iran.

Exiling the Ayatollah

In the 1960s, the Shah was hobbling along with the help of two crutches: SAVAK and the United States. He relied on SAVAK to root out and suppress any dissent within Iran that threatened his power, and he relied on the Americans to deliver economic and diplomatic support—and to look the other way when he imprisoned and tortured political prisoners.

Earlier in the 1960s and 1970s, SAVAK did its job well. It was able to isolate and crush the disparate dissenting groups inside the country. However, one group of dissenters could not be cowed and could not be eliminated: the *mullahs*.

What's It Mean?

The **mullahs,** as a group, were the religious authorities in Iran. The word *mullah* simply means "clerical figure" or "preacher"; it is often used to refer to a member of the clergy who has not yet been granted authority to deliver judgments on Islamic law. Mullahs preached at the mosques and oversaw religious education in Iran, and they were able to preach fundamental Shiism with the Shah's approval.

The United States continued to operate to support the Shah, by both overt and covert means. The Shah was too important as a tool in the Cold War and friendly ally in the Middle East for the United States to challenge him on his abysmal human rights record. This policy of accommodation only solidified the hatred of the mullahs and, ultimately, the Iranian "man in the street" toward Uncle Sam—with disastrous consequences in the latter half of 1979.

Preaching Gets Political

Well into the 1960s, the Shah indulged the mullahs' preaching of fundamentalist Shiism because he wanted to provide some outlets for the Iranian people. He also realized that Islam was a force to be respected, so he gave the mullahs a great deal of latitude.

There were limits, however. The Shah appears to have believed that he could control the influence of religion by exiling key religious figures. He exiled the Ayatollah Ruholla Khomeini, a vocal opponent of secular rule, by refusing to allow him to return to Iran in 1968 after the *ayatollah* had been traveling abroad.

What's It Mean?

A mullah who has reached the next highest level in the Shiite religious hierarchy is called an **ayatollah.** Ayatollahs may deliver judgments on Islamic law. The mullahs designate those who achieve the level of ayatollah.

The Ayatollah Khomeini took up residence in An Najaf, the Shiite holy city in southern Iraq. The two holiest sites of Shiism, An Najaf and Karbala, are located in southern Iraq, and the southern part of Iraq is predominantly Shiite. So the ayatollah was able to exert a strong influence on the Iraqi and Iranian Shiites from his residence at An Najaf.

"We'll Always Have Paris"

In 1977, facing internal pressures and the incoming administration of Jimmy Carter, the Shah agreed to some internal reforms. He remained wary of the Ayatollah Khomeini's influence over the Shiite faithful in Iran. In 1978, hoping to diminish that influence, the Shah asked the Iraqi government to do him the great favor of getting the ayatollah out of the area. The job of exiling the ayatollah fell to none other than Saddam Hussein, then the number-two man in the Iraqi leadership.

Saddam was all too happy to oblige. The Iraqi leadership was wary of influences upon its own Shiite population. The Shiites made up the majority of the Muslim population in Iraq, yet they did not control the country. The Sunni Muslim minority ran the country, the military, and the economy. So it was with some pleasure that the Iraqi government saw to the removal of an influential Shiite cleric.

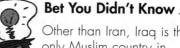

Bet You Didn't Know

Other than Iran, Iraq is the only Muslim country in which Shiites are the majority of the population. In Iraq, the Shiite Arabs are 60 percent of the population, and Sunni Arabs are about 25 percent of the population. The Kurds are about 13 percent of the population. Assyrians and Chaldean Christians make up the rest.

Sunni Muslims, we must remember, make up roughly 95 percent of all Muslims worldwide. With the exception of Iran, all of Iraq's neighbors are Sunni Muslim (Turkey, Syria, Jordan, Saudi Arabia, and Kuwait). These countries would not tolerate a Shiite Muslim–controlled country on their borders. When the British were carving countries out of the old Ottoman Empire after World War II, they took care to keep the Sunni elites happy and in power throughout the region—and gave them a leading role in the new nation of Iraq.

Hussein responded to the Shah's request by exiling the ayatollah to Paris. This deed did nothing to endear the future leader of Iraq to the future leader of Iran. As we will see in Chapter 14, the bad blood between Saddam Hussein and Ayatollah Khomeini led to one of the bloodiest conflicts of the twentieth century.

So Far Away

Booting the ayatollah out of Iraq did not have the effect the Shah wanted. He continued to exert a powerful influence on the Shiites in Iran from his Parisian exile, and he continued to preach his message of liberation and rebellion. The pressures within the country increased, and the mullahs formed a powerful—and influential—network of organized opposition.

As it happened, the ayatollah's ability to spread his message was only enhanced once he got to Paris. The fact that secular governments had gone to such great lengths to remove him from Shiite communities only added to his stature and authority.

Bootleg Sermons

Once in Paris, the ayatollah was able to get his messages printed in publications that found their way back to Iran. In addition, the ayatollah was able to record his messages to the faithful back in Iran on cassette tapes. These cassettes were smuggled back into Iran and then were copied and distributed across the country.

The cassettes were an easy and effective method of distributing his message, since tape recorders and cassettes were universally available across the country, and the cassettes themselves were easily hidden or camouflaged with innocuous labels. The Shah was aware of the bootleg messages but was unable to do much to counter their effects. His reach did not extend to France, and his own SAVAK was unable to stop the spread of the ayatollah's message through the popular underground.

They Said It

Thirty million people have begun to move. Only a few hundred people have not joined the movement, and they are the hirelings of the regime. This roaring flood of people is on the move now, and neither Russia nor America can stop it. This is a just act. This is the hand of God, and no one can stop it. This is an obvious call for justice. A nation is calling out for its freedom, and no one can say they don't have that right. They are human beings, too. The situation is very difficult for the Shah and his regime now, but they cannot continue to confront such a just call with bayonets. Martial law cannot be imposed forever. This regime may not be able to survive a day without martial law, but it cannot be in effect forever.

In any case, you must explain the situation to these foreigners. Give your friends the facts. If you attend schools over here, speak to the people who attend with you and tell them what is really happening. Form groups; gradually they will increase and you will become preachers and speakers, telling the people about the problems of Iran. If you do this, a wave of public opinion will come about which the reporters will not be able to counteract; then it will be the people here who stand up to the false propaganda. This is a service that we who are abroad can do now for the nation of Islam.

I beseech God the blessed and exalted to assist you and to grant you success.

May he keep you safe from harm and protect you.

—From a recorded sermon of Ayatollah Khomeini, Paris, October, 1978

Partying at Persepolis

As the situation in Iran grew increasingly tense, the Shah continued to behave as if all was well. He threw a lavish gala at Persepolis to celebrate 2,500 years of the Persian regime. This celebration angered the Iranian populace on several levels. First, the Shah was not the direct descendent of Darius and the great Persian kings of old—far from it. In fact, he was the son of a former army general, Reza Khan, who had seized power in 1923. Second, the fete at Persepolis further angered the mullahs. From Paris, the Ayatollah Khomeini bitterly observed that while the Shah was spending enormous sums for his guests on the party, many less well-connected people were starving in Iran.

The Shah Goes on Vacation

As 1978 wore on into 1979, the Shah's grip on power loosened. The fundamentalist mullahs were becoming more openly critical of the Pahlevi regime, and the Ayatollah Khomeini was a more powerful symbol than ever of Iranian resistance to the Shah's oppressive regime. From Paris, the ayatollah called for general strikes to protest the pro-Western nature of the Shah's regime and the many abuses he perpetrated against his people.

As January 1979 came around, these strikes were paralyzing the Iranian economy. Rioters took to the streets, and despite the best efforts of SAVAK to suppress the dissent, the size and fury of the gathering made the transition from mob to uprising. Finally, on January 16, 1979, the Shah announced that he and his wife were taking a vacation. He never returned.

Too Little, Too Late

In an attempt to preserve some sort of order and preserve the privileged position of his followers, the Shah had appointed an opposition leader (but not a fundamentalist mullah) to take over as prime minister: Dr. Shapour Bakhtiar, a man the Shah had once jailed, was thus in charge of the government in early 1979. Bakhtiar was the leader of the National Movement of Iranian Resistance, which represented a secular alternative to the mullahs. He was thus acceptable to the Iranian elites.

Uncle Sam Caught Off-Guard

The speed with which the Shah's hold on power dissolved took the U.S. government by surprise. Despite warnings within the intelligence community, the Carter administration was unprepared to adapt to the new reality that was unfolding in Iran. The

United States transferred its support from the Shah to Bakhtiar, which tainted Bakhtiar with the same pro-Western brush that the mullahs had smeared on the Shah. Bakhtiar was losing the battle for Iranian hearts and minds.

Persian Perspectives

Shapour Bakhtiar (1915–1991) was born in Iran but educated in Lebanon and France. He received a Ph.D. in political science from the Sorbonne. Bakhtiar fought in the French Resistance and later in the Orlean Battalion. In 1951, Bakhtiar served as deputy minister of labour during Mossadeq's administration. Due to his criticism of the Shah's regime, particularly after the fall of Mossadeq, he was imprisoned for 6 years and was restricted from leaving Iran for another 10 years after that.

The Ayatollah Returns

With the Shah gone, the new prime minister Bakhtiar and the Iranian army were left to deal with the emboldened fundamentalists and the rampaging mobs in the streets. Bakhtiar believed he could build a lasting government and new society in Iran. As it turned out, his government lasted only 37 days.

Persian Perspectives

The Iranian military had closed airport facilities in an attempt to keep the ayatollah from returning from Paris. In response, an army of irate citizens descended on the airport, demanding that it be opened. The military relented, and the airport was reopened before the ayatollah's return.

Good Intentions Aren't Enough

Bakhtiar did not sit idly by, watching the mullahs trying to take over and doing nothing. He believed he headed the legitimate government in Iran, and he moved swiftly to change the government according to his principles. Bakhtiar ordered the infamous SAVAK to be disbanded. He opened the prisons, freeing all the political prisoners jailed by that same SAVAK, and also lifted restrictions on the press.

Perhaps most important, Bakhtiar tried to establish a relationship with the ayatollah, and he made gestures that suggested he was interested in a summit meeting of sorts. It never took place, and the tide of popular discontent, which had been building for many long years, swept him from power. There simply was not enough time for Bakhtiar's reforms to take hold because the mullahs were working against him as aggressively as they had worked against the Shah.

A Triumphant Return

Following the mullahs' policy of hostility to any authority (internal or foreign) that was not Shia Islam, the ayatollah simply refused to acknowledge the legitimacy of the Bakhtiar government and deliberately avoided contact with him. Even then, with the ayatollah rebuffing his efforts to meet, Bakhtiar instructed the air force to not interfere when the ayatollah was preparing to fly back to Tehran.

Finally, on February 1, 1979, the Ayatollah Khomeini returned to Iran for the first time in 15 years. While the military stood by, the mullahs and the mobs rushed to the runway, enraptured now that the "holy one" had returned.

Upon his arrival, the ayatollah went from the airport to Behesht-e Zahra, the Tehran Cemetery. There, among the tombstones, the ayatollah laid claim to the future of Iran. He declared that the true path for Iran was through a return to Islam, not through following the example of pro-Western regimes. No amount of reforming would change his opinion on this matter. And the Iranian people appeared to agree with him.

This Town Ain't Big Enough for Two of Us

The Shah was gone, but that hardly seemed to matter to the mullahs. Their goal was not just the overthrow of the Shah, but the overthrow of any pro-Western, secular authority in Iran. The Ayatollah Khomeini set the tone by refusing to meet with Bakhtiar. By avoiding Bakhtiar, the ayatollah challenged the legitimacy of his government.

The ayatollah himself went to the Alavi School in Tehran, where he took up station and began to direct affairs. Rather than simply ignore Bakhtiar and his government, the ayatollah named his own prime minister, Mehdi Bazargan. He promised to create a provisional government as soon as possible, and he appointed Bazargan to run the new government. In reality, the ayatollah called the shots for the provisional government. Bazargan made regular round-trips to Alavi to get his directions from the ayatollah.

The Ayatollah Khomeini refused to recognize the Bakhtiar government as the legitimate authority in Iran, but Bakhtiar refused to step aside. For a time, there were two governments in one country, neither recognizing the authority of the other. The situation was clearly untenable, and it was tearing the country apart. Already pro-ayatollah forces were running the city of Esfahan. At the same time, Bakhtiar was in control of Tehran.

Persian Perspectives

Mehdi Bazargan (1907–1995) was deputy prime minister under Mossadeq. Bazargan founded two opposition groups (which were sympathetic to the Shiite mullahs): the Liberation Movement of Iran and the Iranian Human Rights Association. For his trouble, he was jailed several times during the 1960s and 1970s, but he earned his stripes with the mullahs. Because of Bazargan's combination of opposition credentials and fundamentalist beliefs, the Ayatollah Khomeini selected him to create a new government after the Shah left Iran.

The key to control was the army. Gradually, the cadets and rank and file began to gravitate toward the ayatollah and away from their officers and Bakhtiar. Finally, on February 9, the air force cadets joined an uprising at the Doshan Tappeh barrack against the Imperial Guards.

The violence quickly spread the following day, and Bakhtiar decided to call out the army to quell the violence. However, the commander of the armed forces had decided that the army would remain neutral, in an effort to avoid further bloodshed. Bakhtiar found out about this only when he heard the announcement on the radio, along with everybody else.

Bakhtiar accepted the inevitable and resigned in favor of Bazargan. The pro-Western authority in Iran was gone for good, and the Islamization of Iran had begun in earnest.

The Least You Need to Know

◆ After years of brutally suppressing his own people, the Shah found himself unable to hold on to power in the face of rising popular discontent.

◆ The Ayatollah Khomeini, exiled in 1964 and sent to Paris in 1978 by Saddam Hussein, only gained power and prestige in absentia.

◆ The Shah left on a (permanent) vacation in January 1979.

◆ The democratic "experiment" of the Bakhtiar government was doomed to fail before it started because it lacked the blessing of the mullahs and the Ayatollah Khomeini.

◆ The ayatollah set up his own government when returned from exile, led by Bazargan, which immediately destabilized the Bakhtiar government.

Chapter 12

The Fork in the Road: The Hostage Crisis

In This Chapter

- ◆ The seizure of the American Embassy
- ◆ Secular leadership takes a back seat
- ◆ The ayatollah exhorts the students
- ◆ The formal launch of the Iranian theocratic state

In early 1979, unprecedented civil protest against the Shah's rule led to a powerful mass movement that forced the Shah into exile. The Shah's departure, however, did not slow the pace of change in Iran. The continuing destabilization of the country's existing institutions became obvious when the armed forces officially pronounced themselves neutral in the political arena—thus severely undercutting the Shah's choice as prime minister, Bakhtiar, who promptly resigned.

The ayatollah's choice, Mehdi Bazargan, seemed to hold out the possibility that some form of secular government was still an option in Iran. But the fall of the Shah's choice was actually the first sign of a new era of leadership in Iran. The emerging government was, in fact, being formed by

Khomeini's Islamic Revolutionary Council, a body that had no use for secular influence. It envisioned a government in which clerics exercised not only practical control over street demonstrations, but ultimately control over the affairs of state.

The formal declaration of an Islamic republic took place in April 1979 after a popular referendum, but the first dramatic global expression of the new regime's outlook and attitude took place in November of that year, with the onset of what came to be known as the Iranian Hostage Crisis. You'll be learning about this fateful period in this chapter.

Carter's Worst Call

The hostage crisis—if one can call a standoff that lasted for 444 days a "crisis"—unfolded as the direct result of a serious miscalculation on the part of the Carter administration. It was, of course, only the most recent in a long series of American miscalculations involving Iran. But this error had consequences that profoundly affected the focus of American foreign policy and at least one U.S. presidential election. As it turned out, the error also solidified the clerical hold on power in Tehran.

Where to Land the Shah?

After the Shah's departure from Iran, President Jimmy Carter faced a difficult choice: Should he allow the ailing former leader of Iran into the United States? Many in the foreign policy establishment insisted that loyalty to an old ally required not only that the United States offer refuge to the wandering Mohammed Reza Shah, but also that it make every effort to win back his throne for him. The argument of this group of policymakers went that the geopolitical interests of the nation demanded that America show allegiance and respect to all those who had helped it to oppose Soviet influence, even if they were having a little trouble at home. This wing of policymakers cautioned that the spectacle of a trusted ally being abandoned would not be lost on other figures in the Middle East and elsewhere in the world.

The opposing view, argued by what might be called the more pragmatic wing of the American diplomatic establishment, held that the most important thing was developing a constructive relationship with the new regime. As this reasoning went, the clerics could perhaps just as easily be played against the Soviets as the Shah had. This group of foreign policy experts insisted that any show of support for the man recently reviled in the streets of Tehran as an American puppet would destroy the opportunity to turn the tide of anti-American feeling that was sweeping Tehran—and perhaps win an ally.

For some time, Carter sided with the pragmatic group. Then came the news that the Shah had been diagnosed with terminal cancer. Carter then chose to allow him entry to the United States, and he was admitted into a hospital in New York in October for treatment.

In protest, a group of Iranian students made plans to seize the U.S. Embassy in Tehran in order to conduct a sit-in. They demanded that the United States return the Shah to Iran for trial.

Bet You Didn't Know

President Jimmy Carter's choice to admit the former Shah into the United States for medical treatment meant that he overruled urgent pleas from American Embassy staff in Tehran that he keep the Shah off American soil. The Embassy, they warned, was vulnerable—it had been briefly occupied in February 1979, and the diplomatic corps feared a repeat performance.

A Sit-In Becomes a Siege

With the seizure of the American Embassy, it became clear who was really in control in Iran. It was not Bazargan, the nominal head of state, but the clerics who controlled Iran's Revolutionary Committees—and their leader was Khomeini.

The seizure of the American Embassy compound—so clearly foreseen by its occupants that they had been busy shredding classified documents—quickly escalated into a hostage drama. Of the roughly 90 people in the embassy at the time of its seizure, about 40 were released for humanitarian or propaganda reasons. The remaining 52 Americans were held captive by the students, who quickly found themselves backed by the clerical establishment.

A remarkable wave of Iranian popular support for the occupation of the embassy apparently took the students by surprise. Backed by the religious leaders whose power was growing with every passing day, the students stood their ground and insisted that they would not release the hostages until the United States capitulated.

An Extended Confrontation with the Americans

The "sit-in" quickly became an important domestic political event and an expression of Iranian national will. The demands of the students eventually evolved: The United

States had to return the Shah for trial, return his wealth to the people of Iran, apologize for committing crimes against the Iranian people, and promise never to interfere in Iranian affairs. The U.S. government briskly rejected these suggestions, and the crisis dragged on.

Over a period of months, the White House launched a series of efforts to secure the release of the hostages through standard diplomatic channels. They accomplished nothing. The world media, in general, and the American media, in particular, began to take an obsessive focus on the latest "news" regarding the hostage situation— which was, all too often, that there was nothing new to report.

What the Crisis Did for the Clerical Establishment

The seizure of the U.S. Embassy, which proved to be wildly popular among the Iranian people, accomplished three important objectives for the clerical establishment in Iran:

- ◆ It neutralized secular opposition and consolidated popular support for a theocratic state. Prime Minister Bazargan, who had met with American National Security Adviser Zbigniew Brzezinski just a week before the sit-in, was suddenly out of favor with the people. Bazargan resigned shortly after the crisis began.

- ◆ It allowed the clerics to put the world's focus on the excesses and inhumanity of U.S. intelligence operations in the region, and on the abuses of the Shah.

- ◆ It gave the clerics an international forum to circulate the teachings and viewpoints of the Ayatollah Khomeini. Although he was reviled in the United States and elsewhere in the West, Khomeini's global prominence was a source of enduring pride in Iran. His letters and speeches were circulated widely, and his open letter to the Pope received especially close attention.

Shortly after the seizure of the American embassy, the new Iranian constitution was ratified. It established both an elected president and a religious Supreme Leader who would exercise ultimate authority in the country. The Iranian theocratic state was a reality.

Persian Perspectives

Your Excellency's message expressing anxiety over the worsening of the relations between the Moslem country of Iran and the United States has been received. I appreciate Your Excellency's goodwill and draw your respected attention to the point that our militant, noble nation took such cutting-off of relations as a good omen and celebrated it with rejoicing and illuminations. I thank you for your prayers to Almighty God for our militant people but should mention that Your Excellency should not be worried about the greater and more dangerous problems mentioned in your message because the Moslem nation of Iran welcomes the problems which may result from the cutting-off of relations and is not afraid of those greater dangers.

That day will be dangerous for our people on which relations such as those existing during the former treacherous regime are re-established, but God willing, they will not be re-established. I want Your Excellency, in view of the spiritual influence you have among Christian people, to warn the U.S. government of the consequences of its tyrannies, its imposition of force and its plundering, and advise Mr. Carter, who will be confronted with defeat, to treat the nations which want absolute independence and do not want to be affiliated with any power in the world, according to humane criteria, to follow the teachings of Christ (may God's blessings be on him) and not expose himself and the U.S. government to further scandal.

I pray to Almighty God for the prosperity of the oppressed of the world and hope they may be freed form the hands of the oppressors.

—The Ayatollah Khomeini's open letter to the Pope, April 16, 1980

Carter Runs Out of Options

In the United States, a sense of futile rage grew ever more intense as the days of the crisis turned into weeks, and the weeks turned into months. Representatives of the American government found themselves sputtering endlessly that supporting the seizure of the diplomats was a violation of international law. That much was certainly true, but it was also true that the emerging powers in Tehran didn't much seem to care whether international law had been violated.

Carter froze some $8 billion of Iranian assets. He ordered a complete embargo on Iranian oil. He imposed sanctions. He tried to work through back channels. Nothing seemed to make any difference.

Having drawn a great deal of attention to the importance of freeing the hostages, and having then shown himself utterly unable to do so, the president of the United States found himself with few options. He had a problem on his hands. It was a problem of his own making, a problem that eventually helped to bring down his presidency.

Bet You Didn't Know _____

December 12 and 14 (approximately): On December 14 I was taken out doors for the first time for exercise—my 41st day of captivity! Although I had been exercising in my rooms by pacing back and forth as much as possible, being out in the fresh air for the first time made me feel almost as though I had just gotten up from a hospital bed for the first time after a long period in the hospital! I actually felt rather weak and wobbly! One of the guards asked me why I didn't jump around and exercise more vigorously rather than just walk around in the yard, but I actually couldn't—just felt too weak. … I had to request paper, envelopes, and a ballpoint pen from the guard on duty each time and had to return the pen and any unused paper as I wasn't permitted to retain them. At that moment, I was the only one in my room to receive mail. I felt badly about this as I knew that, Bruce German in particular, was very worried about his wife and children.

—Diary entry from Robert C. Ode, American hostage

A Rescue Attempt Ends in Failure

With negotiations, economic sanctions, and oil embargoes yielding nothing, President Carter severed all relations with Iran in April 1980. Shortly thereafter, he authorized the military to conduct a rescue attempt of the hostages in Iran. The project was known as *Operation Eagle Claw.*

It was a fiasco. Three of the eight helicopters intended for use in the mission malfunctioned, and eight American servicemen were left dead on the ground in Iran when a helicopter ran into a refueling plane. Carter assumed full responsibility for the mission, and the hostage crisis attracted yet another period of media saturation in the States.

What's It Mean? _____

Operation Eagle Claw was a top-secret attempt to rescue the American hostages from Iran. Its utter failure in April 1980 marked what was arguably the low point of the Carter administration.

The failure of Operation Eagle Claw to attain its goal marked a fresh point of futility in the American government's attempts to resolve the hostage crisis. For many in the United States, it served as an emblem of incompetence that reinforced Carter's many domestic political difficulties. Not surprisingly, the mission's failure was greeted with jubilation in Iran. Images of an upbeat, robed cleric perusing the ruins of the operation circulated around the world.

Bet You Didn't Know

A few days ago, the president made a very courageous decision as he ordered us to execute the rescue operation as we tried to free our Americans held hostage in Teheran. It was not a risk-free operation—there is no such thing as a risk-free operation. ... We all shared considerable disappointment that we were not successful. But let's not be despondent about that. Our job is now to remain alert, to look for those opportunities, times when we can bring our Americans out. Our job is to stay ready.

—Admiral Thomas B. Hayward, chief of Naval Operations, April 1980

Moving Toward an Endgame

In July 1980, the former Shah (who, by this point, had been shuttled off to a series of exotic destinations) died in Egypt. While returning the former ruler to Iran for trial was now out of the question, the Iranian government insisted that the other demands remained in effect. The world began to wonder whether the ongoing "crisis" would, or could, ever end. While all of this was going on, the Iranian government was releasing sensitive documents that it had discovered on the grounds of the U.S. Embassy in Tehran. These documents had actually been shredded, and the Iranians had painstakingly reassembled them prior to publicizing them. While these documents did not get much attention in the U.S. media, they created a sensation in Europe and elsewhere in the Middle East.

Then in September, Iran was invaded by Iraq (see Chapter 13). A new war was underway, and the theocratic powers in Iran found themselves with a new set of challenges to address.

Meanwhile, in the United States, President Carter was engaged in an uphill battle to secure re-election. His opponent, Ronald Reagan, spoke of ringing terms of pride in country, of restoring respect for the nation's military institutions, and of ending a long period of stagnation and decline. All of these appeals resonated powerfully with a populace weary of bad news from abroad and economic downturns at home.

Carter, for his part, had chosen to make his handling of the hostage crisis a central element of his campaign, perhaps believing that emphasizing his role as commander-in-chief would secure support for his cause. Whether or not that was his intent, the decision to place the hostage issue front and center during the campaign backfired badly, and he went down to emphatic defeat against Reagan in November.

Persian Perspectives

Abolhassan Bani-Sadr was elected the first president of the Islamic Republic of Iran in 1980. The Ayatollah Khomeini, however, as Supreme Leader, exercised ultimate political authority in Iran.

Analysts are in general agreement, however, that Carter might well have won the election had the hostage rescue attempt in April been successful or had he somehow been able to engineer an "October surprise" that would have delivered the hostages safely home shortly before the election. As it was, the image of the failed rescue attempt hung over his campaign like a dark cloud.

The leadership in Iran managed to bring down one more final defeat upon the recently defeated Jimmy Carter. After the election, the lame-duck president negotiated tirelessly to secure the release of the hostages through various intermediaries. After months of extraordinary effort, a final resolution of the crisis was arranged, with Algeria acting as the go-between.

As if intending to leave all options open with the new occupant of the White House—an understandable objective, given the state of war that their nation now faced—the Iranians saw to it that the plane bearing the hostages did not take off until after Ronald Reagan was inaugurated on January 20, 1981.

Bet You Didn't Know

Q: How do you feel about that and the fact that they're coming home?

The President: Oh, more pleased than anything I can say. It just was needed to make the day perfect. They've had the refueling in Athens, which should put them by now on their way to Algiers. And whether they try and start immediately for Germany or not, that I don't know. But they will switch to American planes in Algiers .... When we were watching the parade—well, at first, at lunch I learned that both planes had taken off and were in the air. And then I learned here, while we were watching the parade, that they had crossed the border and were out of Iranian airspace. And the next word I got, before the parade was over, was that they were refueling in Athens. The flight from there to Algiers is about 2½ hours.

—President Reagan, discussing the hostage release with reporters, January 22, 1981

So it was that the man whose presidency came to be defined in its final year by the Iranian hostage crisis saw the credit and acclaim for his final diplomatic victory descend on the man who had defeated him. It was a bitter irony, but it was not, perhaps, unjust, given that responsibility for the crisis itself could ultimately be traced to Carter's decision to admit the Shah to the United States.

In the United States, the immediate consequences of the hostage crisis were evident in the priorities of the new Reagan administration: higher defense budgets, greater reliance upon the option of military intervention (a notion in decline in the years immediately following Vietnam), and a renewed commitment to promote American interests throughout the world by means of the media, diplomacy, and covert operations.

In Iran, the consequences of the hostage affair were equally clear: It was the event that saw the consolidation of formal political power into the hands of the clerics. How America would deal with those clerics was a fateful question—one that would, as it happened, tarnish the presidency of Carter's successor.

The Least You Need to Know

- ◆ Jimmy Carter's decision to admit the Shah of Iran to the United States for medical treatment helped to consolidate political control of Iran under the authority of Islamic clerics.

- ◆ The seizure of the American Embassy began as a sit-in by students but eventually galvanized the country and turned into a national expression of Iranian will.

- ◆ The crisis allowed Iranian religious leaders to defeat secular opponents, highlight past abuses by the Shah and the United States, and promote the message of the Ayatollah Khomeini.

- ◆ Shortly after the seizure, the Iranian constitution was ratified, the Ayatollah Khomeini was granted supreme power, and the Iranian theocratic state was a reality.

- ◆ The crisis concluded after Carter's defeat in the 1980 presidential election, but as the result of Carter's intense diplomatic efforts.

- ◆ The Iranian government saw to it that the plane carrying the 52 American hostages did not leave the ground until Carter's successor, Ronald Reagan, was inaugurated.

The Iran-Iraq War: Survival and Revenge

In This Chapter

- ◆ The newly created Islamic Republic is attacked
- ◆ Iraq unleashes mustard gas; Iran unleashes the Human Wave
- ◆ Playing the USA card
- ◆ Stalemate and ceasefire

In this chapter, we trace the first decade of the new Islamic Republic as it fought for its very survival against an ancient enemy: Iraq.

A Fight Waiting to Happen

The Iran-Iraq War—the longest conventional military conflict of the century, and one of the bloodiest—had three motivating causes:

- ◆ Historic and ethnic rivalries and animosities
- ◆ A new, unstable leadership in Iran
- ◆ A new, power-hungry leader in Iraq

The convergence of these forces brought about a horrific conflict that lasted eight years and consumed approximately one million lives.

This conflict saw the use of both terrifying chemical weapons and "human-wave" assault forces that defy comprehension. The Iran-Iraq war was also the backdrop for the Iran-Contra scandal, a disgrace to the American political system that rocked the Reagan administration in the late 1980s.

This war was, then, certainly among the most important military conflicts of the century. It was, in many ways, a fight waiting to break out.

Long Time Coming: Historical and Ethnic Animosity Between Iran and Iraq

Four main things must be kept in mind about the long-standing historical/ethnic animosity between Iraq and Iran:

- Iran and Iraq are ancient enemies. Iran is Persian and Shia Muslim, while Iraq is Arab and is controlled by Sunni Muslims. (See Chapter 2 for a fuller discussion of these divisions.)

- Southern Iraq is the home to millions of Arab Shia Muslims who share a common socioreligious bond with the Persian Shia Muslims in Iran. The two holiest sites for Shia Islam (outside of Mecca and Medina, of course) are located in southern Iraq.

- The border between Iran and Iraq also serves as the border between the Arab world and the Persian world. The Ottomans saw the three vilayets that made up modern Iraq as their bulwark against Persian expansionism.

- There was no small degree of animosity between Saddam Hussein and the Aytollah Khomeini. When still the number-two man in Iraq, Saddam Hussein negotiated the deal with the Shah of Iran that helped to quell Iranian-fueled Kurdish dissent in Iraq. In that deal, signed in 1975, Saddam agreed to move the border between the two countries to the middle of the Shat-al-Arab channel, which effectively gave both countries free use of the waterway. Before that boundary shift, Iran was supposed to pay a fee to Iraq every time its ships used the waterway. In return, Iran agreed to stop supplying the Kurds with military equipment. That détente held until the onset of the war in August 1980.

> **Persian Perspectives**
>
> The Ottoman Empire, which covered much of what is now the Middle East and extended at its height into southeastern Europe, created administrative districts called *vilayets*. After the fall of the Ottoman Empire at the end of World War I, the British combined the three former vilayets of Mosul, Baghdad, and Basra to create the modern state of Iraq.

Supposed Iranian "Instability"

The Iraqi leadership felt that Iran, which had recently undergone its Islamic Revolution, was not prepared to fight against an organized invasion force. Saddam Hussein appears to have concluded that the Iranians were too disorganized to resist him. Iran looked like an easy mark. As the next eight years of war unfolded, the Islamic Republican Iran showed itself not to be the weak target Iraq thought it would be.

Hussein's Lust for Power and Oil

Saddam Hussein came to power in 1979, staging a coup and purge of the former ruling group in Iraq. He was not elected to power, nor was he appointed by the outgoing ruler. Instead, he seized power by placing the former ruler under arrest and killing several of that ruler's highly placed followers.

While Saddam had the tacit backing of the surviving Iraqi elite, he needed to do something to increase his stature, both within Iraq and among the other Arab nations of the Middle East. Attacking Iran and weakening the hated Shiite Persians must have seemed like the perfect way to improve his standing at home and internationally. In addition, the Iranian region he coveted, Khuzestan, has significant oil reserves and a sizable Arab population.

> **Bet You Didn't Know**
>
> Khuzestan is a territory in Iran that borders Iraq. Khuzestan is predominately Arab, in contrast to the Persian majority that exists throughout most of the rest of Iran (excluding the Kurdish areas in the northwest). Khuzestan boasts strategically important oil holdings.

How It All Started: The Shatt-al-Arab

As we have seen, the decline of British influence left Iran and Iraq jockeying for dominance in the Gulf. Before 1975, the two countries had operated under the terms of a 1937 British-mandated treaty governing the Shatt-al-Arab. That treaty placed the international border at the Iranian shore instead of in the middle of the channel. Thus, Iraq had nominal ownership of the waterway. The treaty also required Iraq to maintain the waterway for navigation, while requiring "other nations" (namely, Iran) to pay a transit fee for use. With the British pulling their forces out of the Gulf states, Iran saw an opportunity to exert more influence in the vacuum that departure created.

Abrogating the Treaty

In 1970, the Shah said that Iraq was not fulfilling its end of the agreement and abrogated the 1937 treaty. To prove the point, the Iranians cruised the waterway and did not pay the fees. The Iraqis responded by aiding dissidents in Iran, and Iran returned the favor by aiding the Kurds in Iraq. Not surprisingly, tensions mounted along the border.

In November 1971, the Shah continued his attempts to expand influence. Iranian forces occupied the Gulf Islands of Abu Musa and Greater and Lesser Tunbs. These islands had been controlled by the two of the Emirates that are part of the United Arab Emirates. Without British support, there was little the UAE could do about the move.

The Iraqis, however, viewed the move as a clear challenge; they foresaw Iranian forces trying to take over the Gulf and threaten Iraqi oil shipments through the strategic Strait of Hormuz. But they couldn't do much about the incursion, thanks to a vexing Kurd rebellion back home. (The Shah, we must remember, was aiding the Kurds in this effort.) In other words, the Shah's ploy of aiding the Kurds was working.

> **Bet You Didn't Know** _____
>
> The Persian Gulf is separated from the Indian Ocean by the narrow *Strait of Hormuz*. Tankers and navy vessels going to or from the upper Gulf (where the oil-loading terminals of Iraq, Iran, Kuwait, Bahrain, Qatar, and the UAE are located) must pass through this strait. Iran makes up the entire northern shoreline, and the islands of Abu Musa and the Tunbs are across the Strait. The country that controls these islands can more easily interfere with shipping through the Strait.

The Iraqis sought rapprochement with the Shah in 1975. They had little choice because the Shah's support for the Kurds was threatening the very stability of the Ba'th government in Iraq. By agreeing to move the international boundary to the middle of the Shatt-al-Arab, Iraq got Iran to stop supporting the Kurds. The trade-off worked: The Iraqis were then able to suppress the Kurds, who were left without Iranian arms shipments. For his part, the Shah gained official Iraqi recognition of Iran's right to navigate the Shatt-al-Arab without Iraqi oversight.

The Calm Before the Storm

Relations between the two countries were cool throughout the late 1970s. At one point, however, the Iraqis granted a special request of the Shah: As requested,

Saddam expelled the Iranian Shia cleric, Ayatollah Ruhollah Khomeini, from An Najaf (the Shia holy city in southern Iraq) in 1978. The Shah, as we have seen, was deeply concerned about the ayatollah's fundamentalist influence on the Shia Muslims in Iran. Saddam Hussein, similarly leery of the ayatollah's fundamentalist influence on the Shias in Iraq, was only too happy to comply.

Persian Perspectives

Born in 1900, Ruhollah Khomeini was educated into the Shia faith. In 1950, at the age of 50, he was dubbed ayatollah, or supreme religious leader. The Shia faith places great emphasis on their leadership. Khomeini, like many Shia clerics, was outspoken in his criticism of the secular regime of the shahs. He was exiled from Iran to Turkey in November 1964. In September of the following year, he left Turkey for An Najaf, the Shia holy city in Iraq, where he remained for 14 years. At the request of the Shah, Saddam Hussein deported the ayatollah in 1978. After a year in exile in Paris, the Ayatollah Khomeini returned to Iran during the Islamic Revolution of 1979. He was proclaimed leader of the Islamic Republic of Iran in 1979. The last decade of his life was filled with turmoil, notably the hostage crisis at the former U.S. Embassy in Tehran and the Iran-Iraq War.

When the ayatollah proclaimed the Islamic Republic of Iran and assumed absolute power in 1979, a protracted showdown with the United States over hostages taken in the American Embassy followed (see Chapter 12). A period of profound isolation from the United States followed.

Meanwhile, back in Iraq, Saddam Hussein carried out a coup of his own, overthrowing Hasan al-Bakr and assuming control. Saddam was thus faced with a resurgent Shia ruler in Iran whom he had booted out of the most holy Shia city scarcely 12 months before. Rather than a secular, pragmatic, if belligerent, shah, Saddam found himself face to face with a hostile, fundamentalist cleric who commanded the attention, if not the allegiance, of over half the population of Iraq—and virtually all the Shias in Iran. On the other hand, Saddam recognized that Shiite Islamic fundamentalism also isolated Iran from its former American ally—and had only deepened existing divides among Muslims in the Middle East.

Why Saddam Attacked

To understand the war Saddam waged against Iran, you have to understand the challenges and the opportunities he faced once the ayatollah assumed power in Iran.

The challenges:

 ◆ Saddam Hussein feared that the ayatollah would resume arms shipments to the Kurds in the north and, worse, maybe even to the Shias in the south. Already, Iraqi Shias were rioting, thanks to the government's refusal to allow a procession of Shias to cross into Iran to congratulate the ayatollah.

 ◆ To make matters worse, Saddam's secret police had uncovered a Shia group led by the Iraqi Ayatollah Muhammed Baqir as Sadir. This group was named Ad Dawah al Islamiyah (the Islamic Call), and was usually referred to as Ad Dawah. Sadir called for an Iraqi fundamentalist Shia state—on the Iranian model.

 ◆ The ayatollah's regime was every bit as despotic and aggressive as Iraq's. (Already, Iranian Shia leaders were preaching expansionist themes.)

The opportunities:

 ◆ By attacking a (supposedly) weakened Iran, Saddam could improve his standing within Iraq (to Sunni elites, at any rate) and within the Arab world by beating up on the *non-Arab* Shias in Iran.

 ◆ What's more, shutting down the ayatollah meant shutting down the Kurds. Saddam had not really put the Kurd problem to bed, and a Kurd truce was vital to his personal hold on power.

 ◆ The oil-rich Iranian region of Khuzestan, which borders Iraq and has (it bears repeating) an Arab rather than Persian majority, was a tempting target.

Countdown to Battle

In April 1980, the Al Dawah attempted to assassinate Iraqi foreign minister Tariq Azziz and, a short time later, made an attempt on the life of the Minister of Culture and Information, Latif Nayyif Jasim. The attempts failed; Saddam responded by deporting thousands of Shias with Iranian blood to Iran and jailing Al Dawah leaders. Baqir as Sadir, the Al Dawah leader, was executed, as was his sister. Things remained tense, and in September 1980, Saddam decided to make his move.

A Pretext for War

The Iraqi government took the position that the 1975 Algiers Agreement—the one that had given Iran joint control over the Shat al Arab—was only a truce, not a permanent treaty. In late September 1980, Saddam officially rejected the Algiers Agreement and announced that the Shat al-Arab had reverted to full Iraqi authority. Iran was incensed at the change of terms, and almost immediately both sides went to a war footing. On September 21, the Iraqis lobbed artillery into Iran, which responded in kind. The next day, both sides sent aircraft on bombing raids into each other's territories. On the day after that, Saddam sent troops into Iran, and the fighting was underway.

The Early War

In the early stages of the war, it seemed as though the Iraqi army would win in a walk. It was well equipped with Soviet weapons, had high morale, and was ably led. It had 12 mechanized divisions, with tanks, to throw at the Iranian army.

The Iranians, on the other hand, had low morale; most of their experienced officers had been purged during the Islamic Revolution, and they were now led by clerics with no military experience. Their mechanized equipment (obtained during the Shah's rule from the United States) had not been maintained, and there was little hope of getting spare parts from the Americans in the war's early stages.

Originally, the Iranians had two divisions in the central border region, but these had been degraded to the point that they had only some poorly outfitted battalions and a handful of undermanned tank companies. The rest of the Iranian equipment was not operational, due to lack of parts. The Iranian air force still was operating some of the latest American fighters and had shown that it could use them during the foiled hostage rescue attempt in April 1980.

The Iraqis attempted a massive air strike against Iranian airfields on September 22, 1980, but the strikes were ineffective. The Iranians quickly responded with air strikes of their own.

Initially, things went well for Saddam. On September 23, six Iraqi army divisions invaded the Iranian territory of Khuzestan. Saddam wanted at least to be able to carve out this section of Iran, and he hoped the Arab minority would rebel against the ayatollah. This did not happen. However, the initial Iraqi attack drove 8 kilometers into Iran within a matter days.

To the north, an Iraqi mechanized mountain division took the Iranian border town of Qasr-e Shirin. In the center, the Iraqis drove on Mehran and severed the main north-south road along the Iranian side of the border.

What's It Mean?

The **Basji** were referred to as the "Army of Twenty Million" or the People's Militia. They eventually numbered in the hundreds of thousands. The Basji were poorly trained and equipped, but they were religious zealots. Many went into combat carrying their own shrouds because they expected to die in battle and achieve martyrdom.

The invasion in the south pushed over 80 kilometers into Iran after only a few weeks of fighting. In response, the Iranian president, Bani Sadr, freed many of the fighter pilots who had been jailed due to their loyalty to the Shah. Using the latest American aircraft, these skilled pilots were able to blunt the Iraqi attack.

By November 3, 1980, Iraqi forces reached the city of Abadan but were stopped there by an Iranian Revolutionary Guard unit, called the Pasdaran. At its height, the Iraqi army had secured the Shat al Arab and occupied a 40-kilometer swath of Iranian border territory. However, the Iranians stopped all the talk of a quick Iraqi victory by calling on the Pasdaran military units and a new force, called the *Basji* (or *Basij*).

Stopping the Iraqi Advance—and Launching the "Human Wave"

Iran's counterattacks finally stopped the Iraqi advance. Iran also responded by convincing Syria to close the Iraqi oil pipeline and by threatening to seize the Iraqi oil terminal in al-Faw. The Iraqi army began to dig in and build an impenetrable defensive line.

What's It Mean?

Iran's **human wave** tactic used humans in huge numbers to attack the Iraqi enemy. The resulting casualties were enormous. An East European reporter watching a battle in the mid-1980s wrote that he "saw tens of thousands of children, roped together in groups of about 20 to prevent the faint-hearted from deserting" during the attacks.

Saddam offered a peace settlement to Iran early in the war. The offer was rejected, and Iran began to counterattack by January 1981. The first attacks were clumsy and unsuccessful.

In late 1981, at the Karun River, the Iranian clerics unleashed their *human wave* tactic that used thousands of Basij to break the Iraqi positions. The Iranians had forced the Iraqis out of their northern and central occupations by December 1981. However, the Iraqi army proved unwilling to endure the thousands of casualties that the Basij were willing to take and so did not mount a serious counteroffensive. To make matters worse, the Iranian air force had almost total control of the skies and was able to bomb any target it could find inside Iraq.

Iraq Retreats

The Iranians launched Operation Undeniable Victory in March 1982. The attack forced the Iraqi army to retreat, and it wrecked three Iraqi divisions in the process.

By May 1982, the Iranians had the Iraqis on the run all over the front. Saddam ordered the Iraqi army to return to the national border. He hoped that Iran would be happy to go back to the status quo, and he even repeated his offer to negotiate a peace settlement in June 1982. Iran again refused to negotiate and instead launched a major offensive—this time penetrating Iraqi territory.

Once again, the Iranians used the human wave strategy and, after suffering enormous casualties, succeeded in capturing a small slice of Iraq. Throughout 1983, Iran continued to use the human wave as a new tactic and had some success. Still, with its superior armor, Iraq was able to stop the Iranians. By the end of 1983, about 120,000 Iranians had died, compared to about 60,000 Iraqis. Iran appeared to be prepared to fight and win a war of attrition with Iraq.

In April 1984, Saddam offered to meet personally with the ayatollah, but the ayatollah once again refused to negotiate with the Iraqi leader.

Chemical Weapons

Then, during 1984, there was a change in strategy. Iraq concentrated on defending its own territory rather than on attacking Iran. As part of this effort, Iraq resorted to chemical weapons in 1984, in an attempt to stop the Iranians. Some experts state that the United States actually supplied Saddam with the chemical weapons technology, out of concern that the Iranians would win the war.

The use of chemical weapons on the Iranians had had little practical effect. To all appearances, the Iranians were still willing to take the immense casualties, and the Iraqis were not. The Iranians plunged into a war of attrition in the hope of pressuring the Iraqis to accept defeat.

In just two days, between February 29 and March 1, more than 25,000 men died on both sides during one of the largest battles of the war. In this battle, the human wave performed a new role: It ran in front, through the minefields, to clear a path for the Iranian tanks.

Horrific Casualties

Finally, the ayatollah started to use regular army units instead of his Pasdaran and Basij volunteers. Still the losses mounted. During one four-week stretch, the Iraqis lost 9,000 troops and the Iranians lost 40,000.

On February 9, 1986, the Iranians succeeded in taking al-Faw, where Iraqi oil was pumped into waiting tankers. The Iraqis attacked furiously and finally regained al-Faw in 1988. However, the oil facilities were out of commission. The land fighting continued, although it was basically a stalemate. Both sides then extended the war to the Gulf, and both sides attacked neutral ships carrying supplies to the belligerents. The "tanker war" eventually involved more than 111 neutral ships in 1986 alone.

In January 1987, Iran launched Operation Karbala Five, aiming at the Iraqi city of Basra. By the time that battle was over, Iraq had lost 20,000 men and 45 planes. For their part, the Iranians had lost over 65,000 men.

Despite coming close to breaking the last-ditch defense of the Iraqis, Iran called off the offensive on February 26, 1987. Heavy fighting erupted in the north in May 1987, but no definitive gains were made by either side.

Global Concerns

The attacks on oil shipping were making Western countries nervous—and increasing a feeling of grievous instability in the region. Although both sides attacked oil tankers, experts estimate that Iraq attacked three times the number of ships as Iran during this period. Iraq had antiship missiles in its arsenal and knew how to use them. Finally, Iraq began attacking Arab-flagged shipping that was moving Iranian oil. The Kuwaitis had ships that were attacked, and they appealed to both the Soviet Union and the United States for help.

Both countries charted some tankers, and the United States sent some naval vessels into the region as well. On May 17, 1987, the Iraqis accidentally hit the USS *Stark* with an antiship missile, killing 37 crewmen. Iraq apologized and did not attack U.S.–flagged ships or naval vessels after that.

Within a few weeks of the *Stark* incident, the Americans drafted UN Security Council Resolution 598 on the Gulf War, which the Security Council passed unanimously on July 20. Tehran rejected the resolution because it did not meet Iran's terms for ending the war, and instead insisted that Iraq should be punished for initiating the conflict. By the beginning of 1988, 10 Western navies and 8 regional navies were patrolling the area.

Back in 1985, the United States had been arming Iran in order to counter earlier Iraqi successes. These clandestine arms shipments eventually came to be known as the Iran-Contra Affair and constituted a huge political problem for the administration of Ronald Reagan. But as fortunes shifted, so did superpower support.

After Iran began to make military progress through 1986, the United States and the Soviets became increasingly concerned about regional stability. Both countries began to arm the Iraqis during 1987 and stopped arming the Iranians. The superpowers were concerned about the possibility of a pro-Iranian Shia state forming in southern Iraq. Such a state, they reasoned, could create serious instability in the region and perhaps bring about another seemingly endless war.

Endgame

The land war remained static; the superpowers were putting a damper on tanker attacks. It was in this environment that the Iranians launched missile attacks on Baghdad, the capital of Iraq.

This was the war's bloody endgame. In what later was called the War of the Cities, some 190 missiles were launched by Iraq into Iran in response to the Iranian missile attacks on Baghdad. The ongoing stress of these missile attacks and the fear that the Iraqis would launch chemical warheads against civilian populations helped to bring the Iranians to the negotiation table at last.

There were other reasons the Iranians came to the table. One was that the Iraqi army, now re-equipped with Soviet and French equipment, was a much more effective fighting force than it had been four years earlier. During the first half of 1988, Iraq defeated Iran in four major battles. In the battle to retake al-Faw, the Iraqis used chemical weapons yet again. Facing those defeats and the continued missile terror, the Iranians submitted to the notion of negotiating a peace settlement with Iraq. By this time, the Iraqis had regained the momentum, but Saddam Hussein, too, had had enough.

The war lasted nearly eight years, from September 1980 until August 1988. It ended when Iran and Iraq accepted UN Security Council Resolution 598, calling for a ceasefire on August 20, 1988.

A Return to the Status Quo

When it was all over, the issues that led to the war were still unresolved. The borders were the same, and the combatants were bloodied but unbowed. Iraq did come out of the war with a military superiority over Iran, but that superiority was lost after Iraq's Gulf War defeat three years later.

Iraqi casualties numbered about 375,000 people in the war with Iran, a staggering figure for a nation of 16 million. Iran may have endured as many as one million dead or wounded. To put those numbers in perspective, consider that Iran had 60 million people in 1988.

Iran Turns Inward

At the end of the Iran-Iraq War, the two belligerents went two very different directions. Iraq owed billions to other Arab nations and found itself looking for ways and means to maintain an army of more than one million men. (It eventually embarked on yet another disastrous expansionist campaign, this one against Kuwait.) Iran, on the other hand, turned inward and focused on its efforts on rebuilding its ravaged country and economy.

The Least You Need to Know

- Iraq picked a fight with Iran for a variety of reasons, including historic rivalries, a perception that Iran was weakened, and Saddam Hussein's desire to establish himself as a great Arab leader.

- Iran reeled under the initial Iraqi onslaught that began in September 1980, but it managed to reverse the tide and almost overwhelm the Iraqis in the mid 1980s.

- The two sides reached a stalemate on land and then moved the war to each other's oil-producing and -exporting facilities.

- When the war began to threaten oil shipments, the United States and the USSR got involved and, operating through the UN Security Council, mediated a ceasefire in 1988.

Chapter 14

The Islamic Republic Meets the Real World

In This Chapter

- ◆ Consolidation after the Iran-Iraq War
- ◆ The clerical establishment's built-in advantages
- ◆ Islamic law takes hold
- ◆ Rumblings of discontent

The founding of the Islamic Republic in Iran in 1979 constituted one of the boldest social and political experiments of modern times. It was the first unapologetic theocracy established in the modern era. It was the first attempt in centuries to govern an entire society—both the "secular" and "religious" realms, to use Western terms—by means of an Islamic governmental structure dominated by clerics. And it had been endorsed by an overwhelming majority of the Iranian people. However, this experiment had no real examples to follow. It was the first of its kind, certainly in modern times. Around the world, both detractors and supporters of the revolution that had just been concluded watched in fascination to see how the experiment would play out. Then came the war.

Almost immediately following the establishment of the Republic, Iran found itself attacked by Iraq, and its people were forced to confront issues of war and peace, assault and defense, deprivation and survival. With the country on a war footing and facing sacrifices that few in the developed world could imagine, the country had no choice but to set aside, in the interest of survival, the important question of precisely what kind of society would emerge in Iran. In August 1988, with the horrific war finally behind them, the Iranian polity finally set about the business of determining what normal life in the republic would look like.

To understand what happened and how the clerical establishment overplayed its hand in the postwar period, it's important to get a working knowledge of the structure of the Iranian system of government. It is a system founded, at least in theory, on principles of democracy.

Is the Islamic Republic Really a Democracy?

A common observation from Americans and Europeans is that the Iranian governmental model does not pass muster as a pluralistic democracy by Western standards. By the same token, it's important to understand that the constitutional structure that emerged from a war footing in the late 1980s in Iran does feature nominally democratic elements. There are elections, although clerical institutions have so much power that the elections amount to the populace selecting from a roster of approved candidates. Still, the inclusion of even a little democracy was a fateful step for Iran, as will become clear in the next chapter.

How Much Freedom Is Too Much?

Any discussion of democracy in the turbulent region of the Middle East must begin with a warning: The idea of an open democratic society along the American or European models is not always viewed with gleeful anticipation in this part of the world. Where Westerners tend to see the potential for traditions of, say, tolerance for religious minorities, an independent judiciary, or a more-prominent social and political role for women, Muslims—even reformist Muslims—may associate a very different set of traditions with Western-style democracy: satellite TV channels drenched with hard-core sex, disrespect for Islamic traditions, and the potential for drug abuse, alcoholism, broken families, and other social problems. However, a movement toward greater democratization in an Islamic context has emerged and has, remarkably enough, expressed itself through the structures established in the aftermath of the revolution of 1979.

The Hybrid

The form of government that emerged after the revolution can be thought of as an unsteady hybrid ice cream cone: two large scoops of Islamic fundamentalism atop one small scoop of carefully controlled democratic influence. While the Republic is not by any stretch of the imagination a pluralistic democracy with a tolerance for free expression or dissent, it is a fascinating and (so far) unique balancing act that incorporates a certain limited amount of popular input within an Islamic governing structure.

Why do the ruling clerics tolerate any kind of popular dissent? Perhaps the reason is more practical than dogmatic. From 1900 to 1979, popular unrest forced the Shah to flee the country on more than one occasion. Public protest also was the vehicle that brought the clerics into power, despite the best efforts of the SAVAK to suppress them. The clerics realize the power of the people, try to keep that power in control, and align it with their goals. To do this, some popular dissent and debate must be allowed, or next time the clerics might be taking a flight from the Tehran airport for an unnamed "vacation" destination. Rather than go down that path, the ruling clerics have established a blueprint for maintaining their power and sustaining the goals of the Islamic Republic.

Let's look very briefly at the specifics of that governmental blueprint now.

Six, Not Three

The federal government of the United States can be divided into three branches—executive, legislative, and judicial—each with checks and balances on the other two. The system in Iran is a little more intricate and is designed not so much in terms of checks and balances, but to favor the clerical forces that played an important role in winning the revolution.

There are not three, but six institutions to keep in mind when considering the Iranian government. Here's an overview of all six.

The Big Guy: The Supreme Leader

The Ayatollah Khomeini, the hugely popular leader of the revolution, originated the role of Supreme Leader. When Khomeini died in 1989, the Ayatollah Ali Khamenei succeeded him. Khamenei inherited an office of immense political and religious influence, an office that clearly embraces the supreme administrative and executive authority in the country.

Theoretically, the populace selects the Supreme Leader. In reality, he is elected by the Assembly of Experts, a body not unlike the College of Cardinals of the Catholic Church or the Electoral College in the United States. The Supreme Leader, however, is not accountable to the people for election or anything else; he can be dismissed only by the Assembly of Experts. Otherwise, he serves for life. In many ways, the role's selection process resembles that of the General Secretary of the Politburo in the old Soviet Union.

The Supreme Leader holds many executive responsibilities. He controls the armed forces, he decides who will run the state-controlled radio and television outlets, and (perhaps most important) he appoints the head of the judiciary and half of the members of the Council of Guardians. (You'll hear more about those two institutions later in this chapter.) The Supreme Leader is the single most powerful representative of Islamic orthodoxy in Iran.

The Judiciary

The judiciary in Iran has always had its share of political influence. Heavily dominated by the clergy until the early twentieth century, it was eventually secularized. However, since the 1979 revolution, the head of the judiciary has served at the pleasure of the Supreme Leader. Since then, and partly due to the backing of the Supreme Leader, the judiciary has emerged as a powerful social and legal force in Iran.

From the early days of the revolution until the death of the Ayatollah Khomeini in 1989, the judiciary was dominated by radical forces and left-wing elements. The judiciary was more progressive and willing to explore new interpretations of law. After Khomeini died, however, the conservatives gained a great deal of influence—an influence they retain to this day—and the judiciary leaned toward a more rigid interpretation of Islamic law.

The Parliament

The Iranian parliament is known as the Majlis and has been in existence since the early 1900s, when the Constitutionalists first convinced the shah to approve it. It cannot be dissolved. The Majlis is elected every four years by the people, and constitutionally authorized minority groups may be represented. Elections to fill it were dutifully held even while the war with Iraq was raging.

After the revolution, the Majlis was inherited by the clerics. Perhaps the clerics realized that doing away with the Majlis may have been going too far, or perhaps the clerics viewed the Majlis as a useful tool for exerting power while giving the man on the street a chance to speak his mind. Either way, the Majlis survived the revolution and the war that followed.

In practice, reformist legislators have come to dominate the Majlis. But that does not mean that the reformists have gained much practical political power. If Iran had a structurally powerful legislature like the United Kingdom or the United States, the dominance of the reformists there would mean that legislation designed to loosen certain social restrictions and increase the influence of the voting public might stand a realistic chance of becoming law. In Iran, however, this is not the case, in large measure because of the influence of a powerful 12-man group known as the Council of Guardians.

The Council of Guardians

The Council of Guardians is made up of six theologians selected by the Supreme Leader and six jurists selected by the judiciary and approved by the Majlis. The Majlis does not have the right to suggest any candidates; it simply must approve (or possibly disapprove) of the ones offered to it.

The Council of Guardians is probably the single most powerful institution in Iran and has the power to reject any legislation that it considers to be incompatible with the constitution and Islamic law. What's more, no law goes on the books without its approval, and decisions of the council are final. It is controlled by conservative clerics who are hostile to reformist movements and the expansion of democracy in Iran.

The President

Under the Iranian constitution, the president is elected directly by the people every four years; he can serve a maximum of two terms. His powers, however, are severely limited. As noted earlier, he does not control the military, the media, or appointments to the judiciary or the Council of Guardians; those are all under the control of the Supreme Leader. The Iranian president is, however, technically responsible for ensuring that the constitution is faithfully observed and executed in practice.

Precisely what tools he is to use in completing this task, however, is sometimes unclear. And his position as defender of the constitution is not helped by his essential powerlessness over the Council of Guardians and the judiciary.

When the president reflects the philosophies and goals of the Supreme Leader, there's no problem. And perhaps this was, in fact, the routine outcome envisioned by the framers of the constitution. However, if the president does not reflect the philosophies and goals of the Supreme Leader, the situation gets more interesting, though less certain.

The Cabinet

The inherent difficulties of the president's job become painfully clear once you examine the stated—and actual—responsibilities of his cabinet.

The president is responsible for nominating ministers to key posts. And the elected parliament has the right to confirm them. But because the Supreme Leader, not the president, controls the armed forces and much of the governmental apparatus, many ministers end up reporting to the Supreme Leader, despite the fact that they are technically accountable to the president.

Ministers in charge of cultural or social affairs are (like, let's face it, the rest of the country) monitored closely by conservative forces for any tendency to undermine orthodox Islamic teachings. If any such tendencies are identified, the conservatives can put pressure on the president, via the experts to the Supreme Leader, to have that minister removed.

And as a Special Added Bonus ...

There is a seventh element, the one supposedly guiding the six basic building blocks of the Iranian government. It is the population of Iran itself. Although the people theoretically are in control of the state by means of direct election of the Assembly of Experts, the parliament, and the president, large chunks of the public at the end of the war with Iraq had little reason to cheer the onset of "freedom, independence, and the Islamic Republic," as the revolutionary slogan of the decade before had read. To the contrary, intellectual and political freedom that attempted to find expression in the form of opposition parties—or any form of organized dissent from the orthodox line—were ruthlessly crushed. As Amnesty International was quick to note, the regime of the Shah had no corner on human rights abuses in Iran.

The Bottom Line: Clerics Rule

As it emerged from the bloody and prolonged war with Iraq, Iran appealed to repression with the same instinctive desire to shut down opposition viewpoints that had guided the Shah. The hard-line clerics were firmly in control of the machinery of the new republic, and the holder of the presidency was, one way or another, going to serve as the subservient executor of the wishes of the Supreme Leader.

Here's a condensed timeline of the key events in the country after the Iranians accepted the UN–brokered ceasefire in 1988:

◆ **July 1988:** Persecution of Iranian dissidents intensifies.

◆ **February 1989:** The Ayatollah Khomeini issues a fatwa, or religious ruling, condemning the author Salman Rushdie's novel *The Satanic Verses* as blasphemous, and calling for the author's death. The ruling causes an international uproar.

◆ **June 1989:** The Ayatollah Khomeini dies; images of tens of thousands of frenzied mourners are circulated around the world. He is succeeded by Ayatollah Ali Khamenei.

Bet You Didn't Know

For Khomeini, there was no difference between prayer and politics. But when it came to the crunch, he put the survival of the Islamic state above religious principles—as, for example, when he authorised the mass execution of opponents, even though this contravened the basic concept of Islamic justice.
—From the BBC's 1989 obituary of the Ayatollah Khomeini

◆ **Mid-1989:** Former speaker of the Iranian parliament Hashemi Rafsanjani is elected president. He is a Shiite cleric and a founding member of the Islamic Republican Party. He receives 95 percent of the vote.

◆ **Late 1989:** The United States releases a huge sum of previously frozen Iranian assets; in 1990, a series of hostage releases takes place. Attempts by Rafsanjani to make economic overtures to the West, however, are undercut by the clerical establishment.

◆ **Early 1991:** Radicals in Iran use the American-led campaign to oust Saddam Hussein as a means of inflaming anti–U.S. sentiment in the country.

◆ **Summer and fall of 1991:** Economic hardship (from low oil prices and heavy war-time debts) leads to unrest and causes Rafsanjani to try to implement a series of economic reforms.

◆ **Late 1991:** Eight members of a group known as the Freedom Movement are imprisoned for composing and publishing a letter to President Rafsanjani, calling for human rights reforms.

◆ **Late 1991:** Seeking to extricate itself from involvement in the Lebanese civil war, Iranian leaders help to coordinate the negotiated release of a number of Western hostages.

- **1991 and 1992:** The leadership makes continued attempts to reconstruct the war-shattered Iranian economy. They meet limited success, even in the critical oil industry.

- **April 5, 1992:** Iranian air attacks the opposition group, called the MEK, bases in Iraq.

- **April 1992:** Hard-liners suffer serious setbacks in the parliamentary elections.

- **May 1992:** Urban riots in Meshed, Shiraz, Tabriz, and Arak break out; a number of people are eventually executed for their involvement.

- **April 1993:** The U.S. State Department condemns Iranian involvement in Islamist movements in the Sudan, Egypt, Algeria, Lebanon, and the West Bank, including Hezbollah and Hamas terrorists.

- **May 1993:** More air attacks take place on opposition bases located in Iraq.

- **June 1993:** Rafsanjani is re-elected as president, but this time with 63 percent of the vote, compared with an overwhelming 95 percent in his first campaign for the office.

What Was Going On?

In the early 1990s, social and economic pressures related to the country's slow and painful recovery from the Iran-Iraq War finally resulted in what would become the first signs of real, practical political trouble for the Islamic clerical forces who had engineered the revolution. The economic problems were severe. The main income source, oil, was experiencing low prices on the world market, which translated into lower than normal income for Iran. On top of that, debt issued during the Iran-Iraq War was coming due. Iranian central bankers and the leadership handled the balance of payments crisis in two ways. First, they limited imports of consumption items, paying debt through forced savings, in a way. Second, they rescheduled much of the outstanding debt with the international lending institutions that were seeking payment. The process ultimately worked (assisted by increased oil prices later), but at great social and economic cost to a population already fed up by eight years of war-time sacrifice.

There was no longer a tyrant to oust; there was no longer a military danger to the homeland. Instead, there was a low but detectable rumbling from the people for reform, a rumbling that somehow only intensified in the face of repression. The hard-liners were about to face a popular, impossible-to-ignore challenge to their authority for the very first time. And that challenge was going to unfold in what must have appeared to them to be the unlikeliest of ways: as the result of a winning campaign for the presidency of Iran.

The Least You Need to Know

- ◆ Hard-line clerics enjoy built-in advantages under the Iranian constitution.

- ◆ Although the Islamic Republic of Iran flunks any meaningful test for a democratic society, it is a fascinating and (so far) unique balancing act that incorporates a certain amount of popular input within an Islamic governing structure.

- ◆ Repression of opposition groups intensified immediately after the conclusion of the war with Iraq.

- ◆ Social and economic difficulties related to the country's recovery from the Iran-Iraq War resulted in popular discontent that would eventually coalesce into a sustained reform movement.

15

Dreams Deferred: The Reform Movement

In This Chapter

- ◆ A stunning electoral victory for the reformers
- ◆ The landslide without a mandate
- ◆ The question of women
- ◆ Possible splintering of the reform movement

Something extraordinary happened in the 1997 presidential elections in Iran, and it had a lot to do with teenagers.

Back in 1979, young people had, of course, played an important role in the overthrow of the Shah and the later occupation of the U.S. Embassy. When the time came to formulate a new constitution, the leaders of the revolution took an interesting step: They extended the vote to people of 16 years of age and older. When the constitution was ratified by the people, this extension of the franchise meant that the young would play a major role in shaping the direction of the new Iranian republic.

In 1997, a new generation of young voters—people born after the revolution who had never experienced any other form of government—would help to spark a conflict over the nature of the Iranian state itself. They knew of the Shah and the previous regime only through what they were told, yet they were in conflict. For all the facts and fictions about the "Great Satan" (the United States), these young people could be pro-Western. For all the teaching on the one path of the Islamic state, these young people wanted more of a voice. They were in conflict, both within themselves and with the regime that had raised them. As of this writing, this conflict is still unresolved.

Rafsanjani Bows Out

Rafsanjani's second term had been marked by military activity abroad (another series of attacks launched in 1994 against Iranian rebels based in Iraq) and economic challenges at home. His efforts to improve the economic situation were not much aided by a U.S. ban on all trade with Iraq (1994). Another potential hurdle was the attempted imposition of U.S. sanctions to any company not of American origin that dared to invest in Iran or Libya (the Iran and Libya Sanctions Act of 1996). This latter measure was challenged by the European Union, however, and the sanctions were largely unenforced. The fully integrated nature of the global economy and the outright refusal of companies from countries such as France, Russian, and China to honor the sanctions made it difficult to enforce the act.

Highlights of the Iran-Libya Sanctions Act include the following:

Purpose: The Iran and Libya Sanctions Act of 1996 imposes new sanctions on foreign companies that engage in specified economic transactions with Iran or Libya. It is intended to:

— Help deny Iran and Libya revenues that could be used to finance international terrorism;

— Limit the flow of resources necessary to obtain weapons of mass destruction;

The Sanctions: The bill sanctions foreign companies that provide new investments over $40 million for the development of petroleum resources in Iran or Libya … These sanctions include:

— denial of Export-Import Bank assistance;

— denial of export licenses for exports to the violating company;

— prohibition on loans or credits from U.S. financial institutions of over $10 million in any 12-month period;

— denial of U.S. government procurement opportunities (consistent with WTO obligations); and

— a ban on all or some imports of the violating company.

This Bill is Another Step in U.S. Efforts to Enforce Compliance from Iran and Libya:

— In 1984, Iran was placed on the list of states that support international terrorism, triggering statutory sanctions that prohibit weapons sales, oppose all loans to Iran from international financial institutions, and prohibit all assistance to Iran.

— In 1987, the U.S. further prohibited the importation of any goods or services from Iran and U.S. naval and air forces struck Iranian naval units on several occasions in response to Iranian efforts to disrupt the flow of oil from the Persian Gulf with naval mines and missile attacks.

— In 1995, President Clinton imposed comprehensive sanctions on Iran, prohibiting all commercial and financial transactions with Iran.

— In addition, the United States has worked with our allies to further isolate Libya both internationally and within the Middle East and to develop new methods to pressure Qadhafi to comply with the U.N. Security Council Resolutions directed at Libya.

Source: The White House

Prevented by law from seeking a third term, President Rafsanjani dutifully stepped aside as the 1997 campaign season unfolded. The strangest thing about his exit, perhaps, was the fact that it was not accompanied by another entrance: that of a front-runner for the office of president. There was a reason for this. The voting public wanted something different this time around.

There was no hard-line candidate who could command enough support to emerge as the obvious successor to Rafsanjani. It came to pass that, for the first time since the founding of the Islamic Republic of Iran, the nation had an election on its hands whose outcome could not be confidently predicted ahead of time. By April 1997, 10 candidates had emerged, and no one had any idea which of them would be occupying Rafsanjani's old post.

A Demographic Dilemma

The conservative clerics in control of the Council of Guardians and the judiciary were in no danger of losing control of the government. They were, however, forced to confront a demographic challenge in 1997 that no one had foreseen in 1979, when the voting age was established as 16. The challenge was this: Roughly two thirds of the country in 1997 consisted of people who were under 25 years of age.

Bet You Didn't Know

As of this writing, there are roughly 8 million voters under the age of 25 in Iran, and they represent the fastest-growing segment of the Iranian population.

These young voters were eager to remove some (although certainly not all) of the restrictions associated with life in a conservative Islamic society; they were eager to establish a social order that included women in positions of greater prominence, and they were ready to loosen the grip of the conservative clerics on the press and other institutions. They were participating in another movement now: a movement to reform Iranian society, modernize the economy, and relax some of the stricter social codes.

Younger voters who had no clear memory (and, indeed, no experience whatsoever) of the revolution of 1979 thus formed what, in a Western-style democracy, would have made up a powerful constituency for some adept politician. What these voters would constitute under Iran's system—other than an irritant to the ruling clerics—was yet to be determined.

As it happened, the two leading candidates to emerge by late May were a hard-liner by the name of Ali Akbar Nateq-Nouri, clearly the favorite of the conservative forces, and a moderate cleric, Mohammad Khatami. Khatami had been forced to resign as culture minister in 1992 for adopting attitudes that the conservatives felt were too permissive for the country's good.

Khatami ran a reform-based campaign, appealed to the youth vote, built a coalition that included intellectuals and (surviving) left-wing activists, and headed up a surprisingly well-organized reform movement. He promised to relax social restrictions in areas such as dating between unmarried couples, increase press freedoms, and expand democratic influence. Exactly how these changes were to come about, given the severely limited powers of the Iranian presidency, was a subject often left for later discussion.

A Landslide—but Not a Mandate

On election day, the reformist coalition of young people, intellectuals, and leftists broke ranks. They voted against the establishment candidate in huge numbers. Khatami took 69 percent of the vote—roughly 20 million votes out of 29.7 million cast—and the reformers believed they had won the first of a series of sweeping victories that would transform the political and social landscape of the country. There were obstacles ahead, to be sure. But surely, believers felt, they could be overcome, just as the official candidate for the presidency had been overcome.

No one believed what some in the West were suggesting about what the election meant: that Khatami embraced a rejection of core Islamic values, for instance, or that the first item on his agenda was going to be a rapprochement with the United States. But there was a group in Iran that felt that Khatami's victory was the first step in another reorganization of Iranian society, a reorganization not unlike that of 1979, but peaceful and built on elections and social activism. There was a group in Iran that believed, in the aftermath of Khatami's stunning victory over the conservative clerical forces, that the country was on the fast track toward radical reorganization of the government, economic policy, and social standards. That group was wrong.

In a Western-style democracy, the winner of the 1997 presidential election would have been the recipient not only of a victory acknowledged as legitimate by the Supreme Leader, but also of a mandate for change. In Khatami's case, the powers that be acknowledged his landslide but denied him his mandate.

They Said It

Under the Islamic system, justice and the welfare of mankind should prevail. To this end, reason and intellect are to be utilized. The best way for the establishment of justice lies in utilizing the best of research and expertise. It is only through the growth of thinking and intellectual forces in the society and free presentation of ideas that the government can choose the best of views and ways and arrive at the proper criteria for "justice and good" in the sophisticated world of today, given the complex mechanisms governing economic, political and cultural relations in the society.

—From President Khatami's inaugural address, August 4, 1997

The Reformers Get Cut Off at the Pass

When he took office, Khatami found the going tough. Remember, the presidency is an office that can carry influence and authority *if* the person who holds it shares the goals and philosophies of the Supreme Leader. If he doesn't, the political options are few. Case in point: The "victory" of Khatami's election was followed by a similarly resounding popular "victory" in the parliament, with the establishment of a strong reformist majority. But it turned out that these were hollow triumphs indeed—at least for those who measure triumph by progress on one's political agenda.

Khatami found himself and his legislative backers blocked on all sides. The fact that a strong majority supported his reform efforts counted for nothing in the overall scheme of Iranian policy and law. Not only did the clerics who controlled the judiciary and the mechanisms of the state ignore the efforts of the reformist coalition to loosen social restrictions and reinforce democratic institutions, but they actually rolled back the clock.

The sense of optimism and all-but-imminent political authority that accompanied Khatami's election faded very quickly. High unemployment was one factor for this. Another was the lack of real-life traction that the reformist agenda showed in a world whose most important institutions were still very much dominated by conservative clerics.

The reformers were forced to watch as a hard-line counterattack stopped any campaign for change before it had the chance to begin properly. The counterattack left both Khatami and the parliament looking essentially irrelevant.

Working for the Clampdown

Among the signposts of the clampdown were the following:

◆ Reformist newspapers and magazines were shut down.

◆ A network of street-roving thugs made a habit of stopping women deemed improperly dressed and assaulting them; accusations of sexual assault were rampant. This was simple state terrorism against the population, as a means of expressing the attitudes of the leadership in another way.

◆ A series of pro-reform student protests was quickly and violently quelled by the Iranian security apparatus, acting in concert with conservative vigilante groups.

◆ The judiciary briskly dismissed efforts at social and judicial reform, and even established a new system of trial under which a presiding judge acted as both prosecutor and sentencer of an alleged offender.

If this was progressive Islam, it looked disturbingly like the status quo—or worse. The bottom line was that, after the reformist "victories," the Iranian government was as unresponsive, doctrinaire, and focused on dismissing the notion of personal freedom as it had been before.

A hard-to-define emotion—one composed of equal measures of impatience, disillusion, and anxiety—came over the reform movement when it became clear that neither Khatami nor anyone else would be able to deliver on the promises of 1997 anytime soon.

The Question of Women, the Question of Equality

Among the most stark differences between the hard-liners and the reformists in Iran is their concept of the role of women. In the years following the revolution, the conservative clerics have repeatedly emphasized the importance of women maintaining their traditional role, a role defined primarily or exclusively through their role in the family.

President Khatami and his reform allies, on the other hand, insist that, under Islam, men and women are equal before God and should be considered equals in Iranian society. Khatami and the reformers hold, for instance, that there should once again be female judges with full authority to decide cases, as there were during the Shah's regime; the conservatives vigorously disagree and see such innovations as a sign of unacceptable Westernization. No prizes for guessing whose position has carried the day so far. (It should be noted, though, that women do serve today in an advisory role in some Iranian court settings.)

In 1999, a reform-minded cleric, Ayatollah Yosef Sanei, set off a national debate when he suggested that there was no obstacle to a woman serving as president of the country or even Supreme Leader. The debate, not surprisingly, goes on.

> **They Said It**
>
> Smiling in the street is prohibited (to Iranian women). Women are banned from pursuing higher education in 91 of 169 fields of study and must be taught in segregated classrooms. A woman may work with her husband's permission, although many occupations are forbidden to women .... Punishments (for "immodest" activity) range from a verbal reprimand to 74 lashes with a whip, to imprisonment for one month to a year. Stoning to death is a legal form of punishment for sexual misconduct.
>
> —From "Women and Reform in Iran," article by Donna Hughes, available at www.uri.edu/artsci/wms/hughes/reform.htm

That Old-Time Religion

On the issue of women, as on many other issues, Khatami should be understood not as a proponent of "liberal" social reforms that would make Western politicians, corporate leaders, marketers, advertisers, and broadcasters happy—but as a spokesman for a view of Islam that embraces its existing egalitarian and progressive elements. Many non-Muslims are unaware of these elements, but that fact alone does not mean that the elements do not exist.

It comes as a surprise to some non-Muslims to learn, for instance, that Islam …

- Explicitly acknowledges all believers as being spiritually equal before God, regardless of gender.

- Guarantees women the right to make contracts, launch businesses, earn money, and possess property independently.

- Calls on men and women alike to pursue knowledge and education.

- Guarantees both women and men the right to freedom of expression.

> **Persian Perspectives**
>
> And their Lord has accepted (their prayers) and answered them (saying): "Never will I cause to be lost the work of any of you, be he male or female; you are members, one of another."
>
> —The Qur'an, 3:195

Surprising as it may be to Westerners, the fact is that many of the obstacles that exist to gender equality in Iran (and in other Muslim nations) have far more to do with recent legal trends, cultural predispositions, and long-standing social tradition than they do with the verses of the Qur'an or the teachings of the Prophet Muhammad.

President Khatami's role as a "reformer" should, therefore, not be misunderstood. He is not appealing to undo or reformulate Islam, nor is he attempting to undermine the notion of an Islamic republic in Iran. He is attempting to reclaim a long-ignored heritage of egalitarianism, mutual respect between genders, and intellectual openness that is at the heart of the faith.

> **Persian Perspectives**
>
> The Khatami era has seen some important changes in thinking in Iran, even if it hasn't delivered the legislative, social, and administrative reforms that Khatami's supporters would have liked. In 1998, for instance, the fatwa against the author Salman Rushdie was effectively lifted, a step that allowed for an improvement of relations with the British and the Americans and allowed Rushdie to resume something resembling a normal life.

Khatami is not—and will never be—interested in promoting Western interests in the region. He is, however, a man many open-minded Muslims believe to be one of the most important figures in the contemporary Muslim world—even if his ability to implement his ideas has been minimal thus far. That his election was acknowledged, and that his views have been the subject of intense public debate, qualifies as something of a success, even if it's not the success young people, intellectuals, and left-wingers had in mind when they voted for him in such huge numbers in 1997.

Quotations from President Khatami

The following are some of the more intriguing public remarks from the remarkable man who holds the impressive-sounding but ultimately less-than-consequential, office of president of the Islamic Republic of Iran:

> Let me declare my belief clearly. The destiny of the religion's social prestige today and tomorrow will depend on our interpretation of the religion in a manner which would not contradict freedom. Whenever in history a religion has faced freedom, it has been the religion which has sustained damage ... when we speak of freedom, we mean the freedom of the opposition. It is no freedom if only the people who agree with those in power and with their ways and means are free.
>
> —Addressing Tehran University students on the first anniversary of his election, May 23, 1998

> One of the ironies of history is that this concept of tolerance, which was adopted by Europeans from Muslims, a consequence of their acquaintance with Muslims, has in our time come to be a moral and political value recommended by Europeans to Muslims.
>
> —Speech at Florence University during a state visit to Italy, March 10, 1999

> When we speak of democratic government, or government of the people, it means that we accept opposition. We cannot possibly have a society with no opposition at all. Such differences of opinion are natural and they are to be found in all societies. We should learn not to allow such differences to turn into confrontation, but to direct them into their legal channels. Certainly, there are elements who are opposing our government, but so long as their opposition is practiced within the provisions of the constitution, we certainly respect them. But those wishing to impose their will against the law will naturally be dealt with through the proper legal channels. We accept both internal differences as well as any opposition that accepts the constitutional framework, even if they openly oppose the government.
>
> —Interview with CNN, January 7, 1998

Outmaneuvered—but for How Long?

By the 2001 elections, it was obvious that Khatami's opponents had effectively outmaneuvered him and would continue to do so for the foreseeable future. Nonetheless, he was returned to office for a second term by an even larger majority, securing 77 percent of the vote.

However, the longer Khatami is unable to accomplish real reform, the greater the likelihood is that the reform movement that elected him will splinter. Those who are impatient for change will split off into a more radicalized group that will add urgency and possibly violence to the pressure for reform. It remains to be seen whether the reformist leaders will be able to control these radicalized protestors.

As this book goes to press, there is some talk that Khatami's enduring popularity has caused something of a split in the conservative ranks, with one wing of the hard-line establishment favoring some form of compromise with the reform majority, and another wing clinging tenaciously to the closed system, the old ways of looking at issues related to gender, self-expression, and the old restrictive social rulings.

If there is such a split for the conservatives, it hasn't exhibited itself by means of concessions to Khatami's agenda. The conservatives are still winning at a game that has, frankly, been rigged to their advantage. The only card Khatami, or any reformer who follows him, currently has the ability to play is popular outrage, and that's a card whose implications are not always easy to predict.

Stay tuned.

The Least You Need to Know

- A coalition of young people, intellectuals, and left-wing thinkers propelled the reformer Muhammad Khatami to presidential-election victories in 1997 and 2001.

- These huge electoral victories did not translate into actual reforms on the economic or social fronts, however, because of institutional advantages clerical conservatives enjoy under the Iranian constitution.

- The mere propagation of Khatami's ideas, however, constitutes a major accomplishment.

- Khatami's brand of reform embraces egalitarian ideas that are at the heart of the Islamic faith.

- If there is a split in the conservative ranks over the question of how to deal with the (still-popular) reform movement, it has not yet yielded any meaningful victories for the reformers.

Part 4

Today: Iran's Relationship with the World

Iran is a work in progress, but change is coming. Fundamentalism drives internal policy and society, but expediency is taking the place of dogmatism in foreign relations. Iran is trying to reach out to the world, but it exports terror along with oil and imports nukes along with food, making for an extremely volatile mix.

The following chapters place Iran into the current world order and explain why its place there is due for significant change.

Chapter 16

Islam and the Challenge of Modernity

In This Chapter

- ◆ The modernity question
- ◆ The Golden Age of Islam
- ◆ "Reversion" to core Islamic values that may surprise you
- ◆ The legacy of conservatism on modern Islam

In this chapter, you'll learn how two important principles—freedom of thought and a desire to avoid religious disunity—helped to define the Islamic faith. You'll also learn how these two forces came into conflict in the twelfth century and how the desire to avoid religious disunity won the struggle, with disastrous ongoing results for Islamic society.

You'll get an overview of the ongoing debate between East and West over whether Islam is "incompatible" with the modern world. This is an ongoing controversy whose resolution is unlikely to come soon but that must be understood to get a sense of the populist movement that may or may not emerge as a potent reformist force in present-day Iran.

What Is a Modern Society, Anyway?

Today many non-Muslims take it as a given that Islam is both ...

♦ Inherently hostile to other belief systems and cultures.

♦ In need of reform, perhaps from the West.

American commentator Daniel Pipes, for instance, wrote in an August 13, 2002, article in *The New York Post:* "Rather than rail on about Islam's alleged 'evil,' ... (we should) help modernize this civilization." After the article ran, Pipes received a huge volume of mail, most of it taking him to task for his supposed naiveté in thinking that Islamic civilizations could ever be modernized.

It should not come as a surprise that most Muslims view such pronouncements with both indignation and alarm. Why? The answer's pretty simple. Any outsider attempting to "reform" the culture, religion, or mores of a group of which he is not a member should be prepared to meet intense resistance. People who are in the group may not be prepared to welcome the helpful (or, perhaps, condescending) advice of outsiders.

The current period of chaos and misunderstanding in relations between the non-Muslim and the Muslim worlds is not going to be resolved by one side's "modernizing" the other. After all, the word itself is loaded with problems: If I attempt to "modernize" you, I am, by definition, defining you as being less advanced than I am. If that attitude didn't produce great results when Europeans interacted with a few million American Indians, it's unlikely to produce great results when contemporary Americans interact with the more than one billion Muslims now alive on Earth. Remember that the cultures of Iran and Iraq, for example, are among the oldest on Earth. They had flourishing cities when European social groups were only just starting. While the recent centuries have not kept up that advanced state, the Muslims in these areas are resentful of the concept of modernization on a pre-Islam basis as well.

When commentators such as Daniel Pipes talk about "modernizing" the Islamic world, what do they mean? In other words, what is this modern society to which the non-Islamic world wants to expose the Islamic world? It seems likely that such social critics are talking about such bedrock Western values as the following:

♦ Equality for women

♦ Active promotion of freedom of thought and intellectual inquiry

♦ Religious and social tolerance

♦ An end to authoritarian governmental models

Most people in the United States and Europe would associate these values with Western society, not with Islamic society. Fortunately for Pipes and the many others in the international community who are eager to bring Muslims into contact with these kinds of values, there is, in fact, a movement in the contemporary Islamic world promoting precisely these initiatives. The following are some intriguing quotes from the leading philosopher of this movement:

On emphasizing equality for women ...

> [Remember, Allah] answers prayers! He says: I will not let the good deed of any worker among you, whether a male or a female, be wasted. You are all the off-spring of one another.

> Anyone who does deeds of righteousness, male or female, and has faith, will enter into Paradise.

On establishing freedom of thought and intellectual inquiry ...

> You must never follow others in matters of which you yourself have no knowl-edge. You have each been given ears, eyes, and a heart—and make no mistake, the way you use these will be taken into account on the Day of Judgment.

> Travel the Earth! Learn for yourself how Allah has brought his creation into being!

On promoting religious and social tolerance ...

> Believers who are among the Jews and the Christians ... whoever believes in God and the Last Day and does good works—these people will have their reward with Allah. They shall have no reason whatsoever to fear or to grieve.

> The person who wants to believe, may believe; the person who wants to reject, may reject.

On moving beyond authoritarian governments ...

> Policy is only [to be] decided after due consultation (with the public).

> The authoritative judgment [of what is right and wrong] belongs to no one but Allah.

> [No leader] on Earth should conduct himself arrogantly .... All [those who do] are hateful in the eyes of your Lord.

These pronouncements are, interestingly enough, not the sentiments of some recent liberal innovator or modern "reformer" of Islam. Every word you just read is a part of the core beliefs of the faith as it was revealed in the seventh century in the Qur'an, the central holy text of Islam. (For the record, the passages cited from the Qur'an are: 3:195, 4:124, 17:36, 29:20, 2:62, 5:72, 18:29, 42:38, 12:40, and 17:37–38.)

Clearly, there is a contemporary movement capable of bringing Islam into contact with (supposedly) "modern" concepts of egalitarianism, freedom of inquiry, religious tolerance, and accountable governmental models. That movement is Islam itself. The question is not whether Islam is capable of "assimilating" these ideas, but whether Islam is capable of living up to its own stated ideals.

Millions of contemporary Muslims believe that the answer to that question is and must be "Yes," and are eagerly advocating reforms from the inside.

And Yet ...

Right about now, you're probably saying to yourself, "Wait a minute. If those are the teachings of the Qur'an, why does the Islamic world look to so many non-Muslims like it is in dire need of reforming or civilizing?" In other words, if Islam really is compatible with the modern world, why does it look so backward?

Of course, there are obvious problems of political repression, gender inequality, and intellectual freedom in the Islamic world today—problems that certainly are not the imagination of outsiders. To get a sense of what these problems are and how they arose, we have to look briefly at a critical social and intellectual debate that took place in the Islamic world about eight centuries ago.

An Enlightened Empire Descends into Darkness

As you saw earlier in this book, the Islamic empire expanded with stunning speed in the century following the death of the Prophet Muhammad. At its high point, the Islamic empire extended from the borders of China to the heart of Spain.

This map shows the geographical reach of the empire, which is fairly well known. What often comes as a surprise to those unfamiliar with Islamic history is the rich cultural, social, and intellectual legacy of the Islamic empire. Not unlike the Roman Empire that preceded it, the Islamic empire used a combination of social flexibility, intellectual openness, and military might to extend into areas that had previously been considered far beyond its reach. As it did so, it made the pursuit of knowledge an essential principle of the empire.

> **Persian Perspectives**
>
> Arabic was the leading language of science for more than 500 years, and Baghdad was a center of learning that reached its zenith in 1000 C.E.

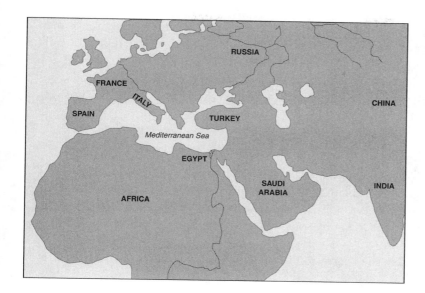

The Islamic empire at its height.

Between the seventh and twelfth centuries—an extraordinary span of time—the Islamic empire was not only a global political force, but also the primary supporter of the advancement of human knowledge and expression. Europe was in the depth of the Middle Ages, and learning there focused on recovering the knowledge that had been lost with the fall of the Roman Empire. At the same time, the Islamic Empire was in its heyday. During this so-called "Golden Age," Islamic artists, scientists, mathematicians, architects, and doctors were the most accomplished on Earth. Some vague idea of their contributions to humanity's heritage of intellectual achievement over half a millennium can be grasped in the following brief list of familiar words, all of which are Arabic in origin and all of which derive from the work of Arabic scientists, mathematicians, doctors, or researchers:

- Algebra
- Algorithm
- Almanac
- Average
- Cipher
- Pancreas
- Zenith

In fact, the extraordinary advances of Islamic culture and science made many of the later scientific advances of the European Renaissance possible.

There came a point, however, when the great tradition of Islamic respect for human knowledge, open inquiry, and intellectual freedom gave way to a preference for religious orthodoxy, rigid dogma, and penalties for those who asked inconvenient questions. This change took place around the twelfth century, and it marked the beginning of a political and social decline from which the Islamic world has not yet completely recovered.

Why the Descent?

A number of theories try to explain why this decline in intellectual freedom took place. Some people say external political and military events played a key role in the descent. Others point to internal divisions within Islamic society. But the best explanation probably has to do with a rise in political power among religious scholars and clerics that made possible the repression of *ijtihad*, which had had a long and proud history up to that point.

What's It Mean?

Ijtihad means independent thought and reasoning. It was a value treasured by Islamic society in the centuries following the death of Muhammad.

Beginning in about the twelfth century, Islamic religious scholars began a movement that basically equated independent thought about social, political, scientific, or religious matters with the crime of sectarianism within Islam. (It helps to understand that the Qu'ran forbids the propagation of separate sects among believers.) Scientific process, which includes skepticism and questioning, was increasingly seen as a threat to unified faith by the religious leadership.

A desire to avoid disunity within the faith led to a clampdown on the traditions that had made Islamic advances in so many intellectual fields possible. And because Islam is an all-encompassing way of life—not merely a "religion" practiced one day out of the week—the movement to repress independent thought had extraordinary implications for believers in all corners of the empire. The success of the clampdown left a lasting—and unfortunate—impression on the faith.

The bottom line was this: Beginning in roughly the twelfth century, a tendency to evaluate *all* questions, inquiries, and disputes in society in terms of the rulings of religious scholars became steadily stronger within Islam. It is probably not a coincidence that the empire that had expanded with such extraordinary speed beginning in the seventh century started to lose its footing at about this time.

As the religious scholars won influence within Islamic society, Islam itself lost much of the open character that had characterized its long "Golden Age"—a period that compares favorably with the similar period of influence and expansion enjoyed by the Roman Empire. Like that empire, however, Muhammad's went into a period of steep decline. And its tradition of free thought, open inquiry, and diversity was lost in a dark fog of orthodoxy (like the *Wahabi*), legalism, social conformity, and intolerance.

That fog, many Middle Eastern analysts hold, is still quite dense in many parts of the contemporary Islamic world. And one could be forgiven for observing that it has been particularly soupy in Iran in recent years.

What's It Mean?

The Saudi Arabian–based **Wahabi** movement, openly dedicated to eradicating the Shia school that dominates countries such as Iran and Iraq, is a particularly intolerant strain of Sunni Islam. Many people see it as the culmination of the emphasis on the clerical/legalistic movement that helped to bring Islam into a period of social and intellectual decline. Perhaps not surprisingly, the intolerant, hard-line Wahabi sect has been linked to al Qaeda terrorist cadres.

Reclaiming the Muslim Renaissance

Contrary to popular belief, there was a "Muslim Renaissance"—a period that celebrated the power and scope of the individual human mind and that gloried in its accomplishments. One problem with this extraordinary period, though, was that it lasted so long and was such an important early component of Islamic society that it was not easy to distinguish from the early phases of the expansion of the empire. Another problem was that the tradition of openness disappeared with such completeness that it has been easy to forget. The fact remains, though, that it occurred.

Persian Perspectives

A native of Iran, Mohammad Targai Ulugh Beg (1393–1449) was a true Muslim renaissance man. The grandson of Tamerlane, Ulugh Beg was a renowned scholar, mathematician, astronomer, wrestler, and statesman. He devoted much time to astronomy and science, and created a famous observatory at Samarkand to carry out his research. His contributions to astronomy were vast. He corrected many errors in Ptolemy's original star observations and became a source of record for European astronomers centuries later.

Ulugh Beg served as a ruler of the Timurid Empire around the city of Samarkand, now in Uzbekistan, administering that region in the name of his father. He later ruled in his own right, but for just two years; he was killed by his own son, who wanted to ascend to the throne. Some scholars argue that the Muslim religious leadership backed Ulugh Beg's son because it viewed Ulugh Beg's questioning and scientific research as a threat. Today Ulugh Beg is a highly respected figure in Central Asian culture.

What most Westerners are clamoring for—a series of "reforms" to make the Islamic world look more like Europe or North America—is highly unlikely. But the possibility of a reclamation of "reformist" values already at the heart of Islam is certainly a realistic goal. When "reform" toward—or, to be more precise, "reversion" to—values of tolerance, open-mindedness, gender equity, and greater democratization come along, they are likely to come as the result of a Muslim insider, not because of any poking, prodding, or agitation on the part of non-Muslim groups or governments.

> **They Said It**
>
> There are some common demands, like democracy. But there are others, like the deep need for people to be allowed to express themselves without pretending something—just freely express themselves.
>
> I think many of our people are going to be secular in this country. They do not have fundamental, strong beliefs in traditional attitudes nor—especially—in Islam. I think they are going to accept Western attitudes and new attitudes.
>
> —Iranian students quoted in a 2002 BBC article on the reformist movement in Iran

Khatami's Corner of the Sky

The populist campaign of Iranian president Muhammad Khatami, ineffective as it may have been in terms of posting practical political gains, may be the most important signpost yet for the emergence of a broad-based Islamic reform movement (see Chapter 21). While it is certainly true that the Iranian reformist movement has thus far been utterly outmaneuvered by the clerical establishment, it is also true that the clerical establishment has been forced to acknowledge the existence of dissenting viewpoints about where the country should be going—viewpoints that are represented by figures within the structure of the Iranian government itself.

That may not exactly constitute a return to the Golden Age of Islam, and Khatami is no Ulugh Beg, but it is nevertheless a small patch of blue sky visible through the heavy fog of clerical authority that has hung over the faith for the better part of eight centuries. It remains to be seen whether the patch of sky will remain an anomaly or will foretell the beginning of a second period of ijtihad—openness, debate, free speech, celebration of intellectual inquiry for its own sake, and expansion of the Islamic experience beyond narrow legalistic and scholarly authority.

The Least You Need to Know

- Islam has a proud history of intellectual freedom. During the Golden Age, Islam contributed much to science, medicine, law, and trade.

- The long-standing tradition of *ijtihad*—independent thought and reasoning—was challenged by the clerical establishment in the twelfth century.

- The clerics won that struggle and brought on a long period of social conformity and acceptance of religious authority that has led to intellectual and social stagnation in the Islamic world.

- The visibility of the reform movement in Iran—despite its lack of success in attaining its objectives—could be a signpost for a significant re-emergence of the tradition of ijtihad.

Chapter 17

Five Compasses

In This Chapter

- ◆ The five most important influences on modern Iranian domestic and foreign policy
- ◆ The impact of Iranian domestic policy on economic life
- ◆ Compromise and competing interests
- ◆ The factors that underlay future uncertainty

Is Iran's foreign policy a destabilizing force—a powder keg waiting to explode in the world's most volatile region? Or is it, as the Iranian government usually insists, a force for international stability, moderation, pluralism, and tolerance in the Middle East? In this chapter, we look at the internal forces at work in Iran today and how they may impact Iran's foreign policy. In Chapter 22, we look at how Iran is dealing with the rest of the world right now.

There is—and is likely to be—no single definitive answer to the important question of which way Iran's foreign policy will go. Important forces are pointing Iran's foreign policy in both directions. In this chapter, you'll learn about five different and influential guidance tools for those leading the Iranian nation, five "compasses" that sometimes seem to point in five different directions. When it comes to issues such as whether to support

Shia revolutionary movements, what kinds of relations to maintain with Gulf states and Central Asian nations, and how to deal with the Americans, these five competing ways of looking at the world are influencing—and will continue to influence—Iranian decision-makers. There are winners and losers as the competing compasses vie for influence in determining the direction of Iran's foreign policy—and there are also some intriguing indications about what the future holds.

Five Key Questions

You can make an argument that Iranian foreign policy is driven by five key concerns, or "compasses":

◆ Fundamentalist, revolutionary Islam and its accompanying ideology

◆ Nationalism

◆ Geopolitical realities

◆ Economic realities

◆ Ethnic realities

Let's look at each in turn.

The First Compass: Fundamentalist, Revolutionary Islam

You probably guessed the compass of fundamentalism yourself. It's the one Americans think of first with regard to Iran and the one they often assume to be guiding the Iranian government. Fundamentalism certainly is an influential point of view, but it's certainly not the only one.

There's a reason that the influence of hard-line revolutionary elements on the formation of Iran's foreign policy is the compass most likely to be noticed by Western policymakers: It's potentially quite dangerous. Fundamentalism is the Iranian school of thought that holds that the Islamic revolution of 1979 was not only a defining moment for the nation of Iran, but also the turning point in modern human history—the beginning of a long-delayed return to theocracy and the beginning of the end for secular government models in the Middle East (and elsewhere, for that matter). Obviously, this approach doesn't sit well with many in America and Europe who envision Western democracy taking hold in the Middle East. Just as the Western democracies once viewed the Communist nations as an ideological threat, now the Iranian model poses another threat.

When using this compass, the arrow always points to supporting revolutionary movements and ideas whose aims parallel those of the 1979 revolution, regardless of whether the U.S. or European governments consider such movements to be "terrorist" in nature.

The following are what this first compass suggests about five important recurrent questions in Iranian foreign policy.

How Should We Deal with the Americans?

The fundamentalist, revolutionary compass suggests that all ties with Americans be severed. They pulled the Shah's puppet-strings, supported Iraq in the 1980s, and are opponents of Islam today. Let them make all the speeches against terrorism they want to; they remain our enemies. Additionally, they must not have cultural influence here.

What Should Our Relations with Nations in Central Asia and the Caucasus Be?

The fundamentalist, revolutionary compass indicates that Iran must find ways to support religious groups that it agrees with in that part of the world. Doing so is a religious obligation. Additionally, the Saudis or Turks should not be allowed to gain too much influence.

What Should Our Relations with the Gulf States Be?

The fundamentalist, revolutionary compass rejects the legitimacy of secular governments and promotes Islamic theocracy as a model; what's more, the Iranian Shia theocracy competes with the prevailing Sunni elites in the region and worldwide for influence and visibility. Wherever possible, this viewpoint holds, Iran must oppose and undercut the puritan Wahabi faction, based in Saudi Arabia, which views all of Shia Islam as heresy. Additionally, all the stops should (according to this viewpoint) be pulled on Iraq; the large Shia population there may be Iran's best bet for setting up a sympathetic Arab Gulf State.

How Much Should We Spend on Defense?

The fundamentalist, revolutionary compass answer to the question of how much to spend on defense depends on whether Iran is under attack. If Iran is not under attack, the answer may be to spend money at home to help build the Islamic state. If it is under attack, that's a different story. Additionally, this point of view suggests, nuclear weapons would counterbalance Israeli and U.S. power.

What Should Our Policy on Revolutionary Movements Outside Iran Be?

The fundamentalist, revolutionary compass points to maintaining strong ties with revolutionary groups that share Iran's view of history and Islam, and doing everything possible to promote the Shia revolutionary model.

The Second Compass: Nationalism

The ancient glories of Persian history, the long series of conflicts with the Arabs, the legacy of religious and social persecution, and the overthrow of the U.S.–supported Shah are some of the defining points in a potent Iranian brand of nationalism that has its share of influence in shaping the country's foreign policy. The guiding ideas here are pretty straightforward: Iran is culturally superior to its neighbors, has taken enough grief from outsiders, and is no longer going to be pushed around. Funny how most countries take this view of themselves in relation to the rest of the world.

When using this compass, the arrow always points toward establishing a leadership position in the region for the Iranian nation. The following sections deal with the second compass direction concerning five important recurrent questions in Iranian foreign policy.

How Should We Deal with the Americans?

The nationalist compass directs the Iranians to oppose Americans openly. The Americans are aggressive, they've oppressed the Iranian people, they're military adventurers, and they're big on subordination. Iran doesn't play second fiddle to anyone—least of all to the meddlers who engineered the Shah's rule and made possible the horrors of Saddam Hussein.

Additionally, with this compass Iran resents American cultural influence, which distracts young people from the true path.

What Should Our Relations with Nations in Central Asia and the Caucasus Be?

The nationalist compass suggests that Iran must find ways to increase its influence in Tajikistan and other areas where Persian culture has a historical role.

What Should Our Relations with the Gulf States Be?

The nationalist compass suggests that Iran must stop following the lead of others—that it deserves to be the dominant power. The leaders of other states in the region, in this view, need to be persuaded to acknowledge openly Iran's leadership role in the region.

How Much Should We Spend on Defense?

The nationalist compass suggests spending a lot on defense. It's seen as the only way to get the rest of the world to show Iran the respect it deserves. Besides, the nationalists would argue, the Americans are encircling Iran.

What Should Our Policy on Revolutionary Movements Outside Iran Be?

The nationalist compass sees ties to revolutionary groups as opportunities to expand Persian cultural influence in the Gulf and Central Asia.

The Third Compass: Geopolitical Realities

Revolutionary Islamic ideology and pride in country have their place, but real events should dictate policy, not abstract principles. This is the attitude of those who have attempted to use the geopolitical compass to shape Iranian foreign policy. The guiding idea here is basically pragmatic. The geopolitical advocates suggest that Iran is part of a very dangerous area of the world. It has a vested interest in developing long-term solutions that are based less on rigid notions of religion or nationalism and more on a flexible approach that doesn't deprive the leadership of options.

When using this compass, the arrow always points toward finding workable solutions that support pragmatic long-term goals. The following points are what the third compass suggests about five important recurrent questions in Iranian foreign policy.

How Should We Deal with the Americans?

The geopolitical compass suggests finding ways to contain American influence but not going out of the way to initiate conflict with them. Iran may not like the fact that the U.S. is a superpower with regional influence, geopolitical thinking would run, but it's what's happening. This compass suggests finding a way to deal with it.

What Should Our Relations with Nations in Central Asia and the Caucasus Be?

The geopolitical compass sees no single overriding threat in the region, other than the chaos that tends to descend upon Iran's neighbors. The focus is to work slowly and steadily to expand economic and diplomatic influence, and to try to avoid worsening existing conflicts, such as that between Azerbaijan and Armenia over border issues.

> **Bet You Didn't Know**
>
> Iran is part of the "six plus two" group. This group consists of the foreign ministers from Iran, China, Pakistan, Tajikistan, Turkmenistan, and Uzbekistan (the six), and the United States and Russia (plus two). This group was formed originally to provide an international forum for coordinating a response to the Afghanistan crisis. Over the past few years, Iran and the United States have been conducting a high-level dialogue via this group.

What Should Our Relations with the Gulf States Be?

The geopolitical compass urges the Iranian leadership not to allow the Americans to take center stage. America's pro-Israel agenda must be undercut, and diplomatic obstacles must be put up against America's expanding authority in the Middle East. Additionally, the best bet in Iraq, according to this point of view, may be simply to undercut American plans by using Iranian influence to support and reinforce the Iraqi Shia majority.

How Much Should We Spend on Defense?

The geopolitical compass suggests a middle course with respect to defense spending. The collapse of the Soviet Union and the eradication of Saddam Hussein's regime mean that Iran faces no direct military threat in the region. By the same token, there are serious border security issues, and a credible military force should be presented to promote Iran's interests in the region. Note, however, that the Americans are encircling Iran with troops and pro–U.S. governments. In addition, this viewpoint counsels, a way has to be found to deal with the pesky guerilla movements—they're causing a tremendous public relations problem.

What Should Our Policy on Revolutionary Movements Outside Iran Be?

The geopolitical compass suggests picking and choosing outside revolutionary movements carefully. It may make sense to maintain connections with certain opposition groups, such as those in Iraq.

The Fourth Compass: Economic Realities

Geopolitical influence is great, but if the economy collapses, Iran's role in the region won't matter very much. The country should be making foreign-policy decisions in such a way as to improve the economic picture at home. This is the attitude of those who have attempted to use the economic compass to shape Iranian foreign policy.

The guiding idea here is based on survival. Iran faces severe economic challenges, and it must keep a large, restless, youthful, and professionally underutilized portion of its population from becoming too disenchanted with the regime. When using this compass, the arrow always points to creating new jobs and improving the economic picture.

The following sections outline what the fourth compass suggests about five important recurrent questions in Iranian foreign policy.

How Should We Deal with the Americans?

The economic compass suggests that the past is the past and that Iran needs to improve its relationship with Washington to get more dollars rolling into the country.

What Should Our Relations with Nations in Central Asia and the Caucasus Be?

The economic compass emphasizes doing whatever must be done to improve trade even further with nations in central Asia and the Caucasus.

What Should Our Relations with the Gulf States Be?

The economic compass says not to anger the Americans, to improve cooperation with the other governments in the region, and to stop making noises about overthrowing or subverting any country that doesn't agree with Iran.

How Much Should We Spend on Defense?

The economic compass suggests not spending much on defense because nothing but a bare-bones defense is affordable. Resources are needed elsewhere.

What Should Our Policy on Revolutionary Movements Outside Iran Be?

The economic compass places special emphasis on two words: trade and stability. Anything that jeopardizes those goals is to be avoided, and so, according to this view, prudence suggests backing away from the whole "supporting-foreign-brothers-in-Islam" thing for a while.

The Fifth Compass: Ethnic Realities

Political issues related to ethnicity will always be important for the Iranian leadership, and they will continue to play a role in the development of Iranian foreign policy.

Simply put, the government knows that it must not establish policies likely to either (a) inflame or agitate the local minority groups, or (b) make them start thinking about independence.

Ethnic minorities, we must always bear in mind, make up close to half of the Iranian population (the Persians being slightly more than half). The minorities include these:

- Azeri Turks
- Kurds
- Arabs

These and other minority groups are predominantly Sunni, although they do not yet constitute a unified social or political force. (There are also small groups of Christians, Jews, and Baha'is in Iraq, but they have not yet emerged as important pressure groups and probably won't.)

The guiding idea here is simple: Avoid foreign-policy initiatives that cause domestic political problems with Iranian minorities. When using this compass, the arrow always points toward avoiding policies that could make ethnic groups angry or lead to instability on the borders. (The minority groups are often clustered in communities near Iran's borders.)

The following ideas are suggestions of the fifth compass with regard to five important recurrent questions in Iranian foreign policy.

How Should We Deal with the Americans?

The ethnic compass suggests dealing with the Americans in a way that does not cause major internal conflicts or make them more likely. So far, Iranian policy toward the United States has not been a particularly important or controversial issue among the minorities.

What Should Our Relations with Nations in Central Asia and the Caucasus Be?

The ethnic compass points to maintaining important connections with the governments in Central Asia and the Caucasus. Separatist independence movements shouldn't, in this view, be allowed to gain any traction; Iran must stop antagonizing governments that are friendly by supporting groups that want to overthrow them.

What Should Our Relations with the Gulf States Be?

The ethnic compass suggests that the Iranian Arabs in Khuzestan should not be angered by antagonizing or alienating the Gulf states.

How Much Should We Spend on Defense?

The ethnic compass does not promote either a pro-defense-spending policy or an anti-defense-spending policy.

What Should Our Policy on Revolutionary Movements Outside Iran Be?

The ethnic compass asks, why antagonize otherwise friendly governments? Ethnic loyalties compete with national loyalties in this part of the world. Overthrowing governments means less stability, more turmoil, and a greater chance of problems with Iran's own ethnic groups.

What's the Direction?

So far, these five competing compasses yield the following recent directions in Iranian foreign policy:

- Resistance to improvement of relations with the United States

- The development of an expanding economic and diplomatic role in Central Asia and the Caucasus

- A continued attempt to improve relations with the governments of the Gulf states

- Support for certain revolutionary groups that share the leadership's world view

How the compasses will interact in the future and what policy results they will produce in an era of American military interventionism are fateful questions that are unlikely to be resolved soon.

The Least You Need to Know

- Fundamentalist, revolutionary Islam and its accompanying ideology is an influence on Iranian foreign policy, but it's not the only influence.

- Nationalism also plays a role ...

- ... as do geopolitical realities.

- Economic realities also influence foreign policy.

- Finally, ethnic realities carry major foreign-policy implications in a nation where nearly half of the country is not Persian.

Chapter 18

Iran and Terrorist Movements

In This Chapter

- ◆ Iran's foreign policy includes terrorism
- ◆ Iran uses terrorist groups to extend its reach
- ◆ The lineup: terrorist movements sponsored by Iran
- ◆ The tepid international response
- ◆ The United States steps up the pressure

In this chapter, we examine Iran's other leading export: terrorism. The U.S. government believes that Iran is a sponsor of terrorism, and it has outlined its case in a series of official statements and publications. Terrorism experts agree that Iran is sponsoring terrorism on a systematic and long-term basis.

Terrorism Is ...

Terrorism may be hard to describe, but we know it when we see it. Normally, terrorist acts are designed for maximum impact. In the words of terrorism expert Brian Jenkins, "Terrorism is theater." Terrorism is deliberate, planned, and calculated for maximum impact. Terrorists are not uniformed soldiers and do not represent a government outright. They represent their organization and its goals, which may coincide with a particular government's goals. As we shall see in this chapter, terrorists may be supported by particular governments. Terrorists are not looking for wealth, but rather are trying to change the existing political situation. This makes terrorists completely outside the pale of society, since their goal is essentially the destruction of certain elements of targeted societies.

On its website, the U.S. State Department defines terrorist activity this way: [A]ny activity which is unlawful under the laws of the place where it is committed (or which, if committed in the United States, would be unlawful under the laws of the United States or any State) and which involves any of the following:

(I) The hijacking or sabotaging of any conveyance (including aircraft, vessel, or vehicle).

(II) The seizing or detaining, and threatening to kill, injure, or continue to detain, another individual in order to compel a third person (including a governmental organization) to do or abstain from doing any act as an explicit or implicit condition for the release of the individual seized or detained.

(III) A violent attack upon an internationally protected person (as defined in section 1116 [b][4] of title 18, United States Code) or upon the liberty of such a person.

(IV) An assassination

(V) The use of any—

(a) biological agent, chemical agent, or nuclear weapon or device, or

(b) explosive or firearm (other than for mere personal monetary gain), with the intent to endanger, directly or indirectly, the safety of one or more individuals or to cause substantial damage to property.

(VI) A threat, attempt, or conspiracy to do any of the foregoing.

—From the Immigration and Nationality Act, 8 U.S.C. 1001, et. seq., as amended by Public Law 101–549 of November 29, 1990

Terrorism has changed over the past decade. The attacks are more infrequent (believe it or not) but of larger scale and impact. In the 1970s and 1980s, terrorists confined their activities to hijackings and kidnappings primarily. However, in the 1990s, the attacks became larger, with more deaths and more public impact.

Bet You Didn't Know

The Council on Foreign Relations provides this definition of terrorism, attributed to Paul Pillar from the Counterterrorist Center of the Central Intelligence Agency:

It is premeditated—planned in advance rather than an impulsive act of rage.

It is political—not criminal, like the violence that groups such as the Mafia use to get money, but designed to change the existing political order.

It is aimed at civilians—not at military targets or combat-ready troops.

It is carried out by subnational groups—not by the army of a country.

So terrorism, as defined by experts, is the pursuit of political goals through violent means without using a uniformed army or conventional battle. Terrorists are those who pursue those aims using unconventional tactics. Certainly, the international community has known terrorism for decades (if not centuries). Since 2001, the United States has become deeply involved in the fight against terrorism, pushing terrorism to the forefront of international relations.

A Word About the Sponsor

Terrorist groups need support in order to function. They need money, weapons, and places to recruit, train, and hide. The larger the group is, or the more ambitious its activities are, the more support it needs. The longer a terror group exists, the more resources and support it requires. At some level, the requirements for the terror group mean that it needs help from a larger scale than a collection of individuals. The terror group needs support from a national government that can marshal the resources necessary to support that terror group at the level and consistency required. Countries that support terror groups on a systematic basis are considered to be "sponsoring" terrorism.

Sponsorship Levels

A nation can sponsor terrorism on several levels, including with cash, arms, training sites, and hiding places.

Money Talks

The sponsoring state can provide money directly or indirectly to the terrorist organizations. Sophisticated financial networks and support structures have been created to enable national governments to channel cash to terrorist organizations. These financial networks are the easiest and least involved way for a state to support a terrorist group. Most states that support terror groups prefer to provide the financial aid secretly, although some leaders try to generate political stature from their support of terrorists. For example, under the former regime of Saddam Hussein, Iraq used to provide a cash stipend in the tens of thousands of dollars to the remaining families of suicide bombers that attacked targets in Israel or the West Bank. However, the movement of larger sums of money into accounts for use by terror groups typically happens in secret.

Arms

States that support terrorists can also provide them with arms and equipment to conduct their operations. Because these terror groups are typically not fighting open conventional battles, the types of weapons provided tend to be small arms and bombs, plus communications equipment or similar operational items. The other type of weapons that states may supply are bombs and bomb-making equipment. If these bombs are conventional, they can create one level of terror on a localized level. However, if the bombs are nuclear, biological, or chemical, the terror threat is dramatically different. One of the biggest challenges in the fight against terrorism today is the need to keep weapons of mass destruction out of the hands of terror groups. Unless the bombs are stolen outright, the only way terrorists can get these frightening weapons is if a sponsor state gives them to the terrorists. One emerging threat today comes from the coupling of a state that may sponsor terrorism with weapons of mass destruction. The fear is that the sponsor state may provide those weapons to the terror groups that it sponsors. With its known sponsorship of terror groups and its program to develop nuclear weapons, Iran falls into this category.

Training

Terrorists are not born with the skills needed to carry out attacks on civilian targets. These groups need training to conduct their armed attacks. The military training is typically received at training camps hosted in sponsor countries. At these camps, the terror groups teach new recruits the basics of fighting and shooting, and more experienced operatives go there to gain new skills. Countries such as Libya and Afghanistan are considered to have provided (and perhaps still provide) terrorist-training facilities. For example, following the collapse of the Taliban regime in Afghanistan in 2001, several training camps for the al Qaeda terrorist group were discovered.

Hiding

Often these training facilities are secret, and the terrorists who use them are able to hide there from prying eyes. The states that host these training camps make sure that others do not find these places by providing security around these facilities. In addition to simply guarding the training camps, a sponsor state can provide safe houses for terrorists, where they can live in relative security while organizing their next attack. In addition, the sponsor government can hide terrorists simply by not trying to root them out of their hiding places within the sponsor state's own territory. By allowing the terror groups to blend in, the sponsor states are supporting that terror group.

New Definitions of Support

In today's world, where terrorism has become a more pronounced method of achieving objectives, the definition of "sponsorship" comes under more intense scrutiny. One question is that of governmental indifference. If a state allows terrorist groups to recruit or raise funds within its territory, is that state sponsoring terrorism? The dividing line between a sponsor of terrorism and a permissive civil society becomes blurred at this edge. For example, the Wahabist schools in Saudi Arabia have and continue to produce recruits for al Qaeda and other Islamic terrorist groups. Does this make Saudi Arabia a sponsor of terrorism? In another example, the Irish Republican Army solicits funds from Irish Americans in cities such as Boston, New York, and Chicago. Does the fact that such funding is provided by some U.S. citizens, and the fact that the U.S. government does not stop it, mean that the United States is sponsoring terrorism? The problem becomes one of definition and perceived civil liberty. Are the groups that are recruiting or soliciting funds perceived to be terrorists or freedom fighters? Should the state monitor or intervene in a private citizen's financial contributions? These questions will continue to be debated, and the line between legal and illegal acts will move as the "war" on terrorism continues.

With these complex points in mind, we can still proceed with our discussion of state-sponsored terrorism by focusing on the activities that most readers and experts will agree are actions of sponsoring terrorism, including the training, funding, and arming of known terror organizations. We will stay at this end of the spectrum of activity when examining Iran's role in sponsoring terrorist organizations.

"The Understatement of the Day": Iran as Sponsor of Terrorism

At the very beginning of this guide is a quote from U.S. Secretary of Defense Donald Rumsfeld, who is responding to a question about whether Iran is supporting terrorism. To repeat a portion of that quote:

... One of the goals ... is to go after the terrorists and to stop them and to stop nations from harboring terrorists. There's lots of ways to do that .... We have not found Iran to be a particularly cooperative country in the war against terrorism. I think that would be the understatement of the day.

Rumsfeld was alluding to the U.S. government's belief that Iran is a sponsor of terrorism. Iran sponsors terrorist groups for the following reasons:

◆ To carry out its goals against its enemies. Unable to exert its policies by diplomatic or conventional military means, Iran has turned to terrorist groups whose goals correspond to its own where its enemies are concerned.

◆ To destabilize regional governments, to shore up its own security: The logic Iran follows is that if neighbors are distracted by internal fighting and policing against terror attacks, those neighbors will not interfere with Iran. Also, the terror groups enable Iran to push its own agenda with these regional powers.

The Rogue's Gallery

Iran is sponsoring a variety of terrorist groups. Some of the most infamous are listed here.

The Hezbollah: Poster Child for Terrorism Against Israel

The Hezbollah (whose name means the "Party of God") is the most notorious terrorist group sponsored by Iran. The Hezbollah also is called Islamic Jihad for the Liberation of Palestine. Other states support the Hezbollah, notably Syria, but none as openly and consistently as Iran.

The Hezbollah first emerged in 1982 in Lebanon as a reaction to Israel's invasion of that country. Several Middle East experts believe that Iran prompted the organization of the Hezbollah as a convenient way to strike at Israel. The organization is Shia Muslim, and its members revere Shiite leaders, including the ayatollahs in Iran. Like other radical political organizations, the Hezbollah has a nonterrorist side that actually has participated in parliamentary elections within Lebanon. The organization is led by its secretary general, Hassan Nasrallah, and has 12 seats in the 128-seat Lebanese parliament.

The U.S. government has identified the Hezbollah as the organization behind several attacks on U.S. interests. These include the suicide truck-bombing attacks on the U.S. Embassy and a U.S. Marine compound in Beirut in 1983, and those on the U.S. Embassy Annex in 1984.

The Hezbollah shares Iran's view. The Iranian leadership is completely opposed to the existence of Israel. Iran does not even officially recognize Israel's right to exist, and it denounces the Israeli-sponsored settlements on the West Bank. The Hezbollah shares this belief. For decades, the Hezbollah has been engaged in a bloody struggle against Israel and has been attacking Israeli military and civilian targets in the West Bank and inside Israel itself. The Hezbollah attacked the Israeli Embassy in Buenos Aires in 1992. During the Israeli occupation of Lebanon, Hezbollah members were among the resistance fighters that attacked the Israeli army inside Lebanon. After the Israeli withdrawal, the Hezbollah continued its attacks on Israeli targets, resorting to terrorist tactics. In recent years, the Hezbollah has mounted a series of suicide bomb attacks on Israeli targets, and Israel has responded with attacks on Palestinian targets where Hezbollah members are considered to be hiding. The cycle of attack and reprisal increases and lessens in intensity, but it does not stop.

Using the Hezbollah to do this "dirty work" enables Iran to attack Israel without using the Iranian military. By supporting the Hezbollah, Iran is supporting the continued attacks on Israel and indirectly is prompting Israel's continued reprisals for those attacks upon the very people Iran is professing to support, the Palestinians.

The net advantage (for lack of a better term) of sponsoring Hezbollah terrorism is threefold for Iran:

- Real terror visited upon Israel, a sworn enemy of Iran.

- Continued destabilization of the region, which keeps Arab focus on Jewish Israel and not on Persian Iran.

- Constant foreign policy nightmare for the United States, which, by its support for Israel, is seen as an enemy of the Arab states. This impedes U.S. efforts to form a political or military coalition to contain Iran.

The risk for Iran is twofold:

- The Hezbollah attacks the United States, or a U.S. interest in the region.

- Stepped-up U.S. pressure on Iran to cease its support of Hezbollah, using this stance as a pretext for further isolating Iran from the international community.

As of this writing, Iran has shown no indication of lessening its support for the Hezbollah. If anything, it seems prepared to continue to encourage the current spate of violence.

Hamas and Islamic Jihad: Fundamentalism in Palestinian Territories

The United States believes that Hamas (Arabic for "zeal") and Islamic *jihad* also receive aid from Iran. Of the two, Islamic Jihad receives more assistance. This may be because Hamas is a larger, more-established organization, with greater access to resources, whereas Islamic Jihad is smaller and thus more open to receiving outside help.

Hamas is a counterweight to the Palestinian Authority (PA), the secular organization that nominally is the civil authority for Palestinians in the West Bank and Gaza. The Hamas charter states the goals of fighting in an armed struggle (rather than politically), destroying Israel, replacing the Palestinian Authority with an Islamic state, and raising "the banner of Allah over every inch of Palestine." The unspoken part of that statement is that Hamas considers all territory of Israel to be Palestine.

What's It Mean?

Jihad is an Arab word meaning "battle." A mujihadin is one who fights.

According to experts, in the past two decades, the suicide bombers of Hamas and Islamic Jihad have attacked civilian targets inside Israel, killing hundreds of Israeli civilians. More than 1,600 Palestinians have been killed in the reprisals. The recruits come mainly from the West Bank and Gaza, and the conditions of suicide bomber attack and Israeli reprisal generate a steady stream of new volunteers. According to experts, the popular support for Hamas among the Palestinians is directly related to the progress of the peace process: The slower the peace process goes, the more support there is for Hamas and Islamic Jihad bomber attacks.

Warning!

Hamas is not the same thing as the Palestine Liberation Organization (PLO) or the Palestinian Authority (PA). The PLO is the secular representative of the Palestinian people. The PLO created the PA in 1993 after signing a peace treaty with Israel that granted some autonomy to the Palestinians living in the West Bank and Gaza. The PA is intended to be the civil authority in the Palestinian territories. Hamas is a fundamentalist Islamic organization with social, charitable, and militant elements. Islamic Jihad is solely a terror group, dedicated to eliminating Israel.

The Islamic Movement of Uzbekistan: The Bellwether for Central Asian Terrorism

The Central Asian republics of the former Soviet Union include Uzbekistan, Kazakhstan, Kyrgyzstan, Tajikistan, and Turkmenistan. These countries were created out of ancient Turkestan by Josef Stalin in the 1920s as a way to divide and so weaken the rebellious Muslim societies that lived there. With the dissolution of the Soviet Union, this region of 60 million people has found itself facing several new realities. The political systems that have emerged are still secular and modeled after the Soviet system that they so recently lived under. The leaders are despots, and there is little to no democracy in the Western sense. The economies are struggling, and war is not far away (including next door in Afghanistan).

This region is Muslim, and with the removal of Soviet power, religious expression has begun to flower. This re-emphasis on Islam, so long repressed, poses difficult challenges for the political leaders of these republics. In Uzbekistan, the largest Central Asian republic in terms of population, the issue of Islam has become violent. Initially focused on creating an Islamic state in Uzbekistan along Iranian lines, the Islamic Movement of Uzbekistan (IMU) has become increasingly polarized against anyone it feels is opposing Islam.

The U.S. State Department believes that Iran provides assistance to the IMU. Among other indicators is the simple fact that Iranian state radio broadcasts the IMU leadership's speeches and messages.

The IMU was significantly weakened after the Coalition victory in Afghanistan, with several IMU leaders killed in the fighting. Also, an increased U.S. military presence in Afghanistan and Uzbekistan may result in U.S. assistance in operations against IMU cells in the area.

Bet You Didn't Know

During this author's travels to Uzbekistan, I would sometimes see armored personnel carriers patrolling Tashkent (the capital city). My driver, an Uzbek, would inform me that there had been an attack on Uzbek or Russian army troops in the Ferghana Valley (the region where most of the IMU activity was taking place at that time). Once I asked how he knew (given that the Uzbek government would not even acknowledge the attacks). He just shrugged and said that everyone knows that "tanks in Tashkent means fighting in Ferghana."

Today, U.S. troops are posted in Uzbekistan, and their continued presence there has been attributed by some observers as a payback to the Uzbek regime for its support of the U.S.-led attack on the Taliban. If U.S. forces remain there, the possibility that U.S. troops or equipment could be used to fight the IMU increases.

The challenge that groups such as the IMU pose in Central Asia is significant. Although they are not as large as groups such as the Hezbollah or Hamas, the IMU and other groups that may be forming in the region could grow if popular sentiment turns against the local, secular despots and their backers (generally Russia and the United States). In many ways, the situation in Central Asia is ripe for upheaval. The political system is repressive, and the standard of living is low. Islam is one of the only means of popular expression available to the common man on the street. A resurgence of fundamental Islam in Central Asia would pose significant challenges for the other countries in the region, including Pakistan, India, China, and Russia.

The Kurdistan Workers Party: Playing the Kurd Card

The Kurds are a significant minority in Turkey, Iraq, and Iran. One of their representative parties is the Kurdistan Workers Party (PKK). Both Syria and Iran support the PKK in its operations against Turkey. According to the experts, Iraq, Iran, Greece, and Syria have provided some support to the PKK for its attacks on Turkey. Iran is known to have transported PKK fighters to safe havens in Kurdish-controlled Iraq on Syria's behalf, in return for Syria's aid to Hezbollah terrorists in Lebanon.

During a massive uprising in the 1980s, more than 35,000 people (PKK, Turks, and Kurd bystanders) died in terror attacks and intense fighting. After the Turkish crackdown and capture of the PKK leader, the PKK has concentrated on attacking Turkish military and security targets, and has attacked Turkish facilities outside of Turkey itself. The Turkish government has fought back fiercely, and it considers the PKK to be terrorists, even if others in Europe see the PKK as freedom fighters resisting Turkish aggression.

At the request of NATO ally Turkey, the Clinton administration labeled the PKK as a terrorist organization, and the Bush administration has reconfirmed that status. The PKK itself objects to the designation and insists that it has abandoned terrorism. However, due to U.S. and Turkish pressure, the European Union has also designated the PKK as a terrorist organization.

Sanctions—U.S. Response to Iran's Sponsorship of Terrorism

Faced with this evidence of Iran's role as a sponsor of terrorism, the U.S. government has responded by imposing a series of sanctions on Iran. The Iran-Libya Sanctions Act, enacted in 1995 as a result of Iran's nuclear program activity, was renewed in 2001 due to both the nuclear program and Iran's sponsorship of terrorism.

The Iranian response, also presented at the beginning of this book, can be summed up in a statement by President Khatami when complaining about the sanctions:

> The fruit of our revolution is that we have freed ourselves from the yoke of our masters, and we will never submit to any new one. Those who put coercive pressure on others and resort to force, and world powers that try to make oppressive pressure the basis of their relations with other nations … they cannot expect anything from the Iranian nation.

Is Uncle Sam a Target?

The big question is whether Iran is sponsoring or will sponsor terrorists that may attack the United States. For example, after attacking U.S. targets in the 1980s, the Hezbollah has focused on Israel and the West Bank. But if the Hezbollah feels that the only way to put pressure on Israel is to put pressure on the United States, it may renew terror attacks against the United States. More likely, the Hezbollah would attack U.S. interests in the region, whether commercial, military, or political targets.

If a terrorist group does attack the Unites States or its interests in the region, there is little doubt that the U.S. response will be swift and powerful. The Bush administration set the precedent with an immediate attack on Afghanistan. In that case, it became clear that the Taliban (which was running Afghanistan at that time) was supporting the al Qaeda terrorist group in the wake of the September 11, 2001, attacks on the World Trade Center and the Pentagon. As with the U.S.–led attack on Iraq in 2003, the Bush administration has also made it clear that the United States will act in its own interest, even if the rest of the international community does not support the action.

Furthermore, the Bush administration has established a precedent for initiating pre-emptive security. With its attack on the Saddam Hussein regime in Iraq, and through statements made before and afterward by Bush administration officials, the U.S. has established a policy of pre-emptive security. This policy is based on the principle that, if given enough evidence of an imminent threat to U.S. interests, the United States will act before the anticipated attack to eliminate the potential threat.

This policy, to date, has been a unilateral one. The United States is not requiring the participation or permission of existing multilateral institutions such as the United Nations and NATO before it acts. This new unilateral approach is requiring the United States, Iran, and the rest of the world to re-examine current and future actions in this new context.

The Least You Need to Know

◆ Iran is a known sponsor of terrorist organizations.

◆ Iran is using terrorist groups to destabilize its neighbors, attack Israel, and keep the United States off-balance in the region.

◆ Iran focuses on supporting Shiite Muslim terrorist groups whose goals overlap its own.

◆ The U.S. government has established a precedent of reacting against governments that sponsor terrorists who attack the United States or its vital interests.

◆ The U.S. government has established a policy of pre-emptive security, in which it may take action against threats to U.S. interests *before* an attack comes.

Chapter 19

Iran and Weapons of Mass Destruction

In This Chapter

- Iran's possible possession of weapons of mass destruction
- Nuclear weapons technology and the difficulty of controlling their proliferation
- Disturbing signs of renewed activity in Iran
- The international response to and support of Iranian nuclear activity
- The potential impacts of Iranian nuclear capability on its neighbors, the region, and the United States

In this chapter, we look at the question of weapons of mass destruction and whether Iran possesses any. We also focus on Iran's nuclear program, which the Iranians claim is for power generation and the United States claims is for making nuclear bombs. We will see that other countries are actually helping Iran develop its weapons, despite the warning signs.

Weapons of Mass Destruction: A Primer

The term *weapons of mass destruction* is applied to nuclear, biological, and chemical weapons. These weapons are able to kill huge numbers of people (military and civilian) both immediately and over time. These weapons are designed to debilitate a population or army over a wide area. The aftereffects of the weapons (nuclear fallout, chemical, or biological residues) can linger for years, causing long-term suffering and death to thousands, if not millions, who may be exposed to them.

> **Bet You Didn't Know**
>
> Ironically, Iran is one of the most recent victims of an attack by a weapon of mass destruction. Saddam Hussein's Iraqi military unleashed chemical weapons on the Iranian army during the Iran-Iraq War (both times on Iraqi soil), killing thousands of Iranian soldiers and an unknown number of Iraqi civilians.

The term *weapons of mass destruction* encompasses all three types because the United States has stated that it sees an attack with one type equivalent to an attack with any type, and can respond in kind. In other words, the United States considers that a chemical attack on U.S. troops would justify a tactical nuclear response from the United States against that attacker.

Weapons of mass destruction are spreading. Until early 2003, the predominant reaction from the international community (particularly the United States) has been to apply sanctions, with limited success. Iran has acquired some.

Iran and Chemical Weapons

The Iranians have experience with chemical weapons. In fact, their army may be the most experienced army today in the aspects of chemical warfare. The Iranians were on the receiving end of chemical weapon attacks during the Iran-Iraq War in the 1980s. The Iranians claim that Iraq used *mustard gas* and other nerve agents up to 40 times during the war.

Iran did not retaliate with chemical weapons, probably because it did not possess any at that time. However, since then, experts agree that Iran has been working to acquire these weapons. The U.S. government believes that Iran has now stockpiled a small cache of chemical weapons, including *mustard gas*, and is working to develop the infrastructure to make chemical and biological weapons on its own.

What's It Mean? _____

Mustard gas is 2,2'-dichlorodiethyl. As manufactured, the chemical agent is an oily liquid that has a garlicky smell. When dispersed in liquid or gas forms, the agent will burn any human tissues that it comes in contact with, including the skin, eyes, and lungs. The agent works slowly enough to allow it to be ingested before it starts to blister and burn. Mustard gas was first introduced in World War I and has been used sporadically since then, including by Italy in Ethiopia in 1936, by Japan in China during World War II, by Egypt during the Yemen civil war in the 1960s, by Iraq during the Iran-Iraq War in the mid-1980s, and again by Iraq (in Iraq) against the Kurds in 1988.

Nuclear Weapons

The big question is not whether the Iranians have nuclear weapons. They don't—yet. The question is how soon the Iranians will have them. Making a nuclear bomb is a complex and time-consuming process that requires several pieces of sophisticated infrastructure:

1. There must be a source of raw uranium, from which fuel will be processed.

2. There must be a reactor, to create spent uranium that is processed into plutonium. Nuclear bombs use plutonium.

3. There must be processing facilities to turn the spent uranium into plutonium.

4. There needs to be a way to deliver the explosive, in some type of bomb attached to a plane or missile.

5. The Iranians would need some outside help. They would need specific pieces of equipment and parts for a working bomb from some outside source.

Bet You Didn't Know _____

Plutonium (or highly enriched uranium) is the fuel for a nuclear bomb. The plutonium is produced in nuclear power plants. When used to generate electricity, nuclear plants use uranium fuel rods that are inserted into the reactor to start the reaction that generates heat to create steam to create electricity. As atomic particles bombard the rods during the reaction, some of the uranium is changed into plutonium. When the uranium is used up (or "spent"), the rods are replaced. The depleted uranium in the old rods can then be "reprocessed" to separate the plutonium from the spent uranium. The plutonium can be manufactured into a bomb using highly specialized equipment.

Disturbing Sign #1: Reopened Mine

Iran has a uranium mine, located at Um, near Yazid. The Iranians had suspended operations there, but the mine has reopened and the Iranians have resumed extraction.

Disturbing Sign #2: Breeder Reactor

The Iranians are developing a nuclear reactor at Bushehr. While the International Atomic Energy Association (IAEA) was aware of the facility, it was under the impression that Iran had mothballed the project due to UN and U.S. sanctions. However, the IAEA has confirmed that Iran has resumed construction, and the reactor is much further along than previously assumed. In fact, it is due to come online in 2004.

Disturbing Sign #3: Enrichment Facilities

Along with the mine at Um and the Bushehr reactor, IAEA director Mohammed ElBaradei reported in late 2002 that Iran was building a uranium-enrichment facility at Natanz. This facility would be a critical part of the nuclear bomb–making chain. The process of enrichment uses specialized gas centrifuges that ElBaradei noted were being produced for use there.

Disturbing Sign #4: Conversion Facilities

Along with the mining, the reactor, and the enrichment facilities, the Iranians are developing a uranium conversion processor. The Iranians are building the conversion facility near Isfahan. The facility makes uranium hexaflouride, a vital gas used in the bomb-making process. If uranium hexaflouride (from Isfahan) is put into the centrifuges (at Natanz), it can create plutonium from the uranium (mined at Um) and transformed into spent uranium (at Bushehr). Experts contend that the only reason for doing this would be to enrich the uranium to create nuclear bomb fuel. In fact, putting the gas into the centrifuges would be a direct violation of the Nuclear Non-Proliferation Treaty (which Iran has signed). According to *Time* magazine, the Iranians have been experimenting with injecting the gas into a centrifuge in recent months. This is a critical step on the path to developing a nuclear weapon—and a clear violation of the Non-Proliferation Treaty.

Disturbing Sign #5: Missile Development

The Iranians continue to develop missiles with increasing ranges. The Shahab-3 can reach 800 miles and is considered to be in production now. The 1,200-mile range Shahab-4 is in development, and Iran is indicating that it is preparing to work on the

Shahab-5 that would reach even farther. If the Iranians are successful in fielding these longer-range missiles, they can reach large portions of the region and threaten U.S. allies and vital oil fields. If the Iranians succeed in mating a nuclear tip to a Shahab missile, the Iranians would dramatically shift the balance of power in the region.

Who Is Helping Iran?

The Iranians need help from a partner to get the parts for the nuclear-production facilities and ultimately for the more intricate parts of a bomb itself. Items such as the triggers for the bombs and specialty aluminum for centrifuges are complicated, expensive, and able to be made by only a few countries, including the United States, Britain, France, China, North Korea, and Russia. In this case, Russia has been providing the technology Iran needs for the Bushehr reactor. Russia, China, and North Korea are providing technology for the missile programs. The U.S. government also contends that China is sending chemical weapons production technology to Iran.

These nations apparently are not threatened by the Iranian program, or they believe the Iranian leadership when it claims to be developing nuclear facilities for making electricity. By the late 1990s, the Russian government was fully engaged in exporting to Iran a *turnkey* nuclear reactor that is being set up at Bushehr. The reactor is supposed to be completed in 2003. Of course, this also raises the question of where the money is going for the purchase of this reactor. Given the loose state of Russian oversight, certainly many takers exist for the cash the Iranians are willing to pay.

Bet You Didn't Know

When a country or company purchases a factory or other facility from another company, the purchaser often requests that the facility be delivered, set up, and made ready to operate. In theory, all the purchaser then has to do is "turn the key," and the facility is ready for operation. "Turnkey" transfers of technology are common when the acquiring party does not possess the knowledge to build the facility itself or is in a hurry.

Who, Us?

Still, despite all the disturbing signs and sanctions against those countries supplying nuclear technology to Iran, the Iranian leadership denies that it is pursuing a nuclear weapons program. The Iranian foreign minister, Kamal Kharrazi, stated in 1997 ...

> We are certainly not developing an atomic bomb because we do not believe in nuclear weapons .... We believe in and promote the idea of the Middle East as a region free of nuclear weapons and other weapons of mass destruction.

The Iranian position is directly referencing the widespread belief among countries in the Middle East that Israel has nuclear weapons. Kharrazi's statement also reflects the belief that (until the conclusion of Operation Iraqi Freedom in 2003) neighboring Iraq was working on its own nuclear program.

So why are the Iranians pursuing a nuclear program? According to the Iranian leadership, they are developing nuclear energy for the time when they run out of oil. According to Foreign Minister Kharrazi …

> But why are we interested to develop nuclear technology? We need to diversify our energy sources. In a matter of a few decades, our oil and gas reserves would be finished and, therefore, we need access to other sources of energy …. Furthermore, nuclear technology has many other utilities in medicine and agriculture. The case of the United States in terms of oil reserves is not different from Iran's. The United States also has large oil resources, but at the same time they have nuclear power plants. So there is nothing wrong with having access to nuclear technology if it is for peaceful purposes ….

Out of Gas?

The argument that Iran needs to develop nuclear energy because it is running low on oil, on the surface, seems very far-fetched. With about 8 percent of the world's proven oil reserves, Iran would appear not to need to worry about alternative energy sources. At the same time, Iran has been unable to increase its daily production because its older, more developed fields are declining, even while the Iranians bring new production online. The problem that supporters of Iran argue is not the amount of oil in the ground, but the amount of oil that can be pumped out. Over time, mature fields will yield lower amounts unless *secondary recovery techniques* are employed.

> **Bet You Didn't Know**
>
> Extracting oil from the ground is called "recovering" the oil. The primary technique is pumping the oil out of the ground. Pumping works as long as the pressure in the field is high enough to force the oil up the pipes.
>
> As the fields are drawn down, the pressure lessens and the flow out of the pipes lessens. Production levels start to drop. There is still plenty of oil in the ground, but it is harder to get it out. For fields like these, **secondary recovery techniques** are used. These include injecting natural gas (or even water) into the oil reservoir, to force out the remaining petroleum. Although this technique can work, the extracted oil can be infused with gas or water, which needs to be removed from the recovered product (thus increasing the cost of extraction).

Although this situation would appear dire, let's remember that the Iranians are still producing almost three million barrels per day. This is a huge amount of oil that far exceeds domestic energy requirements. What is more, working with TotalElfFina of France, the Iranians are about to bring two enormous gas and oil fields online at Assaluyeh and South Pars. These fields will produce up to 25 percent of all Iranian gas output when they come online. Some of the gas will be used to replace domestic oil consumption in Iran (and could be used ostensibly for decades to come for this purpose). In addition, some of the gas will be reinjected into the older fields (as a secondary recovery technique) to boost their output. The rest of the production will be sold in the export market. So, the argument that Iran will need nuclear energy to keep the lights on in 20 years rings hollow.

Lighting Off Bulbs, Not Bombs

Iran claims that the nuclear facilities are part of a program to develop nuclear energy for civilian use. According to the Iranians, Bushehr will be a 500-megawatt reactor for the generation of electricity. This claim, U.S. experts say, is not plausible.

These experts point out that Iran flares (that is, burns off as a wasted by-product) enough gas to make 500 megawatts of electricity each year (remember, Iran produces almost three million barrels of oil per day). If the country needed the extra electrical capacity, it could much more easily and quickly capture that gas and burn it to create the electricity instead of incurring the massive costs to develop the nuclear facilities.

U.S. experts contend that the Bushehr plant is a "breeder reactor," not an electricity-generating plant. Unlike conventional nuclear plants that produce electricity, breeder reactor plants have the ability to create enriched uranium. The enriched uranium is intended for making nuclear weapons.

To review, Iran has or is building the facilities it needs to develop nuclear weapons. It is receiving equipment and support from a sophisticated nuclear power. It has reopened a mine to extract the raw materials, and it is testing missiles—all of this while most of the world was not fully aware of the progress. In the words of the International Atomic Energy Agency (IAEA) director-general Mohamed ElBaradei, the Iranian program is "much further along than previously thought."

What Would Iran Do with Nuclear Weapons?

So if we believe that Iran has or is making weapons of mass destruction, the question becomes, what will they do with them? The Iranians may simply be trying to keep up with the Joneses. There is the possibility that Iran is attempting to acquire weapons

What's It Mean?

The **Coalition** is the name given to the countries that came together to topple Saddam Hussein in Iraq in the spring of 2003. Leading Coalition members were the United States and the United Kingdom, with Australia, Spain, Italy, Poland, and a "coalition of the willing" numbering more than 40 countries in support.

of mass destruction (most notably, nuclear weapons) as a defensive deterrent. Remember that Iran believes that both Israel and Pakistan have nuclear weapons, and it is a fact that Russia has them. Iran sees itself increasingly surrounded by hostile (or, at least, not openly friendly) regimes. Turkey is a NATO member and U.S. ally; Iraq (however chaotic) is now *Coalition*-dominated; Pakistan is a nominal U.S. ally; and Afghanistan, while in disarray, is nominally friendly to the United States. Even Turkmenistan cannot be counted upon as an ally, and Russia (trading partner or not) is a wildcard in terms of how it would react to a U.S.–led action on Iran.

Iran sees itself as cut-off, under sanction, and labeled as a member of the Axis of Evil (see Chapter 1) by the Bush administration. Iran has seen the former Saddam Hussein regime in neighboring Iraq (also a named member of the Axis of Evil) unilaterally toppled by the Coalition, outside of UN auspices. A nuclear Iran would feel more secure, even in an increasingly unstable environment.

More disconcerting is the possibility that Iran would provide nuclear weapons to the terrorist groups its sponsors. As we explore later in this chapter, this possibility is getting increased U.S. attention.

Reining in the Weapons

International conventions, including the 1972 Biological and Toxin Weapons Convention, have forbidden the use of biological and chemical weapons, and almost every country in the world, including Iran, has signed those conventions. These countries all promise not to use chemical or biological weapons. As far as nuclear weapons are concerned, most countries (including Iran) are signatories to the Nuclear Non-Proliferation Treaty. Signers promise not to develop nuclear weapons, to create the facilities needed to make nuclear weapons, or to try to acquire nuclear weapons from other countries. Countries currently possessing nuclear weaponry promise not to sell it or hand it over to other countries.

These treaties, and the overwhelming number of countries that signed them, sound like a strong control. In reality, these conventions are only as strong as the will of the international community to do the following:

- ◆ Impose sanctions or declare war on the transgressor
- ◆ Maintain those sanctions for a very long time

However, willing trading partners on both sides have repeatedly skirted international sanctions. Often in the desire to curry favor or increase a strategic global position, countries initiate trade with the sanctioned country. By opening the doors to the pariah state when all others shut theirs, the trading partner can gain significant advantages in trade and political relations.

The United States has imposed sanctions against Iran on multiple occasions since 1980. Recent sanctions acts are a result of both its sponsoring of terrorism (see the Iran-Libya Sanctions Act in the Chapter 18) and its development of nuclear technology.

The recent nuclear-related sanctions were imposed with the Iran Nonproliferation Act of 2000 and are intended to cut off the flow of nuclear technology to Iran, as well as punish it and potential suppliers for violation of the Nuclear Non-Proliferation Treaty. However, as the actions of Russia, China, and North Korea (a Non-Proliferation Treaty signatory up to 2002 and a fellow Axis of Evil member) show, the Iranians are still getting the technologies they need to pursue a weapons program.

The challenge for the United States is whether it is willing to alter its relationships with Russia or China to enforce unilaterally imposed sanctions against Iran. The United States has other interests in maintaining positive relations with Russia and with China. Russia still possesses a massive nuclear arsenal, and the United States and Russia are slowly dismantling this stockpile. Russia needs U.S. aid to do this, and the United States is not willing to curtail that aid. Also, the United States considers the development of democratic and market institutions in Russia to be vital and thus is unwilling to curtail direct aid for those initiatives. In the case of China, the United States sees positive relations as vital to its long-term interests. China is a major and growing trading partner, as well as the largest domestic market in the world. Chinese reaction to unilateral U.S. sanctions would probably lock U.S. industries out of China. Furthermore, the United States is actually working with China to resolve conflicts in the Far East, including delicate negotiations with North Korea.

In the case of North Korea, it is apparent that the United States has limited leverage with which to sanction that country. Already cut off from U.S. aid for its own nuclear program, North Korea has little to lose in trying to earn more hard currency by exporting missile technology to Iran. Furthermore, the United States is already attempting to limit the North Korean nuclear program, so added pressure due to its exports to Iran mean little.

Will Pressure Force Iran to Peacefully Abandon Its Nukes?

What is the international community willing to do when facing the pending nuclearization of Iran? Even more important, what can the international community actually do? As is clear from the indecision shown in the run up to Operation Iraqi Freedom in late 2002, the existing multilateral institutions of the UN, the EU, and NATO are ill-suited, as presently constituted, to deal with preventative action. However, preventative action is just what the United States and other nations are calling for.

Option 1: Continue the Current Sanctions Program

Will reasserted sanctions from the United States work? The answer is probably no. Iran is already fairly isolated in the world community. It also has a great deal of oil, which the rest of the world needs. It is unlikely that the world oil consumers would agree to boycott Iranian oil, given the well-known consequences of shortages in the oil markets. Aside from that option, the world community can apply little economic pressure on Iran. In addition, the UN Security Council (of which Russia and China are veto-carrying permanent members) will probably not approve more strict sanctions because Russia and China would essentially be punishing themselves. That leaves precious little in the way of options.

Option 2: Blow Up the Stuff

One option that has been discussed is military action. The United States (or a new Coalition) could attack Iran's nuclear facilities to take them offline. The repercussions of such an act are unclear, but they would certainly create divisions among the United States and its allies, as well as within the United Nations, as were so pronounced during *Operation Iraqi Freedom* in the spring of 2003.

What's It Mean?

Operation Iraqi Freedom was launched by a U.S.– and UK–led Coalition and was intended to topple Saddam Hussein for a range of reasons, including violation of UN Security Council Sanctions and possession of weapons of mass destruction. The Coalition acted without UN approval, and old-line U.S. allies such as France and Germany, and new friends such as Russia, actively worked the diplomatic channels to oppose Coalition actions. The diplomatic fallout from these opposed positions is still being felt in the international community.

In this scenario, the United States and some allies would probably send in cruise missiles and bombers, and would follow up with Special Forces to confirm the destruction of the facilities. The act of war would be risky and could backfire or result in full-fledged war if U.S. troops are still stationed in Iraq at the time of the attack. The Iranians might feel compelled to respond by attacking U.S. or Coalition forces inside Iraq and might count on the support of Iraqi Shiites to further complicate U.S. or Coalition resistance.

Option 3: Do Nothing

Given no other sanction pressure, the world community would probably indulge the Iranian program and even aid it (as Russia, China, and North Korea are doing). However, two countries probably will not tolerate Iranian nuclear weapons being completed. Both the United States and Israel, mindful of Iran's sponsorship of terrorists hostile to U.S. interests and to Israel's very existence, would consider unilateral action, either together or separately.

Given Iran's cozy relationship with the Hezbollah (see Chapter 17) and the Hezbollah's history of attacking U.S. targets, there is a distinct possibility that Iran will provide the Hezbollah with a nuclear weapon. However long the odds may be, they are real (at least, in the Bush administration's collective view). This possibility, however remote, may thus require the United States (in keeping with the new Bush doctrine of pre-emptive security) to unilaterally destroy the Iranian facilities.

The other wildcard is Israel's reaction to the existence of Iran's advanced nuclear weapons program. The Israelis are painfully aware that Iran refuses to acknowledge Israel's right to exist and of Iran's support for terrorist groups that have repeatedly attacked Israel, notably the Hezbollah and Islamic Jihad.

Israel also has demonstrated its willingness to act alone to preserve its own interests (and, some would argue, its very survival). When confronted with a nuclear reactor at Osirek in Iraq in 1981, the Israelis bombed the reactor, completely destroying it and setting the Iraqi nuclear program back a decade. Although Saddam Hussein was preoccupied with the Iran-Iraq War and did not react militarily to the attack, it is not clear how the Iranians would react if Israel attacked Iranian facilities.

As we have seen, Iran already has an established channel for attacking Israel: the Hezbollah. If Israel succeeded in destroying the Iranian nuclear program, the Iranian response could very well be an onslaught of terrorist bombing attacks in Israel. There really is very little else Iran could do. It is doubtful that the Arab nations in the region would support a land action that would require Iranian troops to be based on Arab soil, and it is also unlikely that the Sunni Arab countries would rally to support Shia Persian Iran.

Another point to consider: If Iran perceived that the United States was involved in any way in a military strike against its nuclear facilities (by aiding an Israeli attack), that could open the door to Iran funding and supporting Hezbollah attacks on the United States.

The Least You Need to Know

◆ *Weapons of mass destruction* is a term describing chemical, biological, and nuclear weapons, so called because they can kill huge numbers of people and (in the case of nukes) infrastructure.

◆ Iran is generally considered to possess chemical weapons and is working on a nuclear program.

◆ Iran sees Israel, Pakistan, and Russia as nuclear powers in the region and may be trying to acquire nuclear weapons to enhance its own strategic position.

◆ The U.S. government believes that Iran's nuclear program is intended to produce weapons, while Iran maintains that it is for peaceful purposes.

◆ International sanctions against Iran for its work in nuclear weapons have been effectively nullified by Russia, which is providing Iran with critical technology and a nuclear reactor.

20

Oil–the Economy of the Islamic Republic

In This Chapter

- ◆ Selling oil to pay the bills
- ◆ The need for even more oil, but the troubles in getting to it
- ◆ The elusive impact of sanctions
- ◆ Discontent on the home front

We saw in earlier chapters how the clerics took control of Iran in 1979. They inherited a country with a highly developed oil infrastructure, low foreign debt, and a sophisticated middle class that enjoyed a fairly comfortable standard of living, at least economically (remember that the Shah used the SAVAK to keep a lid on things politically). They also inherited a larger segment of urban and rural poor that was still looking for better times. This group would be a significant part of the clerics' power base—and also would become a threat to it.

In this chapter, we look at Iran's economic situation, domestic and international. We look at some of the factors that created it and where it is headed today. This issue is important because domestic unrest is being fueled in part by dissatisfaction with current economic conditions.

The White Revolution: The Shah's Economic Last Gasp

The Shah's regime was secular and capitalist at its core. The system functioned like this: Oil revenues purchased the necessary food and supplies for the population. Industrial ownership was concentrated in a small group of wealthy elites, who were generally aligned with the Shah. Foreign oil companies made sure that the oil was flowing and that the subsidies that generated revenue masked the inefficiencies of domestic industry. However, there were shortages, and many people did without luxuries—or even without the basics. Against this backdrop, the Shah staged an almost obscenely opulent party to celebrate the 25,000th anniversary of the founding of the Persian Empire by Cyrus and of monarchical rule in Iran.

Persian Perspectives

Mohammad Reza Shah's claim of 25 centuries of monarchical rule was incorrect. There were gaps in the line of shah rule, and the Shah himself had fled the country during a time of internal violence. The Shah seemed to be increasingly obsessed with glorifying his rule. At one point, he attempted to have the Iranian calendar readjusted so that year 1 was the first year of Cyrus's reign rather than the established Islamic start date. These moves gave the clerics even more ammunition in their struggle to overthrow him.

The event underscored all that was wrong in the Iranian economy. The Shah and his elite circle squandered millions at a massive gala in the desert, while huge numbers of his subjects went without the basics.

The Shah did attempt some reforms that were known as the *White Revolution*. However, these reforms did not create lasting and lifting prosperity for the majority of Iranians. If they had, one wonders how successful the fundamentalist clerics would have been. It seems clear that one of the reasons the people were turning to radical Islam instead of a more secular version was that the secular model (at least, as manifested by the Shah's regime) was not working for them. The ayatollahs were preaching an ancient message, with a modern context, of liberation and justice. They were, in a sense, the most desirable alternative for the Iranian man on the street.

What's It Mean?

In January 1963, in response to the populist pressures still seething in the country during the aftermath of the Mossadeq era, the Shah launched the **White Revolution**. The elements included land reform, profit sharing for industrial workers in private sector enterprises, nationalization of forests and pastureland, privatization of government factories, and more power to workers and farmers in their enterprise supervisory councils (along the lines of the U.S. Peace Corps). Literacy Corps were set up where young men could teach in the rural areas in fulfillment of military service, and women were given the right to vote.

No Blueprint for the Clerics

As we discussed in Chapter 15, the Islamic Republic was without precedent in modern times. This included reconfiguration of the Iranian economy. The clerics had no guidelines to follow. As the new government created and submitted the new constitution for approval by the Majlis in 1980, it also began to institute a series of economic reforms. In this sense, like the Shah, the clerics were fulfilling the promising of an earlier populism.

The Populism Underfoot

In the early 1950s, a nationalist and very popular prime minister named Mohammad Mossadeq had emerged on the Iranian political scene. Responding to popular demand, Mossadeq pushed for a range of populist reforms. Mossadeq was representative of a growing demand among the Iranian population for better living conditions. As time went on, Mossadeq himself began shifting toward a stance that alarmed the United States and Great Britain as being pro-Communist. In 1953, they intervened in Iran's political system and got Mossadeq removed from power through the covert Operation Ajax. In this operation, the U.S. Central Intelligence Agency "coordinated" Mossadeq's ouster with the Shah and the Iranian military (who opposed Mossadeq's liberal views). The Shah ordered Prime Minister Mossadeq removed from power. He refused, and violence ensued. The situation rapidly escalated, and the Shah fled the country (sort of a habit for him). However, the military eventually prevailed, and the Shah returned to assume control again.

Mossadeq was placed under house arrest, where he died in 1967. The new prime minister, General Fazlolla Zahedi, took over the government. A period of bloody crackdowns on the Iranian Communist Party (known as the Tudeh) and other

Mossadeq loyalists ensued. Still, the Shah read the handwriting on the wall and initiated the White Revolution in the early 1960s, in part to avoid the resurgence of the sentiments that brought Mossadeq to power in the first place.

New Is Not Necessarily Better

The Islamic Republic regime continued the land distribution policies. However, the ayatollah kept a tight grip on industry, placing his own people in oversight roles at most of the larger private enterprises in the country. The Shah's ministers were replaced with Khomeini's designates, and the clerics assumed control over management of the economy. However, unlike the capitalists who ran the companies under the Shah, these clerical appointees were not professionals. The economic situation would not improve through better oversight because better oversight was not put in place.

Investment in nonoil industry was and still is funded by state oil revenues rather than profits from operations. Profitability and efficiency were not required.

In the 1980s, due to the tremendous strain of the Iran-Iraq War, the Iranian leadership issued debt to get the money it needed to finance the war effort. Oil revenues suffered as both sides attacked the other's oil production and export facilities, and then shipping in the Gulf. When the war ended, the clerics continued with the oil-subsidies-for-domestic-industry strategy.

Balance of Trade: Oil Goes Out, Everything Else Comes In

Iran's economy is more self-sufficient than other oil-producing states such as, say, Kuwait or Bahrain. This is not to say that Iran is completely self-sufficient because it is not. When we look at the Iranian balance of trade, we see the ominous structure of oil-dominated production.

> **CAUTION**
>
> **Warning!**
>
> Most Persian rugs are not made in Iran. Many are made in neighboring Central Asia. The term *Persian* was applied to these rugs because they funneled through Persia via ancient trading routes. Western buyers bought them in Persia or from Persian traders, as opposed to the carpet's country of origin.

Iran's leading exports after oil are carpets and rugs, metal products, and specific foods. However, these exports are tiny compared to the value of oil exports. For example, in 2002, Iran exported some $19.7 billion of oil and gas, but only $650 million of fruits and vegetables (its second-largest commodity export) and some $600 million in carpets and rugs.

On the import side, the Economist Intelligence Unit estimates that in 2002, Iran spent about $16 billion on everything from machinery to iron and steel to chemicals and grain. The purchases are financed through oil export revenues, and their volume rises and falls in accordance with oil prices on the world market which are extremely volatile these days.

Iran's biggest export partner is Japan, with China, Italy, and South Korea coming along behind. These four partners account for more than 50 percent of all Iranian exports. So any kind of economic slump in the Asian economy would significantly impact Iran's export revenues.

On the import side, Iran buys the most from Germany. More than 27 percent of Iran's imports come from Germany, France, Italy, and Russia. Interestingly enough, these same countries, with the exception of Russia, could be considered U.S. allies, yet they trade with Iran (and participate in oil deals) despite the ILSA sanctions.

The Role of Oil

Oil drives the Iranian economy. Crude oil accounted for some 82 percent of all Iranian export revenues from 1992 to 2002. This high figure is an average because the price of oil in the world market shifts significantly in relatively short periods, meaning that the actual level of income from crude oil exports shifts wildly with it.

The Iranian oil industry has been producing at its full capacity since the end of the Iran-Iraq War. Trying to rebuild its damaged infrastructure, the greatest level that the Iranian oil leadership has been able to hit is less than three million barrels per day—compared to the eight million barrels per day that Iran produced at its peak in 1974. Unlike other OPEC members, there is not much slack in the Iranian system. The Iranians really cannot produce much more than they currently are, even if they wanted to. What is more, as we saw in our discussion of nuclear power, the Iranians are incurring higher extraction costs in their online fields. They have to invest precious revenues heavily in developing some newer discoveries now, to have that new capacity come online in time to replace the production that is currently declining.

The Role of Foreign Investment

The Shah's oil regime welcomed foreign investment in the oil industry. Already nationalized by Mossadeq, the National Iranian Oil Company still was reliant on foreign investment to develop its industry. Contractual terms were not as advantageous as those under the old concessions, but still they were attractive to foreign oil partners (mainly the United States and Great Britain before the revolution).

Persian Perspectives

National Iranian Oil Company Timeline

1901	Oil concession is granted to D'Arcy to search for oil in Iran.
1909	The Anglo-Persian Oil Company is formed (private, British investors) to extract oil from Persia.
1912	The British government takes a 50 percent stake in Anglo-Persian Oil Company, making it an imperialism tool.
1912	The Turkish Petroleum Company (TPC) is formed to extract oil from Arab lands in the Ottoman Empire.
1914	The Anglo-Persian Oil Company (British owned) takes a 50 percent stake in the TPC.
1935	The Anglo-Persian Oil Company changes its name to the Anglo-Iranian Oil Company.
1951	Mossadeq government nationalizes Anglo-Iranian Oil Company, creates National Iranian Oil Company (NIOC).
1960	Iran joins OPEC.
1974	NIOC produces eight million barrels per day.
1979	The Islamic Revolution forces existing Western oil companies out of the Iranian oil industry.
1980 to 2003	U.S. sanctions and Iranian government policies hurt NIOC's production operations.
2003	NIOC produces three million barrels per day.

After the revolution, the new leadership wanted to set up more-equitable oil partnerships with foreign oil companies. In fact, the Iranian constitution passed in 1980 expressly prohibits granting oil concessions or allowing foreign companies to take direct equity stakes in Iran's oil industry. The concessions to and direct ownership by foreign investors are seen as economic imperialism of the type that was imposed upon Iran before the revolution.

To still encourage foreign investment in the energy sector, the Iranian leadership instituted a program of buybacks. Codified in the Petroleum Law of 1987, buybacks provide a framework for foreign energy investment without direct ownership. In a buyback arrangement, the foreign partner invests the necessary capital and expertise to develop the specific project. The National Iranian Oil Company (NIOC) pays the foreign company with proceeds generated by the project. When the foreign investor is paid, it turns over the project to the Ministry of Petroleum.

However, this policy limits the rate of return for the foreign company, specifies a rapid payback period, and does not guarantee that the foreign company that built the project will be able to win the contract to run it after it is completed. The Iranians bear the list of dropping oil prices. They must sell enough oil or gas to pay the foreign investor its cut. If prices drop, the Iranians must sell more gas or oil to pay, than if prices stayed higher.

The results of the buyback program are that the Iranians do not feel that they are getting the level of investment that they need, particularly now that they need to bring newer fields online promptly. Some changes include lengthening the actual buyback period and adjusting the return levels and how the risk of the deal is shared. Even so, the Iranians are not having as easy a time generating foreign direct investment in their oil infrastructure as they would like.

Caspian Standoff

The Iranians are also looking at oil development under the Caspian Sea. The challenge has been reaching an agreement among the countries that border the sea itself. Before the collapse of the Soviet Union, and before anyone realized just how much oil and gas was under the Caspian, Iran and the USSR had agreed to split equally the proceeds of anything recovered from there. (These treaties were signed in 1921 and again in 1940.)

Today the situation has changed. The Soviet Union is gone, and now five countries (Azerbaijan, Kazakhstan, Iran, Turkmenistan, and Russia) all claim rights to the mineral resources there. As we shall see later in this book, Iran has been less than cooperative with the other regional players in this situation. What is more, people now realize just how much oil and gas is to be had underneath the water there.

Iran wants all five states to share equally in the cost and revenues of developing the sea's floor. Each would receive 20 percent of the proceeds. This is known as the "condominium" approach to allocating the sea bed, and it is based on the original 50–50 concept signed when there were just two *littoral states*, Iran and the Soviet Union.

What's It Mean?

The **littoral states** of the Caspian Sea are the states that border it.

Three of the littoral countries (Azerbaijan, Russia, and Kazakhstan) have agreed to split the Sea using the "equidistant" approach. This method divides the Sea based upon shoreline distance out to the middle points where the abutters' portions would meet. Under this allotment, Iran would not have 20 percent, but more like

13 percent. Understandably, the Iranians are objecting to this plan. Still, even at a 13 percent share, the Iranians would have an estimated 15 billion barrels of oil and 11 trillion cubic feet of gas as their portion—simply huge amounts of energy.

The diplomatic impasse threatens to become more than that. The Iranian Oil Minister announced in March 2002 that Iran would begin working on its 20 percent portion. At one point, an Iranian gunboat took over two British Petroleum prospecting ships in the Caspian, showing that diplomacy was running out of time. As of this writing, the Oil Ministry is promising that Iran will begin drilling in the Caspian by 2005. The problem will come if the Iranians begin drilling in a location that is not inside what would be their equidistant allotment.

Sanctions?

The Iran and Libya Sanctions Act (signed in 1996 and extended five more years in 2001) is intended to limit Iran's ability to develop its oil industry and, thus, its ability to buy weapons of mass destruction or to fund terrorists. However, as the consistent string of energy deals shows, the Iranians have been able to work around those restrictions. Using oil swap deals rather than direct purchases from Iran, foreign oil companies are circumventing the sanctions. Others, including energy companies from France, Canada, and China, simply ignore the U.S. sanctions. Oil is literally a liquid asset. Once in the general pool, it is hard to determine where it came from. So even if the United States does not buy Iranian oil, some other countries will. Those buyers can leave the United States to consume their portion from another producer. The same amount of the same oil is consumed—just by different countries. Nonetheless, the sanctions have made it more difficult for Iran to do business. On top of the systemic problems and the lack of expertise among the clerics who call the shots, the sanctions impact the Iranian man on the street by contributing to the continued lack of economic progress.

Deprivation Leads to Desperation

We have seen just how the economy of Iran is dominated by oil and how that dependence has not lessened under the Islamic Republic regime. The question is how long this situation can last before conditions get too bad or popular patience finally runs out.

Conditions Today—Grinding It Out

The typical Iranian spends a large part of each day working to survive. Iranians focus on getting access to food and water, and making sure they have the money or resources to pay for it. While there are no shortages of basic goods, there are no surpluses, either. Inefficiency still reigns in most of the nonoil sector, and production problems loom in the developed oil patch. The leadership is banking on some big new discoveries coming online soon. Otherwise, oil earnings will decline as output remains level but extraction costs continue to rise in the steadily depleting fields.

Twenty-Five Years of Unmet Expectations

The economic lot of the Iranian people has not improved since the 1979 Islamic Revolution. First, there was the turmoil of the revolution itself, with disruptions in production and management as the clerics took control and the Shah's loyalists were removed from positions of power.

Then came the shock of total war for eight long years. Consider that World War II did not even last that long. The sacrifices and loss on the part of the Iranian (and Iraqi) people were extreme. These countries both were so reliant on oil revenues that any impact on their ability to produce or export it had an extreme impact on their income. As the war ground on, both sides began to attack the other's oil-production infrastructure and oil shipping, and their income plummeted. The Iranians, as we saw, turned to issuing debt to finance the war.

When the war ended, the Iranian leadership applied a forced austerity on imports of consumer goods, to free up cash to pay back war loans. Then, as the 1990s progressed, the oil-production levels hovered just under three million barrels per day. The revenue generated by this level of production is not enough to increase the purchases of consumption items so needed by the man on the street. In addition, investments in facilities and factories that would bring jobs and prosperity are still not coming.

As the 1990s wound down, the dependence on oil did not diminish. If oil revenues slip, renewed deficit spending to finance imports and subsidize domestic industry will no doubt resume. What is more, the persistent popularity of President Khatami is a continuing reminder of the restive Iranian people's desire for a better life.

After 25 years, the Iranian people are getting impatient with the slow pace of progress. They rightly believe that the lack of reform is as much to blame as the apparent mismanagement of economy. They are looking for a better life, and the leadership of the Islamic Republic will have to deliver, crack down on dissent, or leave.

The Least You Need to Know

- The clerics inherited an oil-based economy that was capitalistic and controlled by a small circle of the Shah's elite.

- Oil drives the Iranian economy. High prices mean more money to cover the underlying inefficiencies in the system. Low oil prices mean less money, and the problems of the system come to the forefront.

- Iran managed a debt payment crisis in the early 1990s, but its current account problems could be worse in the coming years, raising the threat of another payments problem.

- U.S.–led sanctions against Iran have had some impact, but Iran is managing to get the U.S.–sanctioned items it needs from countries such as Russia, China, and France.

- Iran's continued economic problems are contributing to rising domestic unrest.

Part  5

The Future: What Happens Next

Internal change is threatening the fundamentalist edifice of the Islamic Republic, and hostile forces are encircling the country. For all their external opening, the clerics show no signs of relaxing their grip at home. At the same time, the United States has adopted a more aggressive and focused foreign policy. The two countries appear to be on a collision course.

The chapters in this section focus on the changes that are taking place inside Iran and on its borders. We also look at the changes that are taking place in U.S. foreign policy and how those changes are having a profound impact on Iran.

Chapter 21

Cracks in the Fundamentalist Edifice

In This Chapter

 ◆ The contest for control between clerics and reformers

 ◆ The agitation of the middle class, women, and students

 ◆ The increasing power of the secular government

 ◆ The polarization of the debate: retrenchment vs. liberalization

We have looked at the history of Iran and the more recent history of the Islamic Republic. The Iranian people have lived in a state of expectation for some time now. From the first constitutional movements at the start of the twentieth century to the too-little-too-late reforms of the White Revolution, to the unmet promises of the Islamic Revolution, the Iranian man on the street has seen hopes for a better tomorrow stay just out of reach. We now turn to the current domestic situation in Iraq.

Who Is Running the Show?

The question of the day in Tehran is, who's in charge? More specifically, the question is, who will be in charge? There is a growing debate inside

Iran on the definition of the society that will exist within the Islamic Republic. The issue comes down to the concept of "progress" and what that means to the various constituencies inside Iran, which, in 2003, include the following:

- The clerics who rule the republic, are the guardians of the revolution, and are represented by Supreme Leader Khamenei

- The reformers who work within the constitutional framework and are represented by President Khatami

- The middle class and industrial workers, who are becoming increasingly frustrated by the lack of progress in the Majlis

- The students, who have all but dismissed the Majlis as a vehicle of real reform in the country

- The rural poor, who tend to support the clerics

- The military, whose high-ranking leadership supports the clerics

- Women, who are becoming increasingly vocal in their protests over oppressive social conditions

At the time of this writing, some 25 years after the Islamic Revolution, these constituencies have adopted different definitions for the term *progress.* The clerics and their supporters see progress as the continuation of the Islamic Revolution, as manifested in the Islamic Republic, and as guided by the Sharia, or the ruling body of Islamic law.

What's It Mean?

The **velayat-e faqih** is the concept that ultimate authority for all aspects of society—political, social, legal, ideological, and economic—rests with the ruling clerics. The clerics are the guardians of the Islamic Revolution, as well as the interpreters and adapters of the Sharia to modern needs.

The reformers and their various factions see "progress" as at least a gradual relaxation of the most oppressive restrictions of the current law and economic reform. At most, the reformers are calling for real democracy and a popular voice in government.

Most in the West view Khatami as the reformer, but this is not necessarily an accurate portrayal. Khatami works within the Islamic Republic's guidelines, which includes the ultimate authority and decision-making power of the clerics. This authority of the clerics is called the *velayat-e faqih,* and it is manifested in the control mechanisms written into the constitution of the Islamic Republic.

Khatami appears unwilling and, at any rate, unable to push real reform through the Majlis and past the Council of Guardians, who must approve any law before it becomes official. He seems content to continue the current efforts, and he does not seem willing to advocate a change in the current constitutionally defined structure of the government. What is more, Khatami appears to support the Sharia that governs modern Iran's political and social discourse.

> **They Said It**
>
> … [T]he defense of law means above all the defense of the *velayat-e faqih*.
>
> —President Khatami, quoted in the *Brown Journal of World Affairs*, Winter/Spring 2003

The Contradiction of Sharia and Human Rights

The *Sharia* and its interpretation by the clerics has resulted in the current body of law in the Islamic Republic, which supporters can argue is the ultimate expression of the Islamic state. On the other hand, Western observers are drawn to the contradictions presented by this societal framework. The code of conduct is particularly rigid, punishments appear extreme, and women are placed in a role that seems unequal and even dangerous.

> **What's It Mean?**
>
> The **Sharia** is the body of Islamic law that lists the rules for governing life consistent with Islam. The source of the Sharia is, first and foremost, the Qur'an. The Hadith and the Sunna (accounting of the sayings and deeds of the Prophet) also contribute to the Sharia, but only in support of the Qur'an.

Social traditions and Islamic law combine to oppress women in Iran. This oppression goes beyond the outward appearance of shrouded females. The legal system favors men over women in most domestic situations, including divorce and domestic relationships. Beyond the legally sanctioned restrictions on women in Iran, there are unequal practices. In one dramatic example, Article 102 of the Iranian Penal Code stipulates that when a man and a woman are convicted of adultery, the penalty is to be stoned. The man is buried up to his waist, and then the mob throws the stones. The woman is

> **Persian Perspectives**
>
> One could, of course, ask [the Islamists], "If you wish to implement the Sharia law in moderate form, how do you more moderately stone a woman to death?"
>
> —Azar Nafisi, Director of the Dialogue Project at the Johns Hopkins School of Advanced International Studies, from "They the People" *New Republic*, March 2003

buried up to her neck, and the same punishment administered. Whereas the man is afforded the opportunity to shield his head with his arms, the woman is given no such chance. This example is a good analogy for the disadvantages put upon women in Iran. The Sharia is tough on everyone, but the men have a better chance of dealing with it than women, who are totally constricted in their legal rights.

New Voices, Old Song

The voices of change are the same as those that spoke out for change in 1979. The middle class and the students are again agitating for change, each in their own manner. Women have joined the dialogue, as well, in response to the oppressive regulations on their social position, domestic life, and economic opportunities. Missing from this group are the Shia clerics who gave voice and structure to the protests in the years leading up to 1979. In the first decade of the twenty-first century, these clerics are "the Establishment" and the ones resisting change.

However, the reform movement is not as simple as the competition between Khatami (the president) and Khamenei (the Supreme Leader). The real reform debate has become a popular movement, and the debate is being conducted among the allies of Tehran, not the aisles of the Majlis. In Iran today, the debate includes groups outside the governmental structures of the Islamic Republic.

The Islamic Republic body of law is built around the Sharia, the strict Islamic code. The Sharia as interpreted by the Shia clerics in the Islamic Republic has resulted in oppressive restrictions on action and appearance. The Western media picks up on the startling statistics, such as 10 women being stoned to death in public between March and September of 2002 (according to the Women's Committee of the National Council for Resistance in Iran) for a range of infractions against the Islamic Republic law.

However onerous and dangerous it may be to live under the Sharia as personified in the law of the Islamic Republic of Iran, the people do practice some freedoms. Mostly, these occur behind closed doors, where drinking, dancing, and dating may go on as they do in most countries. In public, however, these activities—and many others that Westerners would consider commonplace—do not happen.

Religious vigilantes keep an eye out on behalf of the ruling clerics. They have the power to report and even directly punish violators of the rules. Sometimes these punishments are particularly harsh and frighteningly fast. Stories of women being beaten, raped, and even killed for showing even the smallest amount of skin have been meticulously recounted in Western media. Although experts agree that the power of these vigilante groups has waned, the fear of the enforcers remains a powerful tool of repression for the current government. If one lives in almost constant fear of being beaten or punished for slight deviations from Sharia strictures, the likelihood of public compliance with the rules runs high. Most frightening and invasive is the fact that the vigilantes who most often enforce the law are not officials of the state, even though they seem officially sanctioned. So the local thugs are also the local enforcers, and they are just looking for any excuse to take out their frustrations on their hapless fellow citizens. This unregulated threat of terror is a very effective means of policing the people.

We are not suggesting, though, that the entire body of the Iranian people is united against the Islamic Republic in a struggle for liberalization. The existence of the urban vigilante groups, and their allies in the rural regions, is evidence that the Iranian people are not unified in some reformist front. Like many democracies, the political and social movements currently underway in Iran are not monolithic. Instead, the reform movement is made up of a number of parties, each with its own agenda. Arrayed against the reformers is a similar range of groups, each with its own agenda. As we shall see, the longer the debate goes on without some sort of movement, the more radicalized this dialogue will become.

The Outlet Becomes the Catalyst

The Majlis has begun to morph from an outlet for popular opinion into a catalyst for change. This transition did not happen overnight, but it has indeed happened. When crafting the constitution for the new Islamic Republic in 1979, the clerics retained the Majlis. They recognized that the people needed an outlet for popular frustration and some sort of a voice in civil society. After all, the sense of popular disenfranchisement was one of the primary motivations for the overthrow of the Shah. The clerics were not going to make that same mistake. Still, as we saw in Chapter 15, the clerics built in several safeguards, including a Council of Guardians that has the ultimate say over any law passed by the Majlis.

Over the past 25 years of the Islamic Republic, an interesting but not unprecedented phenomenon has developed. The Majlis has evolved from a rubber-stamp organization to a vibrant organ of democracy. Resolutions are debated with vigor, and thoughtful laws are passed. The body of the Majlis has seen a reintroduction of political parties, long outlawed by the Islamic Republic, and it is a representative electorate. However, the Council of Guardians limits the effect of this democratic institution. The council disallows any measure proposed by the Majlis that is reformist in nature. Council members are fundamentalist (even reactionary) clerics who consider their holy duty to be the preservation and defense of the Islamic Revolution. They see the Majlis as a thing to be controlled, not a viable or valued instrument for social progress. The Supreme Leader, Khamenei, supports the council wholeheartedly.

On the other hand, the people elect President Khatami. He has been re-elected twice and enjoyed greater than 70 percent of the vote in the last election. There is little doubt that the people of Iran see Khatami as their voice for change, within the structure of the Majlis. If the Council of Guardians was amenable to this popular will, we would expect to see Iran gradually liberalize and popular protest subside as a more open society emerged.

The Debate Intensifies

However, this gradual opening is not the case. The bloc of support that ordains Khatami is becoming increasingly impatient with the lack of real progress. Each time the Council of Guardians vetoes a Majlis proposal, the voices for change get louder and angrier.

Increasing Polarity

The students are already stepping up the tempo. Student-led protests are occurring with greater frequency and severity in Tehran and other cities. This voice of Iran's youth cannot be ignored for long. More than 65 percent of the population is under the age of 25, and their views are more sympathetic to the West than their parents are. Experts observe that the most popular television show in Iran is *Baywatch*—hardly a model of Islamic thought.

Even more dire for the ruling clerics, recent protests in cities such as Alborz and Arak have included industrial workers and middle-class elements, not just students.

In November 2002, a Tehran University professor and leading dissident named Hashem Aghari was sentenced to death for his statements that exhorted the government to adopt a more progressive stance. About 5,000 student protests in support of Aghari sprouted up immediately in Tehran and spread to Tabriz, Isfahan, Urumiyeh, and Hamedan in the next few days. The protesters demanded not only the release of the professor, but also more democracy.

Suppression Creates Radicalization

The reform movement is becoming more radicalized as it evolves, and the clerics continue to thwart reform. The reformers will splinter, but the overall momentum will grow. The classic signs of reaction are also manifest. In one telling example, *The Wall Street Journal* reported that the Iranian government conducted a poll to gauge whether the people of Iran wanted a more open dialogue with the United States. The results showed that more than 70 percent of the respondents do favor this dialogue. The clerics responded by arresting the pollsters and putting them on trial. The trial began in late 2002 and includes the charge that the pollsters administered a "flawed" poll.

This kind of official response to popular opinion signals an increasing polarization of debate. In this environment, moderate voices on both sides (including Khatami and the Majlis) will be drowned out by the shouts of the more urgent and angry at both ends of the spectrum.

Who Will Carry the Day?

Right now, the clerics hold all the power and are defenders of the Islamic Revolution as they define it. They carried the day in 1979, eventually prevailing over all other reforming elements in Iran that emerged after the fall of the Shah. However, the clerics show no signs yet of an evolutionary view of the Islamic Republic over which they preside. Instead, the Islamic Republic in their interpretation seems an integrated structure that cannot and will not accept outside pressures to change.

Against this edifice we see the groups pushing for change. These groups pushing for change today fall into two camps: the reformers and the liberalizers. The reformers are led by Khatami and are embodied in the Majlis. They are pushing for a gradual opening of society and relaxation of the most onerous dictates of the Sharia, but *within* the constitutional framework that recognizes the ultimate authority of the clerics (the *velayat-e faquih*). The debate methods used by the reformers consist of measures debated and passed by the Majlis that would relax or eliminate the most oppressive regulations of the current laws in force.

The liberalizers, unlike the reformers, are not working within the structure of the Islamic Republic. They are students, women, and, increasingly, the middle class. They are seeking more social and legal freedom, as well as better economic opportunity. These groups are not as concerned with whether their demands are consistent with the Islamic Republic's legal structures. The "debate" methods that this group uses are street protests and demonstrations. The Republic leadership responds by unleashing (or at least, indulging) counterdemonstrators from the most fundamental groups in society. The "debate" being conducted by the demonstrators and counterdemonstrators is happening outside the framework of the constitution, which makes it very dangerous to the clerics who rule the Islamic Republic.

The Coming Changes

It will get worse in Iran before it gets better. The process of reform (meaning a relaxing of the strictest rules of the Sharia, a liberalizing of the economy, and more power to the Majlis) will not be voluntary and will not be quick.

The process will not be voluntary because the clerics are showing no signs of relaxing their grip on power. If anything, the clerics continue to thwart any liberalizing movements by disallowing any liberalizing measures passed by the Majlis and by keeping a tight lid on the people through the police force and the fundamentalist "volunteers" who fight the protesters in the streets.

If history tells us anything, we can be confident that, at some point, the pressure will become too great for the clerics and their constitutional controls and fundamentalist factions to manage. When that pressure point is reached, the question is whether the clerics will give up some controls or go down fighting.

Looking at this eventuality another way, the question is whether the Islamic Republic is fluid or rigid. Is the totality of the Islamic Republic—its law, social system, mission, and values—able to change and still retain those laws, systems, missions, and values? Or will opening up to one small change topple the whole structure? This question is at the core of the future of Iran.

As we have seen, there is no modern precedent for the Islamic Republic. The ruling clerics are operating without a road map. They are following guidelines that were laid out centuries before and are interlacing them with their interpretations of how to apply those guidelines to modern life in Iran. Much of the interpretation is left to the leaders of the state, not the population at large. The democracy familiar to the West, and being demanded by the people in the streets, is not the kind of democracy that the Shia clerics are inclined to accept. Instead, the clerics will probably be forced to approve some liberalizing that is suggested by the Majlis, in an attempt to provide some relief to rising tension in the streets. It is doubtful that this tactic will be enough or will happen in time to stave off more violent protests and demands for reform.

The West and the Coming Changes

Also clear is that the Iranians will be dealing with this question on their own. There is little the West will be able to do to influence the debate. If anything, Western pressure, particularly U.S. pressures to minimize or remove the threats posed by the Iranian nuclear weapons or Iranian-sponsored terrorists, will simply stiffen the resolve of the clerics to resist in the name of defending the Islamic Revolution as they define it.

The clerics have a difficult but unavoidable path to walk. We in the West will watch to see if they will walk alongside the reformers or be pushed along by them.

The Least You Need to Know

- The real reformers are not Khatami and the Majlis, as they operate within the guidelines of the Islamic Republic; the reformers are the students, women, and middle class who are calling for a better life through social and economic liberalization.

- The longer the debate over reform takes, the more polarized the debate becomes, and the potential for violence increases as the radicalized elements become more impatient.

- The students are becoming increasingly violent in their demonstrations, and the basij (fundamentalist "volunteers") are matching them blow for blow in street battles.

- The clerics are the lynchpin in the growing debate over reform in Iran; power and decision-making authority are concentrated in their hands as prescribed in the Islamic Republic's constitution and guiding law, the Sharia.

- The Iranian people will decide the debate over the structure of Iranian society. The West can only watch and wait.

22

Iran in the World

In This Chapter

- ◆ East is East and West is West, and Iran is neither
- ◆ Russia's central role
- ◆ From export of revolution to stabilizing force in Central Asia
- ◆ Ideological foreign policy in the Middle East
- ◆ Meddling on the borders: Iran's quest for security

Some dominant themes describe Iran's relationship with the rest of the world. Economically, Iran's primary interaction with the world is as a supplier of oil. Militarily, Iran supports terrorist groups as proxies for military intervention. We have seen that Iran is alone among the Islamic countries, as the sole Shia-dominated Muslim country. In this chapter, we look at how Iran interacts with the rest of the world on a political and social level.

Iran in the Middle

Iran sees itself as neither Eastern nor Western. Rather, Iran sees itself as a unique people and location, between Asia, the Middle East, and the West. Iran sees this position as an opportunity as much as a threat. Iran is able to reach out to its neighbors through a variety of channels. It has its role in

OPEC as a means of engaging with the oil-producing Arab states. It sees its common heritage as a vehicle to reach out to Central Asia and Afghanistan. Its geographic proximity to Russia presents trade opportunities and security concerns. Across all these opportunities, Iran's approach has gradually shifted from an ideological to a more pragmatic diplomacy.

Iran has long followed the time-honored tactic of destabilizing its neighbors to maintain its own security. Most recently, this "meddling" has occurred in Afghanistan and Iraq. In the case of Afghanistan, Iran's approach is pragmatic. In the case of Iraq, it is more ideological. This difference between pragmatism and ideology underscores Iranian foreign policy toward Central Asia and the Middle East.

Central Asia: Shift from Revolutionary Ideology to Pragmatic Foreign Policy

Immediately after the Islamic Revolution, Iran competed with other Muslim countries to push its own brand of Islam around the world. In the 1980s and early 1990s, Iranian foreign policy was driven by the concept of the umma, or greater community of Islam. The goal was to strengthen the umma by establishing Iran-type Islamic republics that eventually would unite to create a great Muslim state.

In a new twist on the Great Game (remember our discussion of the power struggle between Britain and Russia in Central Asia), Iran competed ideologically for influence against Turkey and Saudi Arabia in the newly independent Central Asian republics. Later, the competition became more grounded in Iranian national interests, and the rivals became Russia and the United States.

Bet You Didn't Know

The Central Asian republics include Uzbekistan, Kazakhstan, Kyrgyzstan, Tajikistan, and Turkmenistan. These "republics" are dictatorships that have emerged from the old Soviet system. For example, the president of Uzbekistan was the former Uzbekistan Communist Party leader under the old USSR. He was elected to a second term as president, with 99.9 percent of the vote. This region is predominately Muslim, as are many of the regions surrounding it, including Afghanistan, Pakistan, and western China.

As the only Islamic Republic, Iran sought strength in numbers and was driven by revolutionary conviction to promote additional Islamic Republics. However, the Iranians wanted to see their brand of Islamic Republic, not someone else's idea of what it should be. Remember, there are really no precedents to follow, so interpretations of what an Islamic theocracy would look like are really up to the group that is creating that theocracy.

The Taliban: Not What the Ayatollahs Had in Mind

The recent *Taliban* regime in Afghanistan is an example of what Iran did *not* want to see as an Islamic state. On the surface, here was another Islamic regime right next door, which would seem to be a good thing. Several similarities did exist between the two states. The Taliban had risen to power by overthrowing an oppressive regime—in this case, a secular, Soviet-backed Afghan government, and established an Islamic theocracy. The Taliban also sponsored terrorists—including al Qaeda, but this is where the similarity ends.

What's It Mean? _____

The **Taliban** emerged in the southwestern parts of Afghanistan as one of the many resistance groups battling first the Soviet military and then the Soviet-backed Afghan government in the 1980s and early 1990s. It gradually increased its power and followers as it achieved victory after victory on the way to Kabul (the Afghan capital). Upon taking power, the Taliban provided support and sponsorship to al Qaeda, the Muslim terrorist group responsible for the several attacks on the United States and U.S. interests. Finally, after the September 11, 2001, attacks on the World Trade Center and the Pentagon, a U.S.–led Coalition (with the support of the rival Northern Alliance within Afghanistan) attacked and removed the Taliban regime. Remnants of the Taliban persist in their traditional home areas in southwestern Afghanistan.

The Taliban was approaching the concept of an Islamic state from a different perspective. It follows the *Wahhabism* variant of the Sunni school.

What's It Mean? _____

Named for its founder, Muhammad bin Abdi al-Wahhab, **Wahhabism** first emerged in the mid-1700s in Saudi Arabia. Basically, al-Wahhab offered his support to the ancestors of the Saudi ruling family in return for their support of his strict interpretation of Islam. Over time, Wahhabism became the dominant version of Sunni Islam in Saudi Arabia and elsewhere. Even today, the Saudi government supports the Wahhabist view of Islam inside of Saudi Arabia and, through international organizations, in other countries.

Wahhabism—the Saudi Version of Islam

The Taliban is not made up of Shia Muslims; its members are Sunnis and, more specifically, Wahhabist. The Taliban had created a strict Wahhabist state in Afghanistan. Under its strict interpretation of Muslim law, punishments for a range of vices were extremely severe, and the role of women was rigidly constrained. The Taliban even destroyed priceless Buddhist artifacts in Afghanistan, including a huge statue of the Buddha. (In a similarly strict interpretation of Muslim law, Wahhabists almost destroyed the Prophet Mohammad's tomb in Mecca in 1926 because Mohammad had specified that his grave should not be a place of pilgrimage.) Ultimately, the Taliban would have considered Iran to be an intolerable regime and would not have tolerated its Shia views any more than it tolerated those of Buddhism or Christianity.

Opposed to the Wahhabist hardliners in Afghanistan, the Iranians provided assistance to the Coalition that toppled the Taliban in 2002. (The secular governments in the Central Asian republics also supported the Coalition against the Taliban. In fact, U.S. troops used a former Soviet base in southern Uzbekistan as a crucial staging point for operations against the Taliban.)

Nonetheless, despite the ambivalence of the Central Asian governments toward Wahhabism, the movement did (and still does) compete for the hearts and minds in the region. Saudi dollars help fund organizations and schools, whose teachers spread the Wahhabist viewpoint. Wahhabism is considered to be a bigger threat than Iran by the Central Asian leaders. This common enemy provides an opportunity for engagement on a nonideological level among all the interested parties. Iran has taken up that opportunity, with some successes.

The Turkish Model—Secular Islam

As a counterweight to the Saudi-sponsored Wahhabism and Iranian Islamism, Turkey was pushing its own version of Islam on the Central Asian republics. Turkish products and companies are very active in Central Asia, as were Turkish-funded mosques and madrasas (schools). However, the future of Turkey's ideology-promotion policy is in doubt for two reasons. First, to some extent, Turkey offered its secular version of Islam in Central Asia as a means of currying favor with the United States. The United States viewed (and still does) the Iranian version of Islam as a threat to U.S. interests. By promoting a secular, democratic, and "acceptable to the United States" version of Islam in Central Asia, Turkey was looking to please the United States. However, the new Turkish leadership is decidedly less supportive of U.S. policies in the region, as reluctance to provide logistical support and bases for U.S. troops in

Operation Iraqi Freedom showed. Second, Turkey lacks the extensive resources that Saudi Arabia has to sustain a large-scale international system to promote the Turkish model of Islam.

Pragmatism vs. Ideology

Given the waning Turkish efforts and the U.S. destruction of and continued vigilance against Taliban-like Wahhabist power in Central Asia, Iran no longer is pushing its ideology as aggressively in Central Asia. Instead, Iran is taking a more pragmatic approach to the countries in the region. Finally acknowledging that its ideological fervor was not translating well to foreign relations, post–Ayatollah Khomeini Iran has softened its stance toward other Muslim countries, particularly in Central Asia.

"Reduction of Tensions" and "Dialogue of Civilizations"

Under President Khatami, the Iranian foreign policy has adopted the two tenets of "reduction of tensions" and "dialogue of civilizations." As they sound, these policies are far less confrontational and less dogmatic. These policies suggest that Iran is willing to set aside ideological arguments in favor of open dialogue on national interests. As we have seen, although the power of the reformers is rising, it is not guaranteed. Still, this softened stance shows that the hardliners are either seeing the benefits of pragmatism or are unable to stop the trend. Either way, Iran as the glowering revolutionary is giving way to Iran as the constructive partner, at least in some parts of the world.

Pragmatic Meddling in Afghanistan

While the Iranians are happy to see the Taliban out of Afghanistan, they are equally unhappy to see a U.S.–backed regime take hold there. Faced with that option, Iran has chosen to attempt to destabilize the Afghan government, to minimize any pressure it could apply against Iran in the future. According to U.S. government officials, Iran has actually harbored survivors of its old foes, the Taliban, and helped them to continue to fight the U.S.–backed Northern Alliance who control Afghanistan. In addition, Iran is sending supplies, weapons, and money to Afghan warlords in western Afghanistan who are fighting against the central government. With these resources, the local warlords can buy and equip recruits to fight for them. The most notorious, Ismail Khan, the warlord in the city of Herat, the old goal of the Persian shahs during the nineteenth century, has received significant support from Tehran. The presence of the strongman in Herat threatens the central government and U.S. forces in Kandahar. However, Iran has been careful not to send any of its own troops into the country. In addition, Khan (a Farsi-speaking Persian) has publicly distanced himself from his Iranian benefactors. He also is facing pressure from other tribal leaders in Afghanistan who do not welcome Iranian activities in their country.

However, Iran has taken to open, cooperative foreign policy moves as well. Iran has formally pledged the most amount of aid to the new Afghan government of any nation (including the United States): $560 million in aid. By comparison, the United States has formally pledged $297 million. (Of course, the United States is committing far greater resources overall to the new Afghan regime.)

From Meddling to Mediation

Along with pledging money and sending arms, Iran has applied diplomacy. Recently, Iran mediated conflicts in Tajikistan between Islamic rebels and the sitting government. In this case, Iran deliberately did not back pro-Islamist rebels, but instead supported the sitting Tajik government. Similarly, Iran has not agitated the Uzbek government over its suppression of Islamic rebels in that country. Iran also tried, albeit unsuccessfully, to mediate the ongoing conflict between Armenia and Azerbaijan in the early 1990s. While that effort failed, the attempt shows how far Iran is taking its more pragmatic approach to foreign relations.

Cashing In on Pragmatism

This constructive dialogue includes taking advantage of geography. Iran has expanded it rail infrastructure to act as a trans-shipment point for goods flowing into Central Asia and southern Russia (much like the strategic role it played in World War II). Rail links to Azerbaijan are in place, and train service from Tehran to Almaty, Kazakhstan, was initiated in 2002. Iran envisions itself as an overland trans-shipment route between Russia and India as well. Nonenergy trade flows between Iran and Central Asia have increased dramatically in the past few years, although no country accounts for more than $1 billion in total trade value.

Iran is the most direct land route to transmit oil and gas from the Caspian Region to the Persian Gulf. The Central Asian republics of Kazakhstan and Turkmenistan are interested in accessing Iran's pipeline network to get their product to market. Iran, wanting the leverage and the transit fees, is pushing for this option. However, U.S. opposition has caused the Central Asian producers to avoid Iran as an export option.

Iran's relationship with the Western powers (including Japan) is driven by those countries' relations with the United States. Trade relations with France, Italy, Germany, and Japan are carried out in spite of U.S. sanctions. Still, trade with these countries is limited due to the sanctions. As U.S. relations with its European allies cool, Iranian relations with those same allies warm, and trade follows. Further opening of relations with the United States would probably result in even greater trade with those countries.

The Russia Factor

As the ideological fervor in foreign policy has died down, the national security focus has increased. Along with the United States, Russia, is a central factor in Iran's foreign policy. Still the giant to the north, Russia, poses a significant challenge to Iranian interests. Part of the softening of the revolutionary tenor in Iranian foreign policy is due to Russian concern over Iran stirring up trouble in the Caucasus and Central Asia. Iran hopes to increase trade and stature in the region by gaining the support of Russia. (Russia asked for Iranian assistance in mediating in the Caucasus.)

Still, Russia (like the United States) will act in its own interests, even when those interests anger Iran. Recall the Caspian Sea oil resource allocation issue. Russia has agreed with the other littoral states to divide the oil in a manner that is less favorable to Iran than the old treaty between Iran and the USSR. Russia deemed it more important to have good relations with those former Soviet republics than to warm its ties with Iran.

Russia has also discouraged Iranian overtures to Central Asia, which it regards as part of the Russian sphere of influence. In addition, Russia tacitly supports the U.S. resistance to Central Asian energy trans-shipments across Iran. Without an Iran shipment option, much of the energy would have to flow through Russian pipelines, increasing Russian revenues and leverage.

However, the fact that Russia supplies the nuclear technology to Iran alarms the United States and the IAEA. Russian weaponry also finds its way into Iranian hands. And Russia is participating in negotiations for a proposed Russia-Iran-India trade link. In the final analysis, pragmatism and power politics describe the Russian-Iranian relationship and probably will continue to do so for years to come.

The Middle East and Israel—the Ideological Approach

Even as Iran's foreign relations with Central Asia and Russia have taken a decidedly pragmatic turn, Iranian relations with the Arab Middle East and Israel (over the Palestinian question) are still decidedly ideological.

Terrorism and the Question of Israel

As we saw in Chapter 18, Iran does not acknowledge Israel's right to exist and actively supports the Hezbollah and Hamas terrorist groups that are dedicated to the destruction of Israeli. Along with support for the Shia Muslim Hezbollah and the Palestinian Hamas groups, Iran has provided support to the Palestinian Authority. In fact, early in 2003, Israeli coastal patrol boats intercepted an Iranian shipment of 50 tons of weapons that were intended for the Palestinian Authority. Procuring this volume of weaponry must have had the approval of Iranian authorities, even if they did not charter the ship themselves.

Iran's relationship with the Arab states is defined by those states' relationships with Israel. The more open to Israel they are, the less friendly Iran's relationship is with those countries. Egypt, for example, is vilified by the Iranians for signing the Camp David Accords. Jordan, too, is castigated for its relationship with Israel.

Iran's relationship with the Persian Gulf States has been menacing, to say the least. These countries financed the Iraqi war effort against Iran during the Iran-Iraq War, which did nothing to endear them to Tehran. Furthermore, the secular, monarchist nature of the regimes outraged the Islamic Republic leaders and inspired antigovernment factions inside those countries. In the 1980s, the Iranian leadership actually branded the sultan of Oman as an "un-Islamic" leader who should be removed from power, and a number of attacks in the Gulf States resulted from Shia groups in those countries taking their inspiration from the Iranian example. A suicide bomber even tried unsuccessfully to assassinate the ruler of Kuwait in 1985. Bahrain's population is mostly Shia, but the ruling family is Sunni, and Iran has consistently challenged the ruling family's authority to rule. Also, relations with the United Arab Emirates are clouded by the Iranian seizure and occupation of Greater and Lesser Tunbs in the Strait of Hormuz when the British withdrew from the region in the 1970s. Despite the common interest in oil production, Iranian relations with the Arab Gulf States are, at best, proper and, at worst, openly hostile.

As hostile as it has been to the monarchies in the Gulf, Iran has been most friendly to Syria. Also hostile to Israel and Iraq, Syria actually cut off Iraqi oil trans-shipments during the Iran-Iraq War. This action supported the Iranians, and Iran responded by providing favorable oil exports to Syria. After the war, Syria opened some to the Saddam Hussein regime. However, with the collapse of that regime and the potential creation of a pro–U.S. regime in Iraq, the Iranian relationship with Syria has shown signs of warming.

Iraq—Old Enemy to New Friend?

The Iranian relationship with Iraq has been the most complex. Recall that Saddam Hussein started a vicious and costly war with Iran in 1980, on the heels of the Islamic Revolution. That war and its aftermath are still being felt by the Iranians, with reduced oil production, missing loved ones, and battle-scarred veterans. There certainly was no love lost between Saddam Hussein and the Ayatollah Khomeini, and that hostility carried forward after Khomeini's death with the current Iranian leadership.

However, with Saddam Hussein now gone and the Iraqi Shias experiencing their first taste of freedom from his oppression, Iran has seized an opportunity. Remember that more than 60 percent of Iraq's population is Shia and that the two Shia holy sites of Karbala and An Najaf are located in Iraq. Iran would welcome a sympathetic, Shia-dominated theocracy in Iraq and has begun to agitate for that.

Iran has long supported the Supreme Council for Islamic Revolution in Iraq (SCIRI) with bases, training, and finance. SCIRI operatives, called the Badr Brigades, have been infiltrating Shiite Iraq in an attempt to unite and direct Shia Iraqis to get the United States out of Iraq, and then to create a Shia Islamic Republic along the Iran model. Many Iraqi Shia clerics had taken refuge in Iran during the Hussein regime and are now returning to Iraq to stake a claim to leadership there. As of this writing, the final structure of the Iraqi government has not been determined. If true popular democracy is created, the Shia majority will become the power to be reckoned with.

More important will be the power of the clerics within the Shia majority. The Iranian clerics were able to seize power in Iran in the chaos that ensued after the Shah fled in 1979. As we saw earlier in this book, the clerics' path to power was not automatic. The Iranian leadership is no doubt applying its experience to the Iraqi situation, with the intention of establishing theocratic authority in Iraq.

It is hard to decide whether the Iranian efforts in Iraq will be successful and whether the Iranian leadership is more motivated by security concerns or ideological fervor. Either way, Iran's relationship with Iraq and its new government will be closer and more engaged. The question is whether the engagement will be constructive.

Uncle Sam and Iran

We have seen that Iran is reaching out to its neighbors and shifting its policy from ideology to pragmatism, with the exception of Israel and Iraq. Iran certainly will be a critical force in the future of those two countries. The other critical force in determining those two countries' future and, indeed, Iran's future, is the United States.

The Least You Need to Know

- ◆ Iran's foreign policy has evolved from revolutionary fervor to more calculating national interests.

- ◆ Iran continues to define its relationship with the Arab Middle East in terms of how those countries relate to its enemy, Israel.

- ◆ Russian–Iranian relations are driven by Russian interests rather than mutual goals.

- ◆ Iran's relationships with European powers are heavily influenced by the United States.

- ◆ The turmoil in post-Hussein Iraq poses a challenge and an opportunity for Iran relative to the majority Shia Muslim population there.

Chapter 23

The West: Rumblings of Change

In This Chapter

- ◆ U.S. presidents define foreign policy doctrines
- ◆ The terror attacks of September 11, 2001, have triggered a fundamental re-examination of U.S. policy
- ◆ The United States' new role as surviving superpower contributes to the current re-examination
- ◆ "Pre-emptive security" and traditional institutions and alignments
- ◆ The first actions under this new doctrine show both doubts and convictions

In this chapter, we examine the fundamental shifts currently underway in U.S. foreign policy. In the following chapter, we examine how the new U.S. policies are affecting the Iranian–U.S. relationship.

Chilled to the Bone: U.S.–Iranian Relations

We have seen how the cracks are appearing in the fundamentalist edifice of the Islamic Republic. We have traced how these cracks are causing the changes in Iran's foreign policy toward neighbors and other countries. We have seen an increase in ties with Europe, an opening with Russia, and even overtures to the Arab states. We have seen support provided to Afghanistan and a less dogmatic approach toward the Muslim Central Asian republics.

The only countries that still have chilly relations with Iran are the United States and Israel. Iran's relationship with Israel is openly hostile, and as long as the Islamic Republic exists, it probably will remain that way. The combination of religious, ideological, and leadership imperatives drives the Iranian clerics to wage a constant terror war on Israel.

Before we examine Iranian–U.S. relations, we should take a look at the change in the policies that both countries employ in dealing with the other and the world in general. We saw in Chapter 22 how Iran has gradually adopted a more pragmatic, less ideological approach to its foreign policy (with the exception of its unceasing hostility toward Israel). This pragmatism has resulted in increased engagement (Khatami's so-called "Dialogue of Civilizations") with Europe, Russia, and Iran's immediate neighbors in Central Asia and the Middle East. At the same time, Iran appears to be following the Ayatollah Khomeini's "neither East nor West" strategy as it pursues its own course in foreign policy rather than adhering to the policies of any pre-existing bloc of countries. (This policy, too, reflects the reality of Iran's unique cultural and ethnic mix. Iran's ethnic similarities to some Central Asian populations have not led to a clear bonding with those populations the way the Arab countries have bonded with each other.)

U.S. Foreign Policy–the Doctrine Phenomenon

Despite the separation of powers as detailed in the U.S. Constitution and the Senate's role in ratifying treaties, mainly the U.S. presidents and their administrations have determined U.S. foreign policy. This power was not explicitly granted to U.S. presidents by the Constitution, but it quickly became clear that the power of the presidency extends to matters of foreign policy.

These presidents react to situations, or seize opportunities, to define U.S. policy to other nations in the world. Often the policies established by a sitting U.S. president do not survive into the next presidency. For example, the Carter administration's overtures to the Soviet Union were replaced by the Reagan administration's overt confrontational approach to the Soviets. Policies shift partly because of ideology. Carter and Reagan came from different ends of the political spectrum.

From the beginnings of the United States to the current day, U.S. presidents are tied with specific policies that relate to U.S. security in the context of international relations.

The Doctrine Develops

As far back as the early 1800s, the United States has outlined policies relating to its security. The Monroe Doctrine basically claimed the Western Hemisphere as being in the young United States' sphere of influence. President James Monroe, through action and word, made it plain that the United States would not tolerate European intervention in its "back yard." Later, President Truman outlined the Truman Doctrine, which pledged that the United States would resist the spread of communism around the globe.

In many ways, the Truman Doctrine was the basis for U.S. strategy throughout the Cold War. We saw earlier in this book how that doctrine played out in Iran. In the late 1940s, the United States was behind the drive to get the Red Army out of Iran and to get the Soviets to abandon their support for two puppet regimes in Azerbaijan and Kurdistan that threatened Iran's territorial integrity. Later, in the 1950s, the United States intervened to remove Mossadeq from power as prime minister when he began to threaten the U.S. position in Iran. Following the Mossadeq episode, the United States supported the Shah as he used the SAVAK to maintain his position.

Old Habits Die Hard

Presidents do create foreign policy doctrines based upon ideology, but they also do so based upon the U.S. position relative to the current power blocs in the world. For the past 50 years, the two power blocs have been East and West. East was the Soviet Union and its satellites and client states. West was the United States, its allies in western Europe and Asia, and its client states (including Iran until 1979). The Truman Doctrine survived and morphed, but it remained a constant over this period. From the Korean War to Vietnam to Afghanistan, the United States and the Soviet Union squared off militarily as well as politically across the globe.

The United Nations became a forum for debate and diplomacy throughout the Cold War, from dramatic confrontations such as Krushchev's speech complete with pounding footwear and the United States' dramatic presentation of photographic evidence during the Cuban Missile Crisis, to more quiet bargaining outside the General Assembly.

As part of the East-West competition, international organizations were created. Both the United States and the USSR created alliances during the Cold War to help them achieve their strategic goals. The most dominant were *NATO* (the United States, Canada, and western European powers) and the *Warsaw Pact* (the Soviet Union and eastern European powers). Economic alliances also were formed. The *G-7* was a union of leading Western economic powers, and the *CMEA* was the Soviet-led counterpart.

What's It Mean?

NATO (the North Atlantic Treaty Organization) is a military alliance that was created in 1949. At the start, it included the United States, Canada, Belgium, Denmark, Iceland, Italy, Spain, Luxembourg, Norway, the Netherlands, Portugal, and the United Kingdom. West Germany, Greece, and Turkey joined later. France joined initially but later left the organization in 1966. NATO has continued to add members, largely from central and eastern Europe in the past decade.

The **Warsaw Pact** was a military alliance created in 1955. It included the Soviet Union, Albania, Bulgaria, Czechoslovakia, East Germany, Hungary, Poland, and Romania.

The **G-7** is an economic group that includes the United States, Canada, Japan, Italy, France, Germany (then West Germany), and the United Kingdom. During the 1990s, Russia gradually became integrated into this group, which in 1997 became known as the "G-8."

The **CMEA** (Council for Mutual Economic Assistance, or COMECON) was founded in 1949. It was an economic group that included the Soviet Union, Albania, Bulgaria, Czechoslovakia, Hungary, Poland, and Romania at the start. East Germany (1950) and Mongolia (1962) joined subsequently.

The U.S. effort to contain communism also resulted in a series of regional alliances and multilateral organizations. Iran was part of the Baghdad Pact (led by Britain, but heavily supported by the United States) that later evolved into the Central Treaty Organization when Iraq withdrew from the group. Across these alliances, the dominant factor was the U.S.–Soviet competition. Everything lined up behind one side or the other.

The End of History—the Start of a New Doctrine

The constant of East-West confrontation changed in 1989. In that year, the Soviet Union ceased to exist. Unable to compete across the military, economic, and domestic realms, the Soviet Union first lost its allies in eastern Europe and then lost its own identity. By 1990, the Soviet Union had dissolved into the *Commonwealth of Independent States.*

What's It Mean? _____

The **Commonwealth of Independent States** (CIS) included all the former republics of the Soviet Union except the Baltic republics of Latvia, Lithuania, and Estonia. The last to be incorporated into the Soviet Union (after World War II) and the first to split off in the late 1980s, these three republics refused to cooperate with the CIS. In May 2003, the U.S. Senate officially ratified their application to join NATO, making them the first former Soviet republics to be so nominated. As of this writing, the other NATO members had not yet approved their membership.

End of History?

Historians referred to the heady days of the early 1990s as "the end of history." Of course, we know that history cannot end, but certainly the history of the preceding 50 years is no longer being made. The Cold War was over. New history was to begin.

Also over were the imperatives that created the alignments and treaties that had defined the Cold War. Now, some 15 years after the collapse of the Soviet Union, new alignments and policies are emerging. The dominant themes are no longer East-West, but something new. The question becomes, what is it? Some experts argue the new global competition is between the haves and the have-nots, others say it is between democracies and dictatorships, others say it is a competition between Islam and the West, and still others say it is a competition between the so-called "civilized world" and terrorism. Perhaps it is best to consider that all of these conflicts are present at the same time in today's world. Indeed, these conflicts were present during the Cold War but were overlaid and dominated by the East-West conflict between the world's two superpowers of the time, the United States and the Soviet Union.

And Then There Was One

The end of the Soviet Union signaled the end of the Cold War and heralded the start of new conflict, mentioned earlier. Most notably, the "war" on terrorism consumes American attention. The other development that came with the demise of the Soviet Union is that the United States is now the world's only superpower. The United States is now the dominant power in the world, the easiest thing to blame for regional and local problems, and the biggest target for those wanting to act on their rage. This dynamic certainly contributed to the hostility that the Iranian clerics exhibited toward the United States during the Islamic Revolution. As part of its East-West competition, the United States had supported the Shah and his violence toward internal opposition groups, including the Shia clerics. The United States also was seen as a friend of Israel and Saddam Hussein, two enemies of the Shia clerics. The list of perceived and real actions by the United States toward Iran before the Islamic Revolution contributed to the Ayatollah Khomeini's label of the United States as "the Great Satan." Today, as the sole superpower in world, the United States conveniently fills that role for other groups and leaders, for ills (real and perceived) done to them or those they favor.

The Fruits of Rage—the Bush Doctrine

At risk of trivializing the terrible fact of September 11, it is clear that the al Qaeda terrorist group (while having no affinity for Shia, Persian Iran) blames the United States for a wide range of crimes against Islam and the Arab people, and its rage at these crimes led to its attacks on the United States. The reasoning and justifications for terrorist groups to attack the United States may be difficult to completely understand or ever justify, but the Bush administration's reaction is not.

Almost immediately after the September 11 attacks, President Bush began to outline his new doctrine. Like Monroe and Truman before him, President Bush is outlining a doctrine that reflects a new global role for the United States. We can look at President Bush's doctrine as the latest to define the U.S. position in the world. In this sense, Monroe's doctrine informed the world that the United States was a force to be reckoned with in the world and staked the U.S. claim to global power. Truman's doctrine recognized the U.S. global power status and its intention of defeating any other global powers that would challenge it. Bush's doctrine is the acknowledgement that the United States is in a position of unprecedented pre-eminence and that it will act to preserve and extend that pre-eminence.

Focus on Terror

One of the tenets of the Bush Doctrine is a focus on combating terrorism. The doctrine specifies that the United States will focus its domestic, foreign policy, and military resources on defeating terrorism (specifically, terrorism that threatens the United States and probably terrorism that threatens U.S. allies). The Bush administration has made it clear that the United States simply will not accept the inevitability of another September 11. This is not to suggest that no other major terrorist attacks will occur on U.S. soil—only that the United States will not wait and hope one does not occur.

Bet You Didn't Know

Today the United States enjoys a position of unparalleled military strength and great economic and political influence .... We will defend the peace by fighting terrorists and tyrants. We will preserve the peace by building good relations among the great powers. We will extend the peace by encouraging free and open societies on every continent.

Defending our nation against its enemies is the first and fundamental commitment of the federal government. Today that task has changed dramatically. Enemies in the past needed great armies and great industrial capabilities to endanger America. Now shadowy networks of individuals can bring great chaos and suffering to our shores for less than it costs to purchase a single tank. Terrorists are organized to penetrate open societies and to turn the power of modern technologies against us.

To defeat this threat, we must make use of every tool in our arsenal—military power, better homeland defenses, law enforcement, intelligence, and vigorous efforts to cut off terrorist financing. The war against terrorists of global reach is a global enterprise of uncertain duration. America will help nations that need our assistance in combating terror. And America will hold to account nations that are compromised by terror, including those who harbor terrorists—because the allies of terror are the enemies of civilization. The United States and countries cooperating with us must not allow the terrorists to develop new home bases. Together we will seek to deny them sanctuary at every turn.

—Commonly known as the Bush Doctrine, from the National Security Strategy for the United States, the White House

Pre-Emptive Intervention

Another tenet of the new Bush Doctrine is that the United States will not wait to react to an attack on itself or its interests, but will move against a threat before it occurs. This policy is new, in that is publicly states the U.S. right and intention of seeking out threats and eliminating them before they harm the United States. What is more, the Bush Doctrine does not limit pre-emptive action to sanctions and diplomacy. Rather, the Bush Doctrine keeps military action (including surprise attack) as a tool of strategy.

Unilateral Action

Along with the willingness and claimed right to act peremptorily, the Bush Doctrine declares that the United States may act alone, if in its best interests. The Bush Doctrine cites the urgency of protecting the United States before any threat materializes that could harm it. Therefore, while multilateral action is still a goal, Uncle Sam will go it alone, if need be.

Urgency

This new doctrine assumes a sense of urgency that the United States must act *now* because terrorists are actively working against the country and its interests constantly. The Bush Doctrine suggests that there is a race of preparedness: U.S. prevention preparedness against terrorist attack or other threat preparedness. This includes the creation of nuclear weapons and other weapons of mass destruction.

Fostering Democracy

The Bush Doctrine also promotes the U.S. goal of fostering democratic, civil societies around the world. These societies are considered allied to U.S. interests and not as threatening or willing to foster terrorism attacks on the United States and its allies. The Bush Doctrine of aggressive forward action suggests that the United States may be more willing to engage with "pro-democracy" elements in nondemocratic governments, just like the United States supported anti-Soviet elements during the Cold War. In an ironic turn, this U.S. policy could be perceived by the Iranian leadership to be a threat, much like its Islamic revolution encouragement could be seen as a threat to other Muslim countries.

Are International Organizations Obsolete?

The United States has signaled a willingness to go it alone (unilateralism), use force first (pre-emption), and aggressively pursue terrorism. This policy has meant working against or around the international institutions and conventions put in place over the past 50 years, despite the objections of those institutions.

It also calls into question the effectiveness of existing multilateral institutions to participate in the global order as defined by the Bush Doctrine (and the reality of U.S. pre-eminence). Already the Bush Doctrine has alienated old allies and marginalized established institutions.

Growing Pains—Operation Iraqi Freedom

The recent episodes surrounding Operation Iraqi Freedom show both the rifts in old alliances and the creation of new alliances. Standbys such as NATO and close allies such as Canada and Germany refused to support the U.S. action against the Saddam Hussein regime. These groups had supported the Coalition-led action against the Taliban in Afghanistan in the immediate aftermath of the September 11, 2001, terror attacks. However, these same groups could not support the United States against Iraq.

The difference is that the attack on the Taliban was in response to an attack on the United States, whereas the attack on Iraq was in anticipation of an attack on the United States (as indicated by the goal of disarming the Hussein regime of weapons of mass destruction). The alliances and institutions of the past 50 years are based upon mutual support in response to threats, but they work best in response to proven threats, meaning an attack. These bodies do not work well when the threat is not proven, as was the case with Hussein's Iraq and the question of his possession of weapons of mass destruction.

At the same time, old enemies have stepped forward to become new friends in this realignment of relationships. Eastern European countries, objecting to the Franco-German domination of the European Union whose membership these countries seek, openly supported the United States. Their support was as much a repudiation of traditional European power politics as an endorsement of the Bush Doctrine. Still, the doctrine opens opportunities for old enemies to become new friends.

Alienation or Strong Leadership?

One of the effects of the Bush Doctrine is the polarity it demands. As President Bush has stated, a country is either with the United States or against the United States. It is either black or white; there is no room for shades of gray. Some have pointed out that, with its definitive positions and unilateral statements of policy, the Bush administration has used up all the goodwill that was provided to America in the aftermath of September 11. U.S. friends and allies are being made to choose between two absolutes and are not being asked or allowed to provide their input to the definition of strategy or strategic goals.

The arguments of those who object to this new tactic have merit if one believes in the methods of diplomacy and alliances that have served the international community since World War II. But if one believes that these methods of diplomacy and alliances have failed because they cannot or will not unite to fight terrorism, the statements of Bush administration officials are simply a reflection of the new reality that will drive U.S. policy for decades to come. Furthermore, supporters of the Bush Doctrine can argue that the United States should be seen as leading the way in this brave new world. Either way, Iran has assumed a new primacy in U.S. policy, both as a potential target and as a potential model for change. In the next chapter, we conclude this book by looking at the options for Iranian–U.S. relations and the most likely outcome.

The Least You Need to Know

◆ U.S. presidents set foreign-policy agendas. Definitive policy strategies become "doctrines" that can survive a sitting president for decades.

◆ The Bush Doctrine is the latest step in the evolution of U.S. security policy, starting with the Monroe Doctrine and evolving through the Truman Doctrine.

◆ The Bush Doctrine places an emphasis on fighting terrorism and peremptorily dealing with threats to U.S. security, such as rogue states developing weapons of mass destruction.

◆ The Bush Doctrine follows unilateral strategy. The United States will act alone if international agreement cannot be reached.

◆ The Bush Doctrine presents significant challenges for Iranian–U.S. relations.

Iranian–U.S. Relations in the Twenty-First Century

In This Chapter

- ◆ Several factors pull Iran and the United States apart

- ◆ An early chance for warming of relations has been lost

- ◆ Current U.S. doctrine has decreased Iranian national security

- ◆ Internal dissent may strengthen liberalization in Iran and improve chances for Iranian–U.S. rapprochement

- ◆ Iran's nuclear program is the wildcard in Iranian–U.S. relations

In the last five chapters, we looked at the current forces affecting Iran. We looked at internal dissent and the pressures for change. We traced the Iranian nuclear weapons program and Iran's support of terrorism. We also looked at the Islamic Republic's first efforts to generate a more open dialogue with the rest of the world and tone down the revolutionary rhetoric. At the same time, we outlined the Bush Doctrine, which, as we will see here, poses significant challenges to the future Iranian–U.S. relationship.

The Ties That Unbind

The United States and Iran have a lot of distance to cover between them before the two countries can find common ground. Many elements are pulling the countries apart. Some of these elements have been in existence since the Islamic Revolution in 1979, and some have emerged only in the last few years. All combine to drive a very large wedge between the two countries.

The Nagging Question of Nukes

The U.S. government is deeply concerned about Iran's nuclear-development program. As we saw in Chapter 19, Iran has been developing its nuclear potential despite signing the Nuclear Non-Proliferation Treaty. The International Atomic Energy Agency (IAEA) has expressed surprise over the relatively advanced state of the Iranian program. Based upon earlier inspections and Iranian declarations, the IAEA had been led to believe that the Iranian program was less far along. However, a recent inspection of the Bushehr and Natanz sites shows that Iran is pursuing its nuclear program. If anything, it appears that Iran is doing so with greater effort than ever.

> **Bet You Didn't Know**
>
> The gravest danger our nation faces lies at the crossroads of radicalism and technology. Our enemies have openly declared that they are seeking weapons of mass destruction, and evidence indicates that they are doing so with determination. The United States will not allow these efforts to succeed. We will build defenses against ballistic missiles and other means of delivery. We will cooperate with other nations to deny, contain, and curtail our enemies' efforts to acquire dangerous technologies. And, as a matter of common sense and self-defense, America will act against such emerging threats before they are fully formed. We cannot defend America and our friends by hoping for the best. So we must be prepared to defeat our enemies' plans, using the best intelligence and proceeding with deliberation. History will judge harshly those who saw this coming danger but failed to act. In the new world we have entered, the only path to peace and security is the path of action.
>
> —From the National Security Strategy for the United States, the White House

Regional Realignments

The Bush Doctrine of removing terrorist threats and the governments that support them has resulted in a significant realignment of alliances in Iran's immediate neighborhood. The hostile Taliban regime in Afghanistan is gone. The Iranian leadership did not have friendly relations with the Taliban. The Taliban is made up of Wahhabi, who follow a strict interpretation of Sunni Islam. The Taliban do not accept the Shia Islam interpretation of the faith. Of course, the Taliban was hostile to the Unites States, too, and supported the al Qaeda terrorists who attacked the United States and U.S. interests on several occasions leading up to September 11, 2001, and afterward. The U.S.–led Coalition that toppled the Taliban has set up a more pro-Western regime in Afghanistan, led by Mohammad Karzai. So, from the Iranian perspective, one undesirable regime has simply been replaced with another in Afghanistan.

On their other border, the Iranians have seen the hostile Saddam Hussein regime in Iraq removed and the strong likelihood that a pro–U.S. government will be installed there. At the time of this writing, the situation is still unfolding, but the fact remains that there are hundreds of thousands of U.S. and Coalition troops in Iraq.

Also, Pakistan and Turkey are nominally U.S. allies (or, at least, friends). Even the Central Asian republics, including neighboring Turkmenistan, are engaged with the United States. The Iranians find themselves increasingly surrounded by pro–U.S. regimes and, in some places, U.S. troops. In fact, despite Iran's softer approach to Central Asia, the United States and NATO are actively working with local governments there. From the perspective of the Iranian leadership, their world has grown less secure, not more so.

Bet You Didn't Know

In early 2003, NATO conducted a joint exercise with Uzbek forces, called Ferghana 2003" in the Ferghana Valley in the far eastern end of Uzbekistan. The Ferghana Valley is the operating base for Islamic groups fighting to overthrow the Uzbek secular regime. The exercise focused on search and rescue, fire-fighting, and damage recovery. Still, the implications for observers are clear. The United States and NATO are making a statement about military preparedness in support of a former Soviet Republic (now a secular Muslim one) that is dealing with fundamentalist Islamic terrorists.

Iran has responded by attempting to assert its own agenda in the region, which necessarily has become an anti–U.S. agenda in many respects. Iran is actively supporting proxy groups in the confusion of post-war Afghanistan and Iraq. It is making more friendly, less dogmatic overtures to U.S. friends in Central Asia, Pakistan, Turkey, and western Europe. And the Iranians are turning to the only counterweights to the United States left on the world stage, Russia and China, for trade and technological support.

As covered in Chapter 19, the Russians and Chinese are supplying vital pieces of the Iranian nuclear program, much to the concern of the United States. However, unlike the pressure being placed on North Korea (which also is supporting the Iranian nuclear program), the United States must tread carefully when pressuring Russia or China because other economic and security factors are at play between the United States and those two countries. Consequently, the set of response options for the United States against those two nations is limited. To date, U.S. sanctions have not been able to interrupt the flow of technology to Iran. As long as the United States encircles Iran with troops and pro–U.S. regimes, and as long as Iran successfully increases trade ties with Russia and China, the United States and Iran will have a difficult time reaching a common ground.

Conflicting Interests

Iran and the United States are also separated by conflicting interests in the Middle East. As we saw in Chapter 22, Iran is aiding certain Afghan warlords in and around Herat to destabilize the U.S.-backed Karzai regime. This program is not to attack the United States indirectly, but to promote the Iranian concept of their own security. They want a sympathetic regime in Afghanistan, at most, and a weak one, at least. Destabilizing the Karzai regime accomplishes these objectives. At the same time, the Iranians have been uncharacteristically restrained in their exhortations to Shia Afghans and have stood quietly by as the United States has attacked the Afghan warlords around Herat.

The situation in Iraq is similar but is motivated also by ideology. Remember that southern Iraq is Shia, like Iran. Also remember that southern Iraq is home to the two holiest sites of Shia Islam, at An Najaf and Karbala. In the confused aftermath of Operation Iraqi Freedom, Iran sees the best opportunity it has had to establish a Shia-dominated government in Iraq. At the very least, Iran sees the opportunity to increase its own security yet again, by having a more sympathetic (Shia Arab) government in Iraq or by simply keeping the Iraqi situation unstable. If so, the United States will be preoccupied with keeping things in control in Iraq and will not be as able to apply pressure (including staging U.S. forces) on Iran from immediately next door.

Israel and Terrorism

Along with U.S. concern over Iranian "meddling" in Afghanistan and Iraq, the reality of Israel constantly pulls Iran and the United States apart. As long as there is strong support in the United States for the survival of Israel and there is strong support in Iran for the destruction of Israel, U.S.–Iranian ties will be strained.

What is more, because Iran's approach to Israel involves terrorism (see Chapter 18 for a discussion on Iranian support of the Hezbollah, Hamas, and Islamic Jihad), the strain on U.S.–Iranian ties is even greater. Ever since the September 11, 2001, terror attacks on New York and Washington, the United States has assumed a more aggressive approach to terrorist groups and the countries that support them. There has been a fundamental shift in U.S. foreign policy as a direct result of September 11.

The U.S. has been sanctioning Iran, with limited effect, for Iran's support of anti-Israel terrorist groups. However, the primary emphasis in the Bush administration on combating terrorism means that the United States will consider itself obliged to continue to sanction Iran. The Iranians, of course, object to the sanctions. The two sides are so tightly bound by their convictions on this issue that it will take skilled and patient diplomacy and a real willingness of the part of the senior leadership of both sides for a shift to occur.

Leadership Antagonism—the Legacy of 1979

One of the undercurrents that makes it difficult for the two countries to carry out a dialogue is the lingering distrust on both sides that was brought about by the Islamic Revolution. It would be hard for the clerics to engage the "Great Satan" in Khatami's "Dialogue of the Civilizations," given the strength of their own ideological convictions.

At the same time, the Bush administration has shown no desire to engage the Iranian leadership in any kind of dialogue. The opportunity to open the door to more open relations between Iran and the United States was presented in the aftermath of the terror attacks of September 11, 2001. Vigils in sympathy toward the United States and the thousands of victims of the attacks sprang up spontaneously around the world, even in Tehran. Significantly, the Iranian leadership indulged the demonstrations. Later, Iran provided unofficial assistance to the U.S.–led Coalition that toppled the Taliban in Afghanistan. However, any opportunity for rapprochement between Iran and the United States was squashed effectively by President Bush during his famous "Axis of Evil" speech.

The reality of the Bush Doctrine, its polemic of black and white, and its focus on promoting U.S. security by proactively and unilaterally attacking terrorism and the proliferation of weapons of mass destruction has no room for the delicate shades of gray required for a warming of U.S.–Iranian relations.

Opposites Attract

Despite the wedge between the countries and the ambivalence of the leadership of both countries toward dialogue, compelling forces are pushing the two countries together.

The Enemy of My Enemy Is My Friend

The strongest force pushing the United States and Iran together is fighting against a common foe. As we have seen, in Afghanistan the Iranians came to the door by providing support for the Coalition, but the Bush administration held it shut.

In Iraq, the United States has followed the Bush Doctrine to the extent of attacking the MEK, the anti-Islamic Republic group operating out of eastern Iraq. The U.S. military attacked and ultimately disarmed the MEK. The U.S. government had characterized the MEK as a terrorist group and has neutralized its threat. One wonders if a trade-off with Iran is at work here. Could the United States be cracking down on the MEK under the pretext of fighting terrorism, in return for Iranian movement elsewhere? Perhaps there is a trade-off concerning Iranian support for the Hezbollah or for the SCIRI (the Iranian-based group pushing for Islamic Revolution in Iraq). It would not be the first time the United States and Iran traded favors behind the scenes. (Recall the Iran-Contra Scandal during the 1980s.)

> **Bet You Didn't Know**
>
> The U.S. government classified the MEK (Mujahedeen Khalq) as a terrorist organization for attacks on U.S. interests in the 1970s. During the late Shah's regime, the MEK mounted several attacks on U.S. military and civilian personnel living and working in Iran. After the Islamic Revolution, the U.S. attitude toward the MEK shifted. Some members of Congress actually openly praised the MEK, and the United States stopped working against it. However, with the fall of the Saddam Hussein regime, the United States has asserted its military control in Iraq by forcing the MEK to disarm.

It is possible that the United States and Iran could covertly cooperate in Central Asia, but only the future will tell. Certainly, any such cooperation is not openly admitted or identified at this time.

I've Got What You Need

One of the most compelling reasons for the United States and Iran to maintain some level of dialogue is simple: oil. The United States is one of the largest consumers of oil, and Iran is one of the largest producers. As the United States seeks to increase the security of its supply of oil, better relations with Iran could help. Iran is a member of OPEC, but the United States refuses to purchase its oil. However, this boycott is weak because the oil all goes into a large global commodity pool, in one sense. So, the United States could buy from other suppliers to the pool, and other countries could buy from Iran instead.

As the United States consolidates its position in Iraq and decouples from Saudi Arabia, it will need to ensure closer ties with other oil-producing countries. Iran could be one of those countries.

Bet You Didn't Know

The Bush administration has stated its intention of withdrawing U.S. troops from Saudi Arabia. The reasoning is that they are no longer needed there with Saddam Hussein gone. Most likely, the United States will redeploy the troops to Qatar and Kuwait, and keep a sizeable presence in Iraq for some time. In fact, as U.S. troops are attacked in Iraq, the likelihood grows that the troops will remain in Iraq for a considerable period. The withdrawal from Saudi Arabia also removes one pretext for al Qaeda attacks on the U.S. interests there (like the suicide bombings of May 12, 2003). Al Qaeda has objected to "infidels" in the land of Islam's holiest sites, Mecca and Medina.

The Lure of Democracy

The Iranian people may end up being the catalyst to opening Iran further to the world—and, thus, to the United States. As we saw in Chapter 21, there are cracks in the fundamentalist edifice. Internal dissent is becoming popular pressure for reform. The symbol of that reform, President Khatami, continues to apply pressure on the ruling clerics and continues to enjoy strong popular support. Emboldened university students have clashed with basji supporters of the Islamic Revolution in Tehran and other major cities. (Remember, the basji are the fundamentalist zealots who formed a human wave during the Iran-Iraq War and since then have been the self-appointed popular guardians of the regime.)

There is a clear indication that the Iranian man on the street does not share the antagonism that the leaders hold toward the Great Satan. The Iranian people are increasingly frustrated with the rigid social structure and depressed economic conditions that show no signs of improving. For reasons both real and imagined, the Iranians look to the West and the United States for inspiration on reform. They want a better life, and they see the United States as part of the solution.

The Clerics' Call

The pressure will be on the clerics to make the first move. The leadership is in a delicate position. It either must accommodate the restive population and seek a peaceful coexistence with the United States, or not. Right now, the jury is out on which way the clerics will go.

Clamp Down

One reaction would be for the clerics to clamp down on the popular dissent and refuse any reform measures that would be passed by the Majlis (the Iranian parliament). The hardliners could call out the basji to fight the protesters that would react to the clampdown and try to retain control against the rising tide. Nicolai Ceauscescu tried this approach in Romania in 1989 when he called out the coal miners to attack the reform protesters in Bucharest. While the coal miners succeeded in their thuggery in the short run, the protesters ultimately won the day. Of course, the clerics have more powerful tools at their disposal, including the pasdaran (armed forces). However, screwing the lid down tighter might just make the inevitable explosion that much stronger when it finally does happen. In addition, by continuing to frustrate reform, the clerics are succeeding in radicalizing their opposition, forcing those groups to act more violently and desperately. If the clerics do read the writing on the wall, a slow but steady opening of this society to the United States—and the West, in general—could occur.

The Osirek Option

When faced with an Iraqi nuclear reactor at Osirek in Iraq, the Israelis unilaterally bombed the reactor, setting back the Iraqi nuclear-development program for at least a decade. This setback had a significant impact on both the Gulf War in 1991 and Operation Iraqi Freedom in 2003. Saddam Hussein did not have a nuclear weapon to threaten the United States or Coalition forces.

There is a real possibility that if Iran does not dismantle its nuclear program, the United States or Israel would unilaterally attack and destroy the Iranian facilities at Bushehr and Natanz. If the IAEA—and, by extension, the United Nations—do not compel the Iranians to react, the United States may follow the precedents of Operation Iraqi Freedom and launch a U.S.–led attack on Iran. As of this writing, the Iranians are pursuing their nuclear program aggressively, and they show no signs of slowing down.

People Power?

The most hopeful scenario is that internal liberalization causes Iran to cease its support for terrorists, abandon its nuclear program, and reach out to the West. This scenario depends on the Iranian people to act in their own best interests, as they have done before. The Shah and his U.S. backers made the mistake of underestimating the Iranian people and their desires. One wonders if the Iranian clerics will do the same.

The Least You Need to Know

- Several powerful forces are driving a wedge between the Iranians and the United States, and many forces could enable a warming of relations.

- The Bush Doctrine and the anti-Western ideology of the Iranian leadership make high-level contacts chilly, at best.

- An opportunity for rapprochement was lost in the immediate aftermath of the September 11, 2001, terrorist attacks on the United States.

- The Iranian people are the biggest wildcard in the future of Iranian–U.S. relations. They are more pro-Western than the clerics who rule them.

- The U.S. or Israeli reaction to the Iranian nuclear program is the other wildcard, with the possibility of unilateral U.S. action to destroy the Iranian nuclear infrastructure.

Appendix **A**

Glossary

Achaemenid   The dynastic name for the Persian Empire that was founded by Cyrus the Great. The name itself refers to one of Cyrus's warrior ancestors.

Alexander the Great   Defeated Darius II and conquered the Persian Empire on his way to building an immense empire of his own. Upon his death, the Seleucid dynasty administered Persian territory.

Anglo-Persian Oil Company   Later called British Petroleum, or BP, this company was founded to search for oil in Persia (now Iran). The Anglo-Persian Oil Company was controlled by the British government and became the principle vehicle for exerting British control over the Iranian oil industry.

Arab   A linguistic group of 256 million people that many experts believe originated in the Hijaz region in what is now Saudi Arabia. The Arabs have spread across northern Africa and the Middle East. Not all Arabs are Muslims; most Muslims worldwide are not Arabs. (Muslims in Iran, for instance, speak Farsi, not Arabic.)

ayatollah   The title for a supreme religious leader of the Twelver Shiites.

Axis of Evil   Three countries identified by President George W. Bush in early 2002 as enemies of the civilized world—Iran, Iraq, and North Korea.

Baha'i   Religion started in 1852 in Persia, based upon the teachings of Baha'u'llah (born Mizra Husayn Ali Nuri). The Baha'i believe that all previous religions are unified and that God has been revealed to humanity at several times and in several ways throughout history. The religion is growing and is practiced in several countries, including Iran.

Bakhtiar   Prime minister of Iranian Republic, appointed by the Shah to rule when he left power.

Bani Sadr   First president of the Islamic Republic of Iran. He resigned after a year in power, due to conflicts with the mullahs.

Basji   Used during the Iran-Iraq War, these were ill-equipped and poorly trained fanatical volunteers, many of whom attacked Iraqi positions armed only with a Qur'an. Many were children, roped together so they would not run away.

Basra   City in Southern Iraq, and heart of the Shiite territory in that country. Chief city of the Ottoman vilayet of the same name.

Bazargan   Prime minister appointed by Ayatollah Khomeini at the same time Bakhtiar was trying to build a government. He resigned the prime minister post eight months after taking the job, due to differences with the mullahs.

Bushehr   Site of nuclear plant used by the current government of Iran to produce enriched uranium, the type that can be used to produce nuclear weapons.

Buwayids   Powerful military clan that originated in Persia and then expanded to rule Mesopotamia from 945 to 1055 C.E.

caliph   Spiritual leader of Islam. (Literally, a successor of Muhammad, the first leader of the faith and the Arabian empire.) The caliphate went through many forms and was abolished in the early twentieth century.

Council of Guardians   A constitutionally defined body (made up of clerics appointed by the Supreme Leader) that determines the legality of any measures passed by the Majlis (parliament). No law can go into effect without council approval. The council consistently rejects any liberalizing measures passed by the reform-minded Majlis, on the grounds that they are not consistent with the Islamic Republic and its guiding body of law, the Sharia.

Cyrus the Great   (580–530 B.C.E.) Persian king who launched the Persian Empire. He followed an enlightened policy of administration and tolerance, including liberating the Hebrews when he captured Babylon in 539 B.C.E.

Darius the Great   Persian king who extended the Achaeminid Empire until his death in 486 B.C.E.

Elamites   First kingdom in ancient Iran. The Elamite Empire emerged from the shadows of its Mesopotamian overlords around 2000 B.C.E. They were centered in the modern region of Khuzestan.

Faw   (pronounced *al-Faw*) Peninsula on Iraq's Persian Gulf coast. Site of major fighting during the Iran-Iraq War, it is a primary loading terminal on the Gulf for Iraq's oil industry. Iran, Iraq, and Kuwait all come together at this strategic peninsula.

Great Game   Cold War fought by the British and the Russians during the nineteenth century across Central Asia and Iran. The British maneuvered against Tsarist Russian to maintain the security of British India. The Russians pushed steadily into Central Asia to expand their own empire and threaten British India.

Greater and Lesser Tunbs   Two islands at the head of the Strait of Hormuz that were seized by Iran and claimed by the United Arab Emirates. By occupying these islands, Iran can potentially interfere with oil shipments through this strategic chokepoint on the Persian Gulf.

Hamas   Fundamentalist Islamist Palestinian group operating in Israel and the West Bank. Hamas is a religious counterpoint to the secular Palestinian Authority. Hamas operates schools and hospitals, and has a large terrorist element that has mounted severe attacks on Israeli targets. Hamas receives some support from Iran. Hamas wants to replace the Palestinian Authority with an Islamist state and wants to destroy Israel.

Herat   City in western Afghanistan. Considered a necessary way point for a Russian invasion of British India, the city was a strategic target for the British, Russians, and Persians during the Great Game.

Hezbollah   Terrorist group operating out of the Bekaa Valley in Lebanon. This Shia Muslim group receives significant assistance from Iran. Hezbollah is responsible for severe terror attacks against Israel in support of the Palestinians.

imam   Name for a most holy leader in the Muslim faith. The majority of Shia Muslims (known as imamites) regard imams as being sinless, with a direct lineage to Ali, the cousin of the Prophet Mohammed. Twelver Shia believe that there were 12 imams, starting with Ali and culminating in Mohammad al-Muntazar, the twelfth imam. Twelver Shia believe that Al-Muntazar occultated (that is, disappeared from human view) in 878 C.E. Twelver Shia believe that the twelfth imam lives to this day and reveals himself at moments of Allah's choosing. This imam is considered by the Twelver to be the only legitimate leader of the Faithful. A smaller Shia sect, called the Ismaelites, acknowledges seven imams.

Iran Islamic Republic of Iran (*Jomhuri-ye Eslami-ye Iran*). Located between the Arab Middle East and Central Asia, Iran is a leading producer of oil and a suspected sponsor of terrorism. The Iranian people are mainly Persian, with Kurd and Arab minorities. The majority are Shia Muslim, with minorities of Sunni Muslims, Christians, Jews, Baha'is, and Zoroastrians.

Iran and Libya Sanctions Act (ILSA) Act intended to hinder Iran's (and Libya's) ability to generate the income needed to purchase or develop weapons of mass destruction or to support terrorists. The act intends to deny money and equipment to Iran, but it is largely unenforceable, particularly to foreign firms that ignore the act. Originally enacted by the Clinton administration in 1996, the act was reviewed and extended by the Bush administration in 2001.

Iraq Comprised of the Ottoman vilayets of Mosul, Baghdad, and Basra, the independent nation of Iraq (*al Jumhuriyah al Iraqiyah*) was established in 1923. The Iraqis are mainly Arab, with Kurd and Assyrian minorities. The majority are Shia Muslims, with a minority of Sunni Muslims (both Arab and Kurd).

Ishfahan Site of a uranium-conversion facility in Iran, part of its nuclear weapons–development program.

Islam Monotheistic religion associated with the Prophet Muhammad (570?–632 C.E.). *Islam* translates as "submission." *Muslim* translates as "one who submits." The emphasis in Islam is on the submission to the will of a single God. The "five pillars" of this great and enduring religious tradition are as follows:

1. Confession of faith in God and his prophet Muhammad ("There is no God but God; Muhammad is the Prophet of God.")

2. Ritual worship

3. Almsgiving

4. Fasting

5. Pilgrimage

Islamic Jihad Palestinian terror group with close ties to Iran. Islamic Jihad has similar goals to Hamas.

Israel Jewish state in the Middle East. Iran does not recognize Israel's right to exist, and it sponsors the Hezbollah and, to a lesser extent, the Hamas and Islamic Jihad, terror groups that are attacking Israel.

Karbala   Holy site for Shia Islam, located in southern Iraq. Karbala is the burial place of Iman Hussein, the son of Ali Ibn Abu Talib, the Prophet Muhammad's cousin. Hussein was killed during a battle with the Sunni army of the Ummayad Caliph Yazid in 680.

Muhammad Khatami   The current president of Iran. He is considered a social moderate and a reformer—but this should not be taken to mean that he is pro-Western. Khatami's practical power is severely limited by members of the religious hierarchy, who still exercise practical political power in Iran.

Ayatollah Ruhollah Khomeini (1900–1989)   The leader of Iran from 1979 to his death in 1989. In 1950, he was named "ayatollah" in recognition of his stature as a learned, religious leader of the Iranian Shiite community. Khomeini was an outspoken critic of the corruption, Western-leaning, and secularism of the regime of the Shahs. In 1964, the Shah exiled him, and the Ayatollah Khomeini moved to the Shiite holy city of An Najaf, in Iraq, where he dwelled for the next 15 years. Still preaching his anti-Shah message from exile in An Najaf, the Shah struck a deal with Saddam Hussein to have the Ayatollah Khomeini expelled from Iraq. Khomeini then traveled to Paris, where his preaching continued with greater force. After a year in Paris, the Ayatollah Khomeini returned to Iran in 1979, and soon was proclaimed the Supreme Leader of the Islamic Republic of Iran. The last decade of his life was filled with turmoil, including a U.S. Embassy hostage crisis, and the bloody Iran-Iraq War.

Khuzestan   Area of Iran that borders Iraq. Arabs make up the majority of the population in Khuzestan, while Persians dominate the population in most of the rest of Iran. Khuzestan has oil and was the touch point for the Iran-Iraq War.

Kurds   Nationality of 25 million people. The Kurds are a distinct ethnic group and are not Persian, Arab, or Turkic. However, their homeland is split among Iran, Iraq, and Turkey. The Kurds have traditionally fought for autonomy, if not outright independence, from the states that control their homeland. The Iranians have supported Kurd insurgents in Iraq, in an attempt to destabilize that country.

Majlis   The Iranian parliament. The Majlis survived the Islamic Revolution of 1979 and has become the legislative voice of the reformers in the early twenty-first century. The power of the Majlis is limited by the Council of Guardians that determines the "legality" of any measure passed by the Majlis, in terms of that measure's compliance with the Sharia.

Manicheism   Religion founded by Mani, as Sasanian, in 274 C.E. Manicheism attempted to unite the best elements of Buddhism, Christianity, and Zoroastrianism.

Mashhad   (Formerly Khorasan) City in eastern Iran that houses the tomb of Reza, the Eighth Imam. It is the only imam's tomb located in Iran.

Medes Central Asian nomads who came to the Iranian plateau around 1500 B.C.E. They were early rivals of the Persians but gradually succumbed to outside invaders.

MEK The Mujahedeen-e-Khalq (or People's Mujahadeen Organization of Iran), a militant group opposed to the Islamic Republic of Iran. Operating primarily from Iraq during the Saddam Hussein regime, Coalition forces actually attacked the group at the close of Operation Iraqi Freedom. The U.S. government has classified MEK as a terrorist organization for its violent attacks inside Iran. However, because of its anti-Iran stance, the MEK has enjoyed support in Europe and in the U.S. Congress.

Mesopotamia From the Greek term meaning "the land between the rivers," this is the ancient name for the region between the Tigris and Euphrates rivers. The region stretches from the Persian Gulf through modern Iraq, into a portion of modern Syria. With abundant water, fertile land, and an agreeable climate, early civilization emerged here. The region was a frequent target for invaders from Persia over the centuries.

Muhammad The great prophet of Islam. Muhammad was born in Mecca (in present-day Saudi Arabia) around 570 C.E. He is believed to have experienced the first of a series of intense religious visions around the year 610 in a cave near Mecca. The Qu'ran, Islam's central religious text, records that encounter and the later revelations of Muhammad, and is regarded as the final and authoritative word of Allah (God). After more than a decade of preaching, Muhammad had been unsuccessful in converting Mecca to the new faith; in 622, he and his followers moved to Yathrib (later known as Medina, the "City of the Prophet"). Muhammad continued to encounter resistance in his effort to spread the word of the new doctrine, but his followers eventually mounted a religious and military campaign that succeeded in unifying Arabia behind this new faith. Muhammad is regarded by Muslims as Allah's final prophet, and Islam is seen as the fulfillment of all previous human religious experiences. Muhammad's birthplace, Mecca, is now regarded as the great Holy City of Islam. Muslims pray in the direction of Mecca, and the city is the destination of an annual pilgrimage by millions of Muslims from across the world.

mullah A term for a member of the Islamic clergy.

Muslim "One who submits." The term for an adherent to Islam.

An Najaf The most revered Shia Muslim holy site, located in southern Iraq, and the burial place of Ali Ibn Talib, the Prophet Muhammad's cousin and son-in-law. The Shiites believe that Ali and his descendents, through their blood kinship with Muhammad, are the rightful leaders of the faith. The name means "High Place" in Arabic, and Shia Muslims hope to be buried there. The Ayatollah Khomeini was exiled here in the 1960s and 1970s.

Natanz Site of a uranium-enrichment facility in Iran.

OPEC (Organization of Petroleum Exporting Countries) Oil-rich countries that control a significant portion of the world's oil reserves and productive capacity. Iran is a member of OPEC.

Ottomans Turkic people who established an empire that first emerged in Anatolia in 1301. They conquered Constantinople (now Istanbul) in 1453 and the Arab Middle East by 1517. The Ottoman Empire stopped at the Iranian (Persian) border. The empire became known as the "Sick Man of Europe" in the decades before World War I. The Ottoman Empire formally ceased to exist at the close of World War I, in 1918.

Pahlavi (Reza Shah) Last Shah to rule Iran before the Islamic Revolution in 1979.

Parthians A group that ruled Persia in ancient times. At the height of its power, the empire extended into Mesopotamia (170 B.C.E. to 224 C.E.) and portions of Central Asia.

Pasdaran The volunteer army of the Islamic Republic. It bore the brunt of the first years of fighting during the Iran-Iraq War. Eventually, as the Iraqi army began to score successes, the Iranian leadership deployed the professional soldiers of the Iranian army (who had been held back due to their connection with the Shah's regime).

Persepolis The capital city of the Achaemenid Persian dynasty. It was razed by Alexander the Great during his invasion.

PKK (Kurdistan Workers Party) Group supported by Iran, among other countries, that has waged terror on Turkey. The United States has classified this group as terrorists.

Qajars (1795–1925) Dynasty that ruled in Persia through the period of the Great Game and into the period of British influence.

Qum Holy city in Iran.

Safavids (1501–1795) Named for their first leader, Ismail Safavi, the Safavids were the first empire that emerged from the Mongol and Turkic invasions of Iran. They established the boundaries and culture that directly trace to modern Iran.

SAVAK The Sazman-e Ettelaat va Amniyat-e Keshvar, the hated secret police (founded in 1954) that kept the Shah in power.

SCIRI   The Supreme Council for Islamic Revolution in Iraq, a Shiite group that is sponsored by and housed in Iran. By sending its Badr Brigades into Shiite Iraq, SCIRI is attempting to establish an Islamist state in Iraq along the Iranian model, following the collapse of the Saddam Hussein regime.

Seleucid   Empire that was carved out of Alexander the Great's empire upon his death. Originally named for Seleuces, the Macedonian general who was given this territory.

Shahab   Name for Iranian missiles. The Shahab-3 and -4 are entering production. If Iran can mate a nuclear weapon to a Shahab-4 (with a 1,200-mile range), it would radically alter the balance of power in the region.

Sharia   The body of Islamic Law, which lists the rules for governing life consistent with Islam. The sources of the Sharia are, first and foremost, the Qur'an. The Hadith and the Sunna (accounts of the words and deeds of the Prophet) also contribute to the Sharia, but only in support of the Qur'an. As time has progressed, the Sharia has been regarded by Westerners to be a rigid code rather than a dynamic set of rules.

Shatt al Arab   Waterway created by the confluence of the Tigris and Euphrates rivers. It flows to the Persian Gulf. The waterway is the border between Iran and Iraq for much of its length.

Shia (also **Shiite**)   Only significant surviving Muslim sect other than the Sunni. Approximately 15 percent of Muslims worldwide are Shia. However, Iran is almost entirely Shiite, as is 60 percent of Iraq. The name is derived from Shiat Ali (Partisans of Ali). The Shias believe that only Muhammad's direct family and descendents are the leaders of the faithful. The Shias were formed when the descendents of Ali (Muhammad's cousin and son-in-law) were not made the leaders of the faithful in the tenth century.

spent fuel rods   The by-product of plutonium reaction. The spent fuel rods are used to make nuclear weapons.

Sunni   The vast majority of Muslims in the world. Unlike the Shia, the Sunnis believed that the caliph does not necessarily have to be one of Muhammad's descendents. They follow a more rationalist approach to Islam.

Tabriz   City in northwestern Iran, capital of the Ilkhanid (Mongol) dynasty in the early fourteenth century.

Tehran   Capital city of Iran, and the central point for political and social debate and activity.

Tunbs, Greater and Lesser   Islands at the opening of the Strait of Hormuz, seized and occupied by Iran and claimed by the United Arab Emirates.

Um   Uranium mine in Iran, near the city of Yazdi. Its reopening is a subject of concern for the IEAA and the United States.

Velayat-e faquih   The concept that ultimate authority for all aspects of society (political, social, legal, ideological, and economic) rests with the ruling clerics. They are the guardians of the Islamic revolution and the interpreters and adapters of the Sharia to modern needs.

weapons of mass destruction (WMD)   Biological, chemical, or nuclear weapons. So called because these weapons have the power to kill huge numbers of people relatively quickly. Experts assume that Iran possesses biological and chemical weapons, and the United States claims that Iran is developing nuclear weapons.

Zagros Mountains   Mountain range in western Iran.

Zoroastrianism   Once powerful religion that originated in ancient times in the region that is now Iran. Based upon the teachings of Zoroaster, the religion spread with the Persian Empire. Zoroastrians saw the world in terms of an epic struggle between the forces of good and evil. The faith had a strong influence on Christianity and is still practiced today in small portions of Iran.

Appendix B

Iran Timeline

4,000 B.C.E.	First human settlements arise on the Iranian plateau.
2,500 to 2,000 B.C.E.	Elamites emerge and settle the city of Susa on the western side of the Zagros Mountains. The Elamites first learn from and are dominated by Mesopotamian cultures; then they turn the tables on them.
2000 B.C.E.	Persians first enter what will be modern Iran, from Central Asia.
1159 B.C.E.	Elamites conquer Babylon and extend their empire into Mesopotamia.
646 B.C.E.	Ashurbanipal conquers the Elamites.
630 B.C.E.	Zoroaster, the founder of the religion of Zoroastrianism, is born.
559 B.C.E.	Cyrus III (the Great) begins to build up the Achaemenid Empire, consolidating Persia and defeating regional rivals such as Lydia and Babylon.
539 B.C.E.	Cyrus takes Babylon and allows the Hebrews to leave their captivity there, if they want.

521 B.C.E.	Darius I (the Great) takes the throne after a brief period of internal rivalry, assassination, and intrigue. He extends the Achaemenid Empire to even greater heights than Cyrus did.
515 B.C.E.	Darius completes an ancient version of the Suez Canal.
499 to 493 B.C.E.	The Ionian Revolt, eventually suppressed by Persian, takes place. A punitive invasion of Greece follows.
490 B.C.E.	The First Persian War takes place. Persians are defeated at the Battle of Marathon.
480 to 478 B.C.E.	The Second Persian War takes place. After the Battle of Thermopylae, the Persians take Athens but eventually are halted by Greek resistance. After the Persian advance is halted, Greek city-states form the Delian League to expel the Persians from Greece.
327 B.C.E.	The rise of the Macedonian Empire takes place. After defeating the Persians in several battles in Anatolia and into Persia, Alexander the Great destroys the Persian capital at Persepolis.
323 to 170 B.C.E.	The Seleucid Empire (named for the Macedonian general who was given the lands) emerges after Alexander's death to control Persia.
170 B.C.E. to 224 C.E.	The Parthian Empire emerges from the collapse of the Seleucid regime.
224 to 651	The Sassanid Empire takes power from the Parthians.
638 to 1100	The Arab Empire brings Islam to Persia.
661	The Shiite schism occurs. Ali ibn Abi Talib, Mohammad's cousin and son-in-law, and last of a group known as the Rightly Guided Caliphs, was assassinated and a nonfamily member was made Caliph. Debates regarding succession led to the development of Shiism, a sect of Islam that recognizes Mohammad's descendants through Ali as the only legitimate heads of the Islamic nation. Shiism eventually took hold in Persia and remains the dominant religion to this day.
770 to 945	The Abbasid Empire controls Persian territory.
945 to 1055	The Buwhayid Empire emerges. (Persia asserts authority over the Abassids, eventually even occupying Baghdad.)

1258 to 1355	The first wave of Mongol invasions takes place. Iranian cities are plundered.
1401 to 1405	Tamerlane invades Persia. Iranian cities are plundered again.
1502 to 1736	The Safavid Empire rises in Persia. This is the foundation for modern Iran. Shia Islam is made the official religion in their empire, and the Persian culture dominates.
1500 to 1918	The Ottoman Empire rises and becomes the rival of Safavids and Qajars over the course of 400 years. Three Ottoman vilayets (administrative districts) are created: Mosul, Baghdad, and Basra. These three vilayets later became modern Iraq, but during Ottoman times they acted as the Arab bulwark against Persian expansion westward into the Middle East.
1736 to 1793	The decline of the Safavids occurs. After the Safavids are toppled by the Afghans, a succession of local empires rules Persia, including the Ashfar and Zand, during this period.
1794 to 1925	The Qajar dynasty rules Persia.
1850 to 1900	In the era of the Great Game (a Cold War between the British and Russian Empires, for control of Central Asia), Persia is a pawn.
1900 to 1905	British interest in Persia begins, first as a land link to India and later as a source of oil. D'Arcy gets concessions to search for oil in 1901.
1906 (August)	After increasing popular discontent with corrupt administration and blatant favoritism toward European economic interests, the elites and tribal leaders in Persia are able to convince the Shah to authorize a constitutional monarchy. The constitution is ratified by the Shah in December, and the Majlis, or parliament, is elected in 1907. The constitutional monarchy is immediately beset by anticonstitutionalists, and civil war ensues for years.
1909	The Anglo-Persian Company is formed.
1914	The Anglo-Persian Oil Company (now owned by the British government) takes a 50 percent stake in the Turkish Petroleum Company. This signals the dominance of investment and extraction in Persia, at the expense of development and extraction in Iraq and other parts of the Middle East.

1914	World War I begins. The Shah tries to remain neutral, but British and Russians invade Persia to safeguard their interests.
1918	World War I ends. Persia emerges from the war with British economic dominance of its oil industry.
1935	Persia officially adopts the name Iran.
1935	The Anglo-Persian Oil Company becomes the Anglo-Iranian Oil Company.
1921	Reza Khan, an army officer, stages a coup, overthrowing the constitutional government.
1925	Reza Khan crowns himself the Shah, launching the Pahlevi dynasty and formally ending the reign of the Qajars. The Majlis' powers are curtailed.
1943	Alarmed by Reza Shah's pro-Axis leanings, Britain again invades Iran and establishes a pro-British government in Tehran.
1941 to 1945	Iran is a critical transfer point for U.S. aid to the Soviet Union during World War II.
1943	The United States, the United Kingdom, and the USSR hold the Tehran Conference, at which they guarantee the independence and territorial integrity of Iran.
1943	Reza Shah is exiled (by the British), and his son, Reza Mohammad Pahlevi, is crowned Shah.
1945 to 1946	At the end of World War II, the Soviet Union attempts to carve out the northern part of Iran, establishing the People's Republic of Azerbaijan and the Kurdish Peoples Republic (both of which claimed portions of Iran). After U.S. and UN pressure, the Soviets withdraw from northern Iran, and the Soviet client states collapse in 1946.
1951	Premier Mossadeq, from the Nationalist Front Movement, compels the Majlis to nationalize the oil industry. They create the National Iranian Oil Company (NIOC). Gradually, the Iranian governments continue to encourage foreign investment in NIOC. By 1975, Iran becomes the fourth-largest producer of oil in the world.

1953	During a period of political turmoil, covert U.S. maneuvering gets Mossadeq out of power and reinstates the Shah (who had fled Iraq the year before).
1957	The Iranian secret police, SAVAK, is formed. It becomes the primary internal vehicle that keeps the Shah in power through 1978.
1957	The Baghdad Pact is formed as a bulwark against Soviet expansionism. Iran is a founding member, and the Shah aligns himself with the United States in the ensuing Cold War. He receives significant U.S. military, covert, and economic support until the early 1970s. Later, when Iraq leaves the pact, it is renamed the Central Treaty Organization, and the headquarters are relocated to Tehran. The Shah moves squarely into the Western camp during the remainder of the Cold War.
1960 to 1970s	The Shah's regime resorts to increasingly oppressive tactics (and U.S. covert support) to stay in power. The United States is increasingly considered to be the enemy by the opposition groups in Iran, including the Shiite clerics.
1960 (September)	Iran joins OPEC.
1964	The Ayatollah Ruholla Khomeini, leader of Iran's Shiite hierarchy, is exiled by the Shah. Khomeini's consistent calls for actions against the Shah have made him dangerous to the Shah's regime. He takes up residence in the Shia holy city of An Najaf in Iraq.
1973	After the Arab-Israeli War, the Arab states stage a boycott of oil exports to the United States. Iran refuses to participate in the embargo.
1978 (August)	More than 400 people die in the Rex Cinema fire in Abadan. Experts agree that the fire was started by fundamentalist students outraged by the "Western decadence" of the theater; however, at the time, the Shiite opposition was able to implicate SAVAK instead. The incident continues to polarize the population for or against the Shah or Islamic fundamentalism.
1978	At the request of the Shah, Saddam Hussein deports the Ayatollah Khomeini. The ayatollah relocates to Paris.

1979	The Shah abandons Iran and appoints Shaphour Bakhtiar as prime minister. The ayatollah returns in triumph to Iran but refuses to recognize the Bakhtiar government; instead, he appoints Bazargan as prime minister and Bani Sadr as president. The two governments operate in uneasy parallel for the next six months. Finally, discovering that the army is now behind the ayatollah, Bakhtiar resigns. However, both Bazargan and Bani Sadr resign their positions in protest to the increasingly heavy-handed clerical rule. By the end of 1980, the clerics take control of the government.
1979 (November 4)	Militant "students" seize the U.S. Embassy in Tehran. Fifty-two American hostages are held for 444 days. The Ayatollah Khomeini insists that President Jimmy Carter resign from office and that the United States unfreeze Iranian assets, as two of several preconditions for releasing the hostages.
1980 (April)	A U.S. attempt to rescue the hostages fails before ever reaching its objective. The rescue helicopters crash during a sandstorm, and the Iranian air force intercepts other elements of the operation.
1981 (January 20)	The hostages are released on the day Ronald Reagan is sworn in as the U.S. president. In return, the United States unfreezes $8 billion of Iranian assets that had been locked up by the Carter administration at the start of the crisis.
1979	The Soviet Union invades Afghanistan. By 1988, some three million Afghan refugees have fled to Iran. Ultimately, the Taliban takes control of Afghanistan. Strict Wahabist Sunnis, the Taliban and the Shia Iranian leadership are hostile to one another.
1980 (September 22)	The Iran-Iraq War begins over a dispute concerning navigation rights on the Shat al Arab waterway.
1982 (June 10)	War-weary Iraq announces a cease-fire, but Iran ignores the offer.
1982 (July 13)	Iranian volunteer troops (called the Pasdaran) make a first push into Iraqi territory.
1983 (July 20)	Iranian troops attack northern Iraq. They unleash a "Human Wave" (Basji) consisting of thousands of unarmed Iranians (many children) who attack wearing only white robes. They are slaughtered by the thousands and do not achieve any real military

success. The Iranian leadership begins to deploy regular Iranian army units (previously held back because of their role in the Shah's regime) in place of the Pasdaran and begin to score successes in the fighting.

1984 (February)	Iraq uses mustard gas on Iranian troops in central Iraq around the Majnoon Islands. Iran claims that the Iraqis used chemical weapons more than 40 times during the war.
1984 (March)	The "Tanker War" (in which Iran and Iraq attack each other's Gulf oil shipping) starts.
1985 (May)	The "Battle of the Cities" phase of the Iran-Iraq War begins. Both sides launch bombing and missile raids on each other's cities.
1986 (August 2)	Saddam Hussein proposes peace in an open letter to the ayatollah. The offer is rejected.
1988 (April)	Iraq begins to make progress in the war; Iran slowly retreats from Iraqi territory.
1988 (July 3)	A U.S. Navy ship, on patrol in the Persian Gulf to protect oil shipping, accidentally shoots down an Iranian civilian airliner.
1988 (August 20)	The Iran-Iraq War ends in a ceasefire, as a stand-off.
1988	The Iran-Contra Scandal erupts. It is discovered that the Reagan administration funneled arms to Iran (via Israel and Syria) for use against Iraq. The money paid by the Iranians is used to fund the United States to support Contra rebels in Nicaragua.
1989	Ayatollah Khomeini dies. Ayatollah Sayid Ali Khamenei, president at the time, takes his place. Ali Akbar Rafsanjani assumes the role of president. His tenure marks a slight warming of relations with the West.
1990 to present	Iran supports the Hezbollah, a pro-Palestinian terrorist group operating from the Bekaa Valley in Lebanon. The Hezbollah is responsible for repeated terrorist attacks on Israeli targets in Israel and the West Bank.
1990s to present	Iran supports the Islamic Jihad and, to a lesser extent, Hamas. These two groups have terrorist wings that repeatedly attack Israeli targets inside Israel.

1991 (January 17)	Operation Desert Storm begins with Coalition bombing that continues for the next five weeks.
1991 (February 24)	The ground phase of Desert Storm begins.
1991 (February 28)	The ground phase of Desert Storm ends.
1991 to 1992	The Iraqi army attacks Kurds; 1.5 million Kurds flee to Turkey and Iran.
1991 to 1992	At the encouragement of U.S. President George H. W. Bush, the Iraqi Shiites rebel against the reeling Saddam Hussein regime. Iraqi troops brutally suppress the uprising, killing thousands of Shiite leaders. The United States does not intervene on behalf of the Shiites.
1993	Rafsanjani is re-elected president, signifying continued opening toward the West (particularly Europe).
1995	The United States suspends trade with Iran as a result of Iranian support of terrorism and pursuit of nuclear weapons. Russia and China ignore the U.S. sanctions.
1997	Mohammed Khatami succeeds Rafsanjani as president. Seen as a moderate, his election signals a growing reaction to the repressive fundamentalism and continued lack of economic progress inside Iran.
1999	University of Tehran students stage pro-democracy demonstrations that are followed by pro-fundamentalist counterdemonstrations.
2001 (September 11)	Al Qaeda attacks the World Trade Center in New York City and the Pentagon.
2001 (October to December)	Never friendly with the Taliban in Afghanistan, Iran provides unofficial support to the Coalition forces toppling the Afghan regime.
2002 (January 29)	President Bush lists Iran as a member of the Axis of Evil, which includes Iraq, Iran, and North Korea. The inference is that these countries foster state terrorism. U.S.–Iranian relations, which had been warming, cool.

2001	Khatami is re-elected president, with an even larger majority. Pro-reform demonstrations and counterdemonstrations occur across the country. Iranian society is increasingly polarizing around the liberalizing ideals (represented by Khatami) and the fundamentalist ideals (represented by Khamenei).
2003 (March to April)	Operation Iraqi Freedom is launched. A U.S.–led Coalition topples the Saddam Hussein regime in Iraq. Iran stays on the sidelines. The United States attacks anti-Islamist regime MEK's Iraqi camps, in return for Iran's neutrality in the war.
2003 (April to May)	The Iranian-sponsored SCIRI (Supreme Council for Islamic Revolution in Iraq) sends operatives and assistance to Shiite clerics in southern Iraq. They are attempting to create an Islamic Republic along the Iranian model.
2002 to 2003	Iran resumes mining uranium at Um, construction on its nuclear reactor at Bushehr, and building of a fuel-processing facility at Natanz. It also continues its missile research. Russia, China, and North Korea provide technology and assistance to the Iranians.
2003 (spring to summer)	Student demonstrations for reform increase in size and locations. More and more nonstudent groups join the demonstrations.
2003 (spring to summer)	Iran continues to refuse access to its nuclear facilities, despite IAEA demands.
2003 (June)	Iran announces the test of a ballistic missile, with a range of 800 miles. This missile is capable of reaching Israel, and U.S. troops located throughout the region.

Dissent and Opposition

Throughout Iranian history, there has been a trend toward dissent and resistance to autocratic authority, sometimes in the face of severe oppression. In the following pages, you'll find some examples of this extraordinary, long-running, seemingly endless drama. It is a drama that has seen the rise of inspiring populist movements for constructive change—as well as dark periods of chaos, division, and bloody recrimination.

You will notice that dominant religious traditions have several roles within this great, long-running Iranian drama:

- ◆ As a personal means of transcending the self and the turmoil and violence of earthly life
- ◆ As a pragmatic social strategy for uniting to action groups that might otherwise never cooperate
- ◆ As a means of silencing dissenting voices

Bloodbath at Karbala

The leadership claim of the Prophet's family is addressed—directly and bloodily.

When: 680.

Who: Hussein, grandson of the prophet Muhammad.

What happened: Hussein was butchered, along with his family and followers, during the sacred month—when military campaigns were forbidden. The violence followed a standoff in the face of an overwhelming force allied with Ali's political opponents.

This horrific massacre took place in Karbala, in present-day Iraq, at a historically critical moment. (The popular Hussein was preparing a campaign to reclaim leadership of Islam from corrupt tribal chiefs who had assumed political control of the empire.)

Whys and wherefores: Hussein and his party were slaughtered because he refused to submit to the opponents who had surrounded his party or to abandon his claim as rightful leader of the Islamic empire.

Aftermath: Incalculable, both for the Shia movement and for Persia/Iran. In one way or another, Shia Islam has been taking part in the same scenes of sacrifice, suffering, mourning, and social opposition ever since.

Among the Shia (whether in Iran or elsewhere in the Islamic world), the symbolically crucial commemoration of the martyrdom of Hussein and his followers takes place on the great holy day of Ashura, when the bloodbath at Karbala is commemorated in great communal gatherings. Participants might wear bloodstained clothes or even show off intentionally inflicted wounds, intending their blood to proclaim their willingness to die as martyrs. The rite of mourning is an integral part of the observance and indeed of Shia belief.

(*A side note:* Shiism—literally, "the tradition of the followers"—is the movement initiated by the "followers of Ali"—Ali being Hussein's father, the fourth caliph, and the son-in-law of the Prophet Muhammad. Ali was assassinated in 661 by political opponents.)

Early Oppression

The early Shia Muslims face persecution and opposition.

When: Decades immediately following the death of Ali, Muhammad's cousin.

Who: Shia partisans organizing in opposition to the established powers of the Islamic empire.

What happened: As the group of Ali's supporters slowly evolved from a political opposition group into a distinct religious movement within Islam, they found themselves violently persecuted on both political and religious fronts.

Whys and wherefores: Opposition from powerful, well-established Sunni elites.

Aftermath: Many competing schools would emerge within Islam in the period following the death of Ali, but only his "followers"—complete with their historic emphasis on mourning, martyrdom, and struggle—would survive. The Shiite movement, ever vulnerable to factionalism within its own ranks, eventually consolidated its position as an alternative to the Sunni expression of the faith.

An Uprising Against the Arabs

Islam gets a Persian makeover.

When: Circa 800.

Who: Abu Moslem Khosasany.

What happened: Khosasany led a successful Shiite uprising in Khorasan.

Whys and wherefores: Factors Khosasany took advantage of included: opposition to Arab dominance in the region, nationalism.

Aftermath: Establishment of an independent Persian Islamic state … for a time.

Invasion

The outsiders descend.

When: Tenth through fourteenth centuries.

Who: Virtually all Persians.

What happened: The kingdom staggered under the respective onslaughts of the Turks, Genghis Khan, and Tamerlane.

Whys and wherefores: The predations of the Turks, the Mongol raids, and Tamerlane's incursions served notice of a seemingly insatiable appetite for conquest by powerful outsiders. The waves of military domination usually left the distracted Persians playing the role of subjugated participants to someone else's dreams of empire. (Khan's authority, for instance, stretched from China to the Black Sea; Tamerlane's reached from Delhi to the Black Sea.)

Aftermath: Chaos and dislocation endured for centuries, but the faith of Islam served as an important form of personal and cultural autonomy.

Shiism Triumphant

The Shia Muslims win formal recognition of their faith.

When: 1501.

Who: Shah Ismail.

What happened: Ismail united Persia under Shiite rule and established Shiism as the state religion.

Whys and wherefores: Ismail's motivations include: establishment, at long last, of clear civil authority; and his own opposition to Sunni Islam, historically antagonistic to Shiism.

Aftermath: Persia emerged with a clear public cultural and religious identity and resumed control of its own affairs.

Challenge from the Shah

Nadir Shah attempts to fuse together the two halves of Islam.

When: Early 1700s.

Who: Nadir Shah, often referred to as the "last great Asian conqueror," had a vision. He believed he could unify the Sunnis and Shiites—by obliterating Shiism in Iran.

What happened: Shia Muslims in Iran resisted and bitterly resented Nadir Shah's attempts to convert the nation to Sunni Islam.

Whys and wherefores: The Shah was led by his own desire to merge a unified Islam state with the Ottoman Empire.

Aftermath: The conversion attempt failed, as Shiism by this point was simply too densely woven into the fabric of the social order, and the populace rejected the attempt to alter their socioreligious traditions.

Nadir Shah later embarked on a series of disastrous military adventures, and his reign ended in a wave of domestic bloodshed. He was assassinated in 1747; three decades of political and social chaos followed.

Challenge from Arabia

A new Islamic reform movement emerges.

When: Late 1730s.

Who: Muhammad ibn Abd al Wahhab.

What happened: In the late 1730s, this Arabian Sunni Muslim returned from studies in Iran to his native land and founded what has come to be known as the Wahhabi movement, a fiercely anti-Shia Islam reform campaign with profound social, political, and religious influence.

Proponents of the movement seek, in essence, to reject all Islamic traditions dating later than about 950, and to re-emphasize Islam's devotion to the oneness of God. Wahhabism's opponents condemn both its intolerance and its eagerness to condemn opposing points of view as idolatrous or blasphemous. Its proponents celebrate its simplicity and its rejection of ostentation and lavish living.

Wahhabism is the religion of the current Saudi Arabian ruling family.

Whys and wherefores: Al Wahhab objected vehemently to certain Shia practices (such as the veneration of the graves of pious men); he also had little patience for Western social influence and innovations.

Aftermath: The Wahhabis would eventually emerge as the chief architects of a modern campaign of global persecution of Shias.

Today, the group is assailed for its persecution of Shia Muslims, for its alleged religious fanaticism, and for its anti-Western, anti-modernist outlook. Detractors of the Wahhabi movement, of which there are many, describe it as a modern-day fascist Islamic faction.

Regardless of the political label one chooses to place upon the Wahhabi movement, its anti-Shia bias is inescapable. The success of the movement in Saudi Arabia and elsewhere has given Shias in Iran and other countries a point of common concern.

Confronting the Baha'is

A new religious movement arises from within Iran's own borders.

When: 1850.

What happened: Mirza Ali Muhammad, one of the central figures of what would eventually be known as the Baha'i movement, was executed in Iran.

Whys and wherefores: Mirza Ali Muhammad, also known as "the Bab," had faced charges of heresy. He had claimed to be on a divine mission, and to be working to prepare the earth for his next manifestation.

Muslims—Shia and Sunni alike—believe that Muhammad was the final prophet of God.

Aftermath: In the period following the execution, the Bab's followers were given the choice of renouncing their faith or facing execution; many chose the latter, and a campaign of terror and persecution followed.

In 1851, government troops attacked the town of Zenjan, a stronghold of the Bab's message. The troops encountered fierce resistance, but eventually laid waste to the town and killed every one of the Bab's followers there—including women and children.

A cadre of Babis attempted to retaliate by hatching an assassination attempt against the Shah; the plot failed, and further brutal persecutions followed.

Amazingly, however, pockets of believers remained steadfast in their new faith, its traditions endured, and the religion did not die out. In the years to come, while a measure of social tolerance would be extended to various minority religious groups in Iran—including local Jews—the story was to be quite different for those who followed the teachings of the Bab and those of his successor.

These new religionists, who would come to be known as the Baha'i, grew from within the Shia tradition itself and rejected certain fundamental tenets of Islam. They periodically face new and brutal campaigns of suppression, but they have somehow managed to endure in Iran.

Indeed, the Baha'i have, despite intense persecution, established their faith as an entirely new global religion. Today, they attract converts from all nations and all walks of life, but they are still regarded with disdain as a heretical schismatic movement by many Muslims. Under the present regime, they are probably the most persecuted faith in Iran, lacking as they do any legal status as an officially protected minority religion under the Constitution of the Islamic Republic of Iran.

The Shah Faces a Popular Uprising

No, not *that* Shah. No, not *that* popular uprising. This popular uprising predates that of 1979 by almost a century.

When: 1891.

Who: Clerics, nationalists, merchants, and activist intellectuals.

What happened: These diverse groups formed alliances in opposition to the government, called protest meetings, and coordinated increasingly impossible-to-ignore street demonstrations.

Whys and wherefores: The new coalition served notice to the government of its opposition to the reigning Shah's decision to grant the British monopolistic concessions on tobacco sales in Persia.

The movement sparked a remarkable public outpouring of opposition to the government's policy, and forced the Shah to cancel the concessions. The growing influence of religious clerics in summoning waves of protesters was decisive; the open participation of women in the protests caused much discussion.

Aftermath: See the following "The Constitutional Revolution" section.

The Constitutional Revolution

The tobacco protests opened the door to demands for broad governmental reforms.

When: 1905 to 1906.

Who: An alliance of clerics, merchants, and others that grew out of the earlier tobacco protests.

What happened: Large-scale protests led to (short-lived) political reforms, limitations on the Shah's power, and an elected representative body (the Majlis).

Whys and wherefores: Effective exploitation of popular discontent with the Shah's mismanagement of financial affairs and the influence of foreign powers in state affairs.

Aftermath: A 1907 agreement between Russia and Great Britain divided the nation into "spheres of influence," and the post-World War I period saw the country plunged into financial and political chaos.

Repression of Opponents, Twentieth-Century-Style

A new leader, Reza Shah Pahlavi, draws the line on open opposition.

When: 1929.

Who: Sayyad Hasan Mudaris.

What happened: Mudaris was imprisoned and eventually (1937) executed.

Whys and wherefores: This eloquent and effective opponent of the Shah was silenced and eventually murdered by forces loyal to the head of state. Those who thought to challenge the Shah's authority, or his "Westernization" campaign, were sent a chilling message: Be prepared to die for your beliefs.

Aftermath: The grim legacy of repression of political opponents got a new lease on life.

The "White Revolution"

Another Shah alienates the clerical establishment.

When: 1963 and years following.

Who: Opponents of Mohammad Shah Reza Pahlavi's Westernization and social reform campaign (the so-called "White Revolution").

What happened: Potential political opponents faced increasingly brutal treatment from the Shah's secret police (SAVAK). Clerics became convinced that objectives such as land reform (with which they agreed) were connected to a general subversion of traditional Islamic values (with which they didn't).

Whys and wherefores: The Shah was eager to implement a reform initiative with which his name would be associated for years—or even centuries—to come. He succeeded, but not quite in the manner he might have anticipated.

Aftermath: Isolation of those who opposed reforms escalated into unapologetic repression or exile of all those who opposed the Shah. By 1971, there was organized underground armed resistance to the Shah's security apparatus.

On the clerical front: In 1964, Ruhollah Khomeini was exiled to Turkey for his brutally frank condemnations of the Shah's policies; in 1965 he moved to Iraq; in 1978 the Shah arranged for his departure from Iraq, imagining that Khomeini would prove less of a threat once he left the Middle East.

This was one of the Shah's most stupendous miscalculations. In fact, Khomeini had ample access to media in his next locale (Paris), and his network of supporters in Iran only grew more committed with his departure.

The Shah Cracks Down

An Iranian dissident group is treated to special treatment from SAVAK.

When: 1972.

Who: Members of the opposition group Mujaheddin-e Khalq.

What happened: Nearly half of the group's membership was arrested by the Shah's secret police. They were not the only real and perceived political opponents of the Shah who were tortured and murdered by (American-trained) Iranian security personnel.

A. J. Langguth wrote in a *New York Times* article published June 11, 1979 ("Torture's Teachers): "A few months ago, I received some clippings of interviews with a former Federal intelligence agency official. That operative ... said that the CIA sent an operative to teach interrogation methods to SAVAK, the Shah's secret police, that the training included instructions in torture, and (that) the techniques were copied from the Nazis."

In 1976, Amnesty International noted that the Shah's Iran had the "highest rate of death penalties in the world, no valid system of civilian courts and a history of torture which is beyond belief. No country in the world," Amnesty International concluded, "has a worse record in human rights than Iran."

Whys and wherefores: The Shah was able to win American military and intelligence aid by opposing Soviet expansionism. But his real purpose appears to have been quelling all domestic dissent at any cost. All too often, American decision makers turned a blind eye to this fact.

U.S. implication in the Shah's humanitarian abuses was sustained and deep. U.S. Senator Hubert Humphrey was attributed with the following remark circa 1976: "Do you know what the head of the Iranian Army told one of our people? He said the Army was in good shape, thanks to U.S. aid—it was now capable of coping with the civilian population. That Army isn't going to fight the Russians. It's planning to fight the Iranian people."

Aftermath: The Shah may have wished to stifle all domestic political dissent, but in the long run he ended up achieving precisely the opposite result.

In an environment of torture and oppression, it was not entirely surprising that popular support for an Islamic revolutionary agenda grew steadily and predictably. In 1978, anti-Shah protesters gathered in huge numbers following the publication of a government-approved article critical of the Ayatollah Khomeini who had been exiled from Iran since 1964 and was currently stoking the fires of revolution from Paris. Khomeini formed the underground Islamic Revolutionary Council and eventually returned to Iran triumphantly.

The Revolution

Meet the new boss.

When: February 11, 1979.

Who: Vast numbers of Iranians including highly visible women (see 1891 and 1905) and university students (see 1999, 2002, and 2003).

What happened: Ayatollah Ruhollah Khomeini assumes political power in Iran.

Aftermath: During this momentous month, revolutionaries stormed Evin Prison to liberate political prisoners held captive by the hated Shah.

Evin Prison today houses political prisoners held captive by the government, which is controlled by Iranian clerical authorities.

Khomeini Cracks Down

When: June through November 1981.

Who: Real or perceived "left-wing" Iranian Muslims.

What happened: It's estimated that, by September of this year, fifty supposed "liberals" were being executed every day by the Iranian authorities. One story has it that a twelve-year-old child accused of participating in a demonstration was put to death.

The actual death toll from this period will probably never be known, but one generally accepted estimate puts the total at 1800. Clerics, Baha'is. government officials, members of the Islamic Republican Party, and not a few innocent civilians were swept up in a tide of violence strongly reminiscent of the worst periods of the Stalinist purges.

Aftermath: A suppressed rival political faction, the Mujahedin-e Khalq (which had been an early and vocal opponent of the Shah), moved from political to military opposition to the government. The group eventually sought refuge in Iraq with Hussein, thus earning the ill will of millions of rank-and-file Iranians.

Clamping Down on the Baha'is

A familiar opponent finds life even more difficult.

When: 1983.

Who: Iranian Baha'is.

What happened: Unlike other recognized Iranian religious minorities, the Baha'is in Iran were stripped of the right to assemble in groups, set up community centers, maintain administrative offices, elect officials, or conduct charitable campaigns.

Aftermath: Further repression of Baha'is in Iran.

Clamping Down on the Sunnis

An even more familiar opponent finds life even more difficult.

When: 1996 and 1997.

Who: Sunni Muslim activists.

What happened: In 1997, the organization Human Rights Watch noted unverified reports of human rights abuses against Sunni Muslim activists in Iran, and began investigations into reports of human rights violations against members of other religious and ethnic groups.

Aftermath: To be determined.

Student Protests, Revisited

Two decades on, the students are restless again … but in a whole different way.

When: July 1999.

Who: Protesters against the clerical establishment begin a series of anti-government demonstrations. Most of the demonstrators have no memory whatsoever of the 1979 revolution; all of them were apparently tired of waiting for promised economic and social reforms.

What happened: Police forces and members of hard-line militias, acting in support of the clerical government, reportedly beat the youngsters bloody in the streets of Tehran, thus ending the demonstration. More than 1,000 demonstrators are placed under arrest.

Aftermath: To be determined.

Female Protests, Revisited

The women are restless again, too.

When: August 2001.

Who: Fatemeh Haqiqatjou, female legislator in Iranian parliament.

What happened: Haqiqatjou was sentenced to prison.

Whys and wherefores: The sentence was for "misinterpreting words of the founder of the Islamic Republic" and other charges, including insulting the head of the Tehran Revolutionary Court. All the charges were associated with her open criticism of the judiciary for arresting a female journalist.

There were brief protests in Parliament from reformists; many lawmakers see the move as an open effort to intimidate the reformist-dominated legislature.

Aftermath: To be determined.

And More Student Protests

The kids take to the streets once again—and pay the price once again.

When: Late 2002.

Who: Leaders of student protestors in Tehran.

What happened: Student organizers were punished for organizing demonstrations opposing the blasphemy conviction of reformist social critic Hashem Aghajari.

Whys and wherefores: Students—and others—had been growing deeply restless at the slow pace of promised reforms in the Iranian political and social system.

Aftermath: See the following "And Yet More Student Protests" section.

And Yet More Student Protests

The story continues.

When: June 2003.

Who: More than 1,000 protesters—Iranian students at Tehran University and others.

What happened: Protesters were again beaten back by security forces and supporters of hard-line conservatives; they were reportedly dispersed by means of iron bars, clubs, and tear gas after four days of demonstrations. Members of conservative vigilante groups are said to have dragged some departing demonstrators from automobiles in order to beat them.

Whys and wherefores: An ad-hoc demonstration against privatization had grown into a larger protest against the Iranian clerical establishment and their chants of "Death to Khamenei" (Supreme Leader Ayatollah Ali Khamenei) were heard, shocking the establishment.

Aftermath: To be determined.

Appendix D

Resources on Iran

Books

Abrahamian, Ervand. *Iran Between Two Revolutions.* Princeton: Princeton University Press, 1982.

Afkhami, Gholam R. *The Iranian Revolution: Thanatos on a National Scale.* Washington, DC: Middle East Institute, 1985.

Akhavi, Shahrough. *Religion and Politics in Contemporary Iran: Clergy-State Relations in the Pahlavi Period.* Albany, New York: State University of New York Press, 1980.

Amirahmadi, Hooshang, ed. *Revisiting Iran's Strategic Significance in the Emerging Regional Order.* New Brunswick, New Jersey: U.S.–Iran Conference, 1995.

Arendt, Hannah. *The Origins of Totalitarianism.* New York: Harcourt Brace Javanovich, 1973.

Bakhash, Shaul. *The Reign of the Ayatollahs: Iran and the Islamic Revolution.* London: I. B. Tauris, 1985.

Buchta, Wilfried. *Who Rules Iran? The Structure of Power in the Islamic Republic.* Washington, DC: Washington Institute for Near East Policy and Konrad Adenauer Stiftung, 2000.

Byman, Daniel L., and Roger Cliff. *China's Arms Sales: Motivations and Implications.* Santa Monica, California: RAND, 1999.

Byman, Daniel, et al. *Iran's Security Policy in the Post-Revolutionary Era.* Santa Monica, California: RAND, 2001.

Economist Intelligence Unit. "Iran: Country Report." London: *The Economist Newspaper,* 2003.

Ehteshami, Anoushiravan. *After Khomeini: The Iranian Second Republic.* London: Routledge, 1995.

Esman, Milton, and Itamar Rabinovich, eds. *Ethnicity, Pluralism, and the State in the Middle East.* Ithaca, New York: Cornell University Press, 1988.

Hopkirk, Peter. *The Great Game: The Struggle for Empire in Central Asia.* New York: Kodansha, 1992.

Jaber, Hala. *Hezbollah: Born with a Vengeance.* London: Fourth Estate, 1997.

Kramer, Samuel Noah. *History Begins at Sumer.* New York: Doubleday & Company, 1969.

Mallowan, M. E. L. *Early Mesopotamia and Iran.* New York: McGraw-Hill, 1965.

U.S. Central Intelligence Agency. *World Fact Book.* Washington, DC: USGPO, 2002.

Websites

Encyclopedia References to Iran

encarta.msn.com
Microsoft's Encarta encyclopedia website

Governmental Sites on Iran

www.un.org
United Nations' website

www.loc.gov
The Library of Congress website, with links to Congressional Research Service reports

www.state.gov/www/global/terrorism/index.html
Website State Department Office of the Coordinator for Counter-Terrorism

www.energy.gov
Website of the United States Department of Energy, with information on OPEC and Iranian oil

Iran-Sympathetic Information

www.president.ir
Presidency of the Islamic Republic of Iran (official site)

www.farsinet.com/news
FarsiNet News

www.iran-press-service.com
Iran Press Service

www.irna.com/en
Islamic Republic News Agency

www.netiran.com
NETIRAN

www.payvand.com/news
Payvand

www.salamiran.org
Salam Iran

www.tehrantimes.com
Tehran Times

Western Views of Iran

www.amnesty-volunteer.org/usa/mideast/reports/iran.html
Amnesty International USA: Human Rights in the Mideast (Iran Report)

news.bbc.co.uk/1/hi/world/middle_east/default.stm
BBC UK: Middle East News

www.countrywatch.com
CountryWatch, which monitors geopolitical developments around the world

www.hrw.org
Human Rights Watch, which monitors human rights around the world

www.foreignpolicy2000.org/home/home.cfm
The Council on Foreign Relations, a think-tank that focuses on a variety of issues affecting U.S. foreign policy

www.kurdistan.org
The American-Kurdish Information Network, which promotes Kurdish causes in the United States

www.rferl.org/iran-report
Radio Free Europe/Radio Liberty: Iran Report

www.rand.org
RAND, a U.S. think-tank

Index

A Little Knowledge Goes a Long Way ...

Check Out These
Best-Selling
COMPLETE IDIOT'S GUIDE

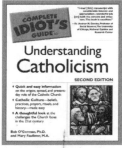

Understanding Catholicism
SECOND EDITION

1-59257-085-2
$18.95

Learning Spanish
THIRD EDITION

0-02-864451-4
$18.95

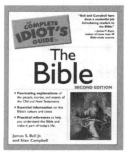

The Bible
SECOND EDITION

0-02-864382-8
$18.95

Feng Shui
SECOND EDITION

0-02-864339-9
$18.95

Playing the Guitar
SECOND EDITION

0-02-864244-9
$21.95 w/CD-ROM

Personal Finance in Your 20s & 30s
SECOND EDITION

0-02-864374-7
$19.95

Creating a Web Page
FIFTH EDITION

0-02-864316-X
$24.95 w/CD-ROM

Digital Photography
THIRD EDITION

0-02-864453-0
$19.95

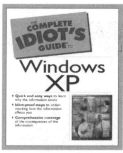

Windows XP

0-02-864232-5
$19.95

More than *400 titles* in *26 different categories*
Available at booksellers everywhere

ALPH